LOOK UP

GAINING INSIGHT AND DIRECTION THROUGH
EXPERIENTIAL LEARNING
For Your Personal, Professional and Civic Life

Joani LaMachia • Jonathan Andrew

Kendall Hunt
publishing company

D0139430

Cover image © Shutterstock, Inc.

Kendall Hunt
publishing company

www.kendallhunt.com
Send all inquiries to:
4050 Westmark Drive
Dubuque, IA 52004-1840

DEDICATION

We wish to dedicate this book to both the co-op faculty members and students whom we have worked with over the years. They have taught us so much and are the inspiration for this book and the work we do every day.

With love and gratitude to my family—Alex, Jeremy, Lucy, Mom and Dad, Honey, David, Peter, Thomas, Stephen, and extended family and friends—I thank my lucky stars for our relationships and experiences together as they continuously teach and remind me of the power of love and taking care of one another—which is at the core of life and learning.

Joani LaMachia

Special thanks to my supportive family and friends. First and foremost Amanda and Eloise, who bring so much joy and love into my life. Thank you for supporting, inspiring, and sustaining me every day! Many thanks to my parents—Wally and Carol—for all you did to support me in all of my educational and life endeavors. Thank you to my siblings and their families: Benjamin and Vanessa, Jillian and Meaghan and Geoff, and all their children for being shining examples in my life, for challenging me and helping me to be honest with myself and others. Many thanks to my family in law: Dr. Ted and Donna, Tasker and Beth, Matt and Robyn, and all their children for being supportive in so many ways while also sharing insights and inspiration for parts of this book. Also to extended family, chosen family, and friends, thank you for all the thoughts, insights on the book, patience, motivation, kind words, fun distractions, love, and support throughout the years and during the writing of this book. I can always count on you when I need it most. You all always push me to accept new challenges and are always there to help me adapt and learn from every new experience.

Jon Andrew

Contents

Content

Foreword

It is a great privilege for me to write the foreword to this incredibly important book, *Look Up—Gaining Insight and Direction through Experiential Learning*. Dr. Joani LaMachia and Jonathan Andrew, both members of the faculty at Northeastern University, are experts in the critically important field of experiential education. Whether you call it an internship, a co-op, a gap year, or a project-based engagement, this book fills the gap for students interested in exploring new ways of learning outside the classroom.

Joani, Jonathan, and I live in the rapidly changing world of higher education. Learning, once confined to the classroom and lab, is happening everywhere: in a physical classroom, somewhere online in cyberspace, and increasingly on-the-job, in the world of experience. This book is written to speak to today's modern learner who is navigating this increasingly complex learning environment.

There is no doubt still much to learn inside the walls of a great university. These are unique places, and the "life of the mind" and "thinking from first principles" are best taught in a traditional bricks, mortar, and ivy environment. We need these institutions of higher education and the quiet spaces they create for analysis, contemplation, and creativity, more now than ever. At their best, universities help build a world of shared values and a deep respect for fact and precedent. At their very best, they drive basic research in all fields of study and expand our knowledge of everything from stem cells to philosophy, from sustainable energy to poetry and theater. Nothing in this book suggests otherwise, and we all believe that the university will be at the heart of higher education for years to come.

However, the world of education is changing rapidly, and our current college students face many daunting challenges. No major or career can be considered future-proof. In fact, many of the most popular majors like computer science and engineering, popular because students think they will lead to secure employment and good jobs, are the ones most likely to be disrupted by new technologies like artificial intelligence. After all, computer languages like Java and Python are designed to be "read" by computers. Unlike French or Chinese, which require memorizing tens of thousands of words or characters, hundreds of rules, and as many exceptions, computer languages can be defined by a few hundred words and a few simple rules with no exceptions. Code-bots will soon be able to write the code that other code-bots love to read, leaving the humans who wrote the original self-organizing scripts with nothing to do. Many engineering careers are not safe either, at least not the analytical engineering jobs that will be the first to be automated. Other college majors, especially in the humanities, are facing an existential threat from technology and everyone on campuses around the globe is asking, "What will a career look like when the robots come?"

On the other hand, one of the things changing dramatically for the better is life expectancy. Many predict that this will be the first generation of college students to live to a healthy 100 years. That means that they can anticipate a working-career of 50, 60, or even 70 years. As responsible educators we have to ask, "What is the best way to prepare college students, in any field of study, for the tumultuous and rapidly changing future of work?" How do we prepare students for jobs that most certainly do not even exist yet, jobs that will appear 20, 30, or 40 years into their professional life? And how do we prepare our students to find meaning and purpose in a life of work? Many of us are turning to experiential learning as one way to go.

The authors point out that we are ". . . living in an interconnected and global society," and this means that learning in the world takes on a heightened importance. "Experiential learning takes on a critical and important role in helping students to gain greater exposure and deeper understanding of complex issues, diverse peoples and various contexts." I couldn't agree more. We are educating students who are digital natives, who spend an average of 6 hours a day on their smartphones, and who live and communicate inside their Snapchat, Instagram, WhatsApp, and Facebook social circles. Experiential learning gets these folks out of their social media bubble and into life. Experiential learning will help teach our students how to make good decisions about their future. It will show them the value and importance of communities of practice and mentors. They will learn how to tell their stories and make sense and meaning of their lives.

Everyone, including students, mid-career professionals, and people entering their encore or retirement careers can benefit from learning through experience. It all starts with self-awareness, knowing what you have to offer the world. Like any good designer, you focus first on empathy, for yourself and your skill set, and for what the world needs to get done. Then there is the experience itself, and staying open to all that you can learn, above and beyond the job at hand. This "being present" in your experience is how we transcend our cultural and personal boundaries and learn deeply about each other. And finally, when you reflect on the experience of the project you've completed, you close the circle on your learning. You extract the meaning from what you've learned—it becomes one of your life lessons. Whether through their innovative SAIL platform or through the Experiential Network, a program through which Northeastern partners businesses with students to complete short-term projects, Northeastern is leading the way in this kind of meaningful and experience-based education. Joani and Jonathan are champions in this field.

You are in great hands with Joani and Jonathan. The detailed research and careful construction that has gone into writing this book is evident throughout. Better than that, they have great empathy for their students' journeys. They will challenge you to think differently about your own learning experiences. They have provided an incredibly valuable toolkit for designing experiential learning. I am sure that you will enjoy reading this book and that it will prove useful as you design your own learning experiences.

It is time to stop discounting the value of learning in the real world. Experiential education can be as rigorous and as structured as learning in the classroom, and it can do so much more. The collision of theory and practice is a powerful formula—it ignites a student's passion and intellectual curiosity and creates a life-long learner. Joani and Jonathan challenge their students to "Be the author of your life." I reframe that as "Be the designer of your life." This is because, as our jobs and our society accelerate through the artificial intelligence and autonomous machine tipping point, we all need to be designing and redesigning continuously. This book is all about one powerful way to educate the leaders of tomorrow and prepare them for the unique challenges of the next 100 years. I invite you to read it and be delighted.

Bill Burnett

Co-author of *Designing Your Life: How to Build a Well-Lived, Joyful Life*

Executive Director of the Design Program at Stanford University

Adjunct Professor, Design, Stanford University

Endorsements

Look Up is a landmark discussion and how-to manual about experiential learning, written by two of its pioneers. Drawing on their hard-won experience with the Cooperative Education Program at Northeastern University and comments from the students themselves, LaMachia and Andrew vividly convey the importance of off-campus, real-world experience for college students—in developing their knowledge of the world, their commitment to making that world a better place, and their understanding of themselves.

Alan Lightman, Professor of the Practice of Humanities, MIT and Founder and Chairman, the Harpswell Foundation, Phnom Penh, Cambodia

Experiential learning is an important bridge between academic learning and the demands and challenges that students will encounter in the workplace and global society. In our experience, students learn not only new skills but also the mechanisms needed to cope with, and manage, fast-changing workplace environments. We have worked with the authors and Northeastern University's Cooperative Education Program for a number of years to great effect. *Look Up* is a timely and useful guide that will help practitioners and students alike to approach this increasingly important and relevant topic in a thoughtful and comprehensive way.

Gerhard Botha, Director of Programs, International Law Institute, Washington, DC

Experiential learning is quickly on the rise within education. Colleges and universities are seeking to develop, implement, and expand student programs and learning "beyond the classroom." Having worked with Northeastern students as co-ops at Foreign Policy Interrupted, I highly endorse experiential learning and have seen the benefits firsthand. With this book, LaMachia and Andrew have given us an indispensable guide for both professionals and students alike. As a professional, I'm excited to use it as a resource for students and young professionals.

Elmira Bayrasli, Author and Cofounder of Foreign Policy Interrupted, New York, NY

Experiential learning is more widely being incorporated into higher education as colleges and universities recognize its value. The authors of *Look Up* have developed a ground-breaking, comprehensive guide for both students and educators. They have captured the essence of how best to harness the power of experiential learning and apply and integrate its lessons in the personal, professional, and civic lives of learners. It is an exceptional resource for educators that includes an impressive array of information and materials to assist them with developing quality programs and advising for their students. *Look Up* is an innovative and significant publication that will greatly benefit the experiential education community.

Veronica Porter, President, Cooperative Education and Internship Association, Associate Professor of Cooperative Education, College of Science, Northeastern University, Boston, MA

Our experience with Northeastern's Cooperative Education Program has been overwhelmingly positive. We found the program to be a great initiative to provide students with on-the-job learning while offering organizations such as ours with high-caliber and dynamic support on specific projects. This book is an important reference for a process that is underresearched and underrated, and it will be of great value to organizations such as ours in maximizing the benefits of experiential learning to all concerned.

Volker Schimmel, Senior Regional Cash-Based Interventions Coordinator, Middle East and North Africa Director's Office in Amman, United Nations High Commissioner for Refugees

TS Eliot once said, "we had the experience but we missed the meaning. And approach to the meaning restores the experience in a different form." This could apply to many students as they participate in experiential education activities, both long and short. *Look Up* addresses ALL the issues that make an experience meaningful for students and guides them in framing the experience to gain the transformation that experiential learning promises. While ostensibly written for students, this should be read by every administrator, faculty member, or industry partner and parent who are involved in helping students navigate experiential education during their college career. LaMachia and Andrew get to the heart of what it means to truly learn from an experience by providing students with information, meaningful and reflective activities, and multiple resources to ensure that students gain the most from their learning outside the classroom.

Donna Qualters, Tufts University, Author of Experiential Education: Making the Most of Learning Outside the Classroom

As an alum, I truly wish *Look Up* was an available tool during my experiential learning process. The insight it provides is critical and will definitely better equip students to become stronger job applicants and leaders. Now as a co-op employer, I value the experiential learning process in a new light and have witnessed firsthand students' transformational growth throughout the program. Experiential learning is truly a win-win for students and employers alike, and I applaud LaMachia and Andrew for creating such a powerful resource on this imperative subject.

Samantha Sheridan, NU Class of 2014, Campaigns Coordinator, Oxfam America

I love teaching public policy to my Northeastern coop students. Why? Because for them it is not some theoretical exercise. They have typically come back from 6 months working in Congress or the executive branch or a state legislature or a city government and eager to hone their skills for public service. What could be better than that? Joani LaMachia and Jonathan Andrew give us an impressive explanation of how we can expand experiential learning throughout higher education and help encourage and train some of the nation's best future leaders.

Michael S. Dukakis, Professor of Political Science, Former Governor of Massachusetts

Experience-based learning is on the rise in both educational and professional settings. Having worked with Andrew and LaMachia in Northeastern's Cooperative Education Program, I have witnessed the benefits first-hand, not only for the student as they gain valuable experience navigating an ever-changing and increasingly collaborative workplace but also from the business side as companies can help rising graduates develop and become capable of making a more seamless transition to that work environment. Look Up is an indispensable guide for those looking to tap into this developmental approach and also for the student as they try to gain a deeper understanding of the method and its payoffs.

Curtis Robinson, PwC Germany

Acknowledgments

There are so many people to acknowledge and recognize in the writing of this book. It has been a genuine experiential learning opportunity as we collaborated and learned together with students, colleagues, and employers. We feel fortunate and deeply grateful for your time and consideration and for assisting us with what we hope is a timely and useful resource for all of us in experiential education.

Let us begin by acknowledging the significant contributions of our peers, associates, and others:

Rebecca Westerling, International Affairs Cooperative Education Faculty, master organizer and curriculum development star. She was the force behind our Toolkit, which she organized and developed from start to finish. This included reaching out to colleagues, setting up meetings, following up on multiple moving parts, collecting and coordinating submissions, filling in the gaps with her own creative ideas and activities, and being the instrumental person in putting together the learning activities into a user-friendly and accessible format for students, faculty, and employers. In our minds, the Toolkit is a unique, distinguishing, and key aspect of the book because of its interactive and self-directed learning activities that are at the core of experiential education. This section would not have come to fruition without the time, energy, and commitment of Rebecca, thank you so much!

Dave Merry, Associate Director for Experiential Integration of the SAIL Initiative at the Northeastern Center for Advancing Teaching and Learning, a thorough research and faculty super star, contributed to the SAIL framework and content on student authorship and integrated learning. His experience and insights in this area are key to experiential learning and as such are a valuable contribution to the book, thank you Dave!

Sarah Klionsky, Rachel Walsh, Gordana Rabrenovic, and Alex Bingham, our editors extraordinaire, contributed their time reading and responding with their timely and important feedback. Their editing of the chapters and giving up of their precious summer time to sit and read and provide us with these needed edits and comments was a true gift and much appreciated.

Leyla Latypova, our student researcher, was an incredible source of support and energy. Leyla worked with us to conduct literature reviews, collected data through in-person interviews (which she both recruited for and organized), and provided us with an important student perspective from her own experiential learning. If you weren't in Dubai, we would take you out for a big café au lait—thank you!

Orianna Timsit, our gifted illustrator, contributed her fun and creative characters and designs to the book. She also worked over the summer on drawings and meeting with us, which is greatly appreciated as her illustrations speak to looking up in interesting ways!

Special Acknowledgments to Our Colleagues for Their Contributions to the Toolkit.

The ideas for activities in this section come from a wide variety of professionals within the co-op community and beyond. The activities often are based upon shared ideas, ideals, and variations of exercises that are updated, adapted, and shifted to fit the audience, time, and focus of the activity—and we hope you will do the same. These activities and case studies would not be possible without the contributions of the individuals named, or without the contributions of the professionals across the strong cooperative education and career design teams at Northeastern University.

With great appreciation and thanks, we would like to acknowledge our contributing colleagues from Northeastern University:

Esther Chewning, Senior Associate Cooperative Education Faculty, D'Amore McKim School of Business

Lisa Cantwell-Doherty, Associate Cooperative Education Faculty, College of Social Science and Humanities

Sally Conant, Faculty Global Co-op Coordinator, College of Engineering

Sarah Klionsky, Associate Cooperative Education Faculty, College of Science

Melissa Peikin, Associate Cooperative Education Faculty, College of Computer and Information Science

Emily Planz, Assistant Director, Employer Engagement and Career Design

Michelle Zaff, Associate Cooperative Education Faculty, College of Social Sciences and Humanities

Other contributors for case study, reality-check, and activity ideas include Mary Carney and Deidre Jordan, Bouve School of Health Sciences; and Jacqui Sweeney, College of Art Media and Design

Special Acknowledgments to Our Students for Their Contributions to the Book.

The aspect of the book that we believe truly distinguishes it from other text books is the focus on and inclusion of the student voice. The concepts presented in each of the chapters came directly from what we heard from students in our classes and advising sessions. In writing the book, we sought to capture the student experience by including individual stories and reflections. We feel so fortunate to have been able to share these student insights and perspectives with you in the book.

With great appreciation and thanks we would like to acknowledge our students from Northeastern University, who contributed insights and reflections to this book:

Michaela Anang

Gabriela Beatham-Garcia

Maggie Burke

Tavish Fenbert

Francesca Giorgianni

Kestral Johnson

Esther Laaninen

Leyla Latypova

Neiha Lesharie

Fernando Loya

Kara Morgan

Vanessa Pena

Olivia Sorenson

Paige Welch

Shelbe Van Winkle

Special Acknowledgments to Our Faculty and Employer Partners for Their Comments and Contributions:

A big shout out and thank you to faculty friends and advisors who provided us with their thoughts and perspectives on experiential education—Susan Ambrose, Barry Bluestone, Jose Buscaglia, Lori Gardinier, Donna Qualters, Gordana Rabrenovic, Rebecca Riccio, Denis Sullivan, Michael Sweet, Cigdem Talgar. Also, special acknowledgment to our Director and Assistant Dean, Mary Mello, who supported our writing and work on the book.

In addition, thank you to our employer partners and partnerships that we have developed over the years. These relationships are critical to experiential education; by working with us they offer high-quality learning opportunities and also support, guide, mentor, and work alongside our students in the workplace and community. Special acknowledgment of partners who contributed to the book through their reflections and anecdotal stories of working in the field—Zoe Gauld-Angelucci, Elmira Bayrasli, Alan Lightman, Ronnie Millar, Cheryl Novak, Marietta Panayopotoulou, Curtis Robinson, Talitha Van Der Waerden.

About the Authors

Dr. Joani LaMachia is an Associate Cooperative Education Faculty member in Northeastern University's International Affairs and Asian Studies Programs. Her area of interest is in preparing students to engage actively in the world as global citizens. Dr. LaMachia has traveled with faculty and students to Northern Ireland, the Balkans, Bali, Cambodia, Cuba, Jordan, and Ghana to develop experiential learning opportunities. Her Doctorate of Education degree at Northeastern University in Higher Education Administration focused on *Integrating Global Citizenship Learning in Undergraduate Education.*

Jonathan Andrew is an Associate Cooperative Education Faculty member with the International Affairs, Spanish and American Sign Language Programs at Northeastern University. He has an MA in International Education from the School for International Training Graduate Institute and a BA in Anthropology from Hamilton College. He has dedicated his career to educating students of all ages through the integration of their in and out of classroom experiences and intercultural dialogue. He currently lives in Wakefield, Massachusetts, with his wife Amanda and daughter Eloise.

Introduction

I am a firm believer that you can't learn in classes what the world can teach you. The best learning experiences are out there, and you have to start exploring by yourself because it doesn't matter how much you learn in a book; when you go into the real world, it is going to be different. (Student Respondent, 2018)

Look up—is the guiding principle that we ask you adopt as you begin reading this book and engaging in experiential learning. The aspects of experiential learning that we observe our students manifest, and which are most transformative to their learning and growth, are their abilities to actively engage, explore, personally connect, seek out, and reflect on the meaning in their experience. It is through a posture of engagement, curiosity, and awareness, where we make the most meaning from our experiences. This is a posture that is dramatically different from what we often see in our daily lives and interactions, where we will most likely see people looking down—occupied on their phones and iPads—missing opportunities to relate, participate, and soak in their surroundings. Growing and developing is at the core of experiential learning, and, in order to maximize this, we want to be sure that your approach allows for you to "take it all in"—to be active and open, to interconnect and integrate, and to be reflective in your learning.

Experiential Learning

This book is written for students to help them frame and understand experiential learning so that it can contribute to their overall learning and distinguish their goals and outcomes. So what exactly is experiential learning? "Experiential learning is a philosophy and methodology in which educators purposefully engage with students in direct experience and focused reflection in order to increase knowledge, develop skills, and clarify values" (Association for Experiential Education, 2011).

Experiential learning that is intentional, integrated, and reflective, and which connects training both in the classroom and through cross-cultural experiences is imperative in helping the students gain the skills, habits of mind, knowledge, and human understanding needed to thrive and contribute in contemporary society. There are many types of experiential learning programs—cooperative education, internships, service learning, study abroad, and research-based opportunities. Fundamental to this learning process is the realization that in an interconnected world community, what you do (and don't do) affects the lives of others and the vitality of our shared humanity and civic sustainability.

We come to writing this book from our collective 20 years of experience as cooperative education faculty members at Northeastern University (NEU) which has historically had a strong emphasis on experiential learning and prepares its students personally and professionally for the reality they will face after graduation. In fact, Northeastern was one of the first universities to incorporate experiential learning by establishing cooperative education as a signature aspect of their education program. In our Cooperative Education Program,

1

students alternate academic and experiential work-place assignments called "co-ops" that provide the opportunity for them to apply their classroom learning in "real world" settings. Typically, students' "co-ops" are 4–6 month placements in organizations that are related to their academic studies and/or field of interest. In addition, our university has been a forerunner in global experiential learning through their Dialogue of Civilizations Program in which faculty lead small groups of students on short-term work and study opportunities.

At Northeastern, we (Dr. Joani LaMachia and Jonathan Andrew) have been involved in experiential learning primarily in our roles as Cooperative Education Faculty. We have also been Faculty Co-leaders on short-term summer study abroad programs and advised students participating in research- and community-based service learning and partnerships. Working as faculty while teaching and advising students for the past 10 years in the International Affairs Cooperative Education Program, we have witnessed the impact experiential learning can have on students' development and opportunities. We have observed how experiential learning has prepared students for a rapidly changing world, created readiness for employment, and helped to develop civic capacity for tackling the social and political challenges that they will experience in their life.

One of the things that we most enjoy about our positions as Cooperative Education Faculty within International Affairs is helping students to learn by doing, through hands-on involvement in their fields of study. Time and time again we see and hear from students that going beyond the classroom—meeting people in diverse places from various perspectives and seeing how issues play out by working with them collaboratively in the community or workplace—presents ideal opportunities to study and grapple with local and global realities.

What we have observed in our faculty advisor roles over the past 10 years is that students' experiences are less campus centric and increasingly nontraditional (beyond the campus classroom)—you are learning online, in various parts of the world on study abroad, in workplaces, on internships, in think tanks conducting research, on campuses that are internationalized to provide opportunities to exchange with peers from local, national, and global locations. Certainly, the once ivory tower that held students on campus for 4 years to be steeped in theory and the classics now looks quite different. In LaMachia's (2017) research conducted on global learning and citizenship, one faculty interviewed articulated it this way: "There's nothing I can say to you, no article you can read to prepare you for the experience of working in the places that we go—the sights, smells, touch, engagement, human contact can only be felt when you are there, and it's touching on the affective learning, not just the cognitive." A student interviewed voiced a similar sentiment: "You can gain these skills here [on campus] but I feel like it's going to take years to have that nuanced approach; I felt it happened with me much more quickly when I'm thrown into a situation." (LaMachia, 2017) Living in an interconnected and global society, experiential learning takes on a critical and important role in helping students to gain greater exposure and deeper understanding of complex issues, diverse peoples, and various contexts. In order to approach learning in this changing world, you will have to be more active in your own educational process and open yourself up to exploring the wide array of possibilities and opportunities that present themselves to you during your lifetime.

As such, one of the big challenges that we see in higher education and beyond is how to maneuver in a global workplace and society that will be more fast-paced, interconnected, and automated. In education, specifically, the issue of automation is widely recognized and debated. According to the American Association of Colleges and Universities (AAC&U, 2007) college and universities have begun revisiting their education protocols in response to the huge changes that globalization, increased technology, and automation have brought to workplaces and greater society. Global experiential learning has become a key aspect of almost every college and university's mission statement and is, indeed, one of the top priorities within higher education (AAC&U, 2007). Some see automation as a threat to jobs; others see it as an opportunity. Whatever you think about it, it is clear that this trend will continue to build with huge implications for education, the workplace, and beyond.

Given NEU's history and experience in cooperative education and preparing students for careers and the workplace, it is not a surprise that Northeastern's President Joseph Aoun was one of the earliest writers contributing to this issue in his book *Robot Proof—Higher Education in the Age of Artificial Intelligence*. In his book, Dr. Aoun addresses the issues of automation, artificial intelligence and robotics, and the need to consider these in educating our students. The key to becoming robot-proof, he suggests, is to focus on human characteristics that machines cannot duplicate, such as being innovative, entrepreneurial, and culturally agile, adaptable, and global. "If the world is changing and there are new fields being created constantly, we are going to become obsolete," he said. "Therefore we need to reeducate ourselves, reskill ourselves, and upskill ourselves. This is going to be essential. To do so, higher education institutions must embrace the notion of lifelong learning and provide programs that are personalized and customizable and meet learners' needs wherever they are" (Aoun, 2017). Also, it is important to note that the future of the workplace will require that students not just develop knowledge and technical skills but also know how to apply them in diverse contexts. The ability to determine when it is appropriate to use machines versus when to use personal connection that only humans can provide is becoming an increasingly important area of knowledge and understanding. In our book, we hope to illustrate ways that technology can serve to complement our human strengths in a way that allows for us to progress beyond what humans or technology can do alone.

One of the aspects of learning that we emphasize in our role as cooperative education faculty is that living in an interconnected and global society, understanding the myriad of global issues and related historical contexts is a fundamental challenge for you and critical for your personal, professional, and civic development. As the world has become more interdependent and complex, it has become even more vital that students widen their lenses to be able to integrate multiple perspectives. The promotion of inquiry-based, experiential learning that engages students as social scientists in their fields of interest and study is essential to increasing your problem-solving capacity, developing higher-order skills, understanding how to work as part of a team, and fostering an open mindset that makes way for lifelong learning.

In considering the impact of globalization, emerging industry trends, and the rapid changes of technology, we recognize our responsibility in aiding you in making meaningful transitions from classroom to workplace to global society. In order to do so, providing opportunities to deconstruct your learning is critical because it is possible to have an experience yet miss the meaning. Thus, integrating reflection as a central aspect of your learning and experience is necessary to help fully process and digest what learning occurred, how it changed your thinking, and why it was important.

How We Found Our Way to Experiential Learning

So who are we, how did we come into experiential learning, and what are our motivations in writing this book? We begin with a quote from Brene Brown to frame our stories.

> *New Worlds are important, but you can't just describe them. Give us the stories that make up the universe.*
> *No matter how wild and weird the new world might be, we'll see ourselves in the stories.* (Brown, 2017)

This quote by Brene Brown captures a sentiment that we hope to convey through the diverse and lively narratives in this book as well as our stories here. The stories presented are not meant to be a reference of how to get from point A to point B to the 'perfect' or 'ideal' student, worker, citizen, or learning experience but rather to provide prompts to consider the small, incremental, and myriad of ways in which we make meaning from our experiences in the "new worlds" that we encounter. We will use this as a jumping-off point to share our own stories and thinking about experiential learning.

Joani's Story:

Who doesn't remember the joy of field trips, those initial voyages to "new worlds" in our young lives? As an elementary school student, the thought of going on an adventure away from school and the classroom was thrilling. Things were more relaxed, yet more exciting. We stepped out of our usual patterns and routines to explore something new. We had "buddies" who we were often assigned to sit with on the bus and to stay with once we had reached our destination. On the bus or while walking, we would talk about our expectations, what we anticipated, and perhaps share something we knew about where we were going. One field trip in particular stands out in my mind—visiting the birthplace of John F. Kennedy. We had studied Kennedy in the classroom and learned the details of his life and of his many challenges and accomplishments as the president. In our discussions with family members and others, we remember talking about him, and how his vision and values reflected our own. Going to Kennedy's house and visiting there, seeing where he lived, the rooms of his house, imagining him playing in the neighborhood with siblings and friends, walking to school, eating dinner with his family, allowed us to see Kennedy in a different way than the books we had read and research we had done. We saw Kennedy as ourselves and related to him as a young boy with similar activities and routines. That is what field trips do; they bring us right to the place to experience it for ourselves, to make a personal connection, to compare our previous thoughts and assumptions with what we actually find, and to reimagine something.

When I reflect on my own learning and teaching, I realize I have always had a tendency toward the field trip approach to learning. This is not to say that the classroom, theory, reading books, or attending lectures are not important. Speaking for myself, when I tally all the years I have "been in school" as a teacher or learner, it is by far the most time I have devoted to anything in my life thus far. Yet classroom learning is just one fragment of where and how we learn. Learning happens everywhere—at home, walking down the street, in the grocery store, talking with a friend, working in the garden, literally everywhere. In discussions with my own students, some of the most powerful learning experiences that they share with me occurred outside of the classroom. In education, more and more we are coming to understand, appreciate, and value learning that extends beyond the classroom and integrates the academic with the experiential.

This book for me grew out of those initial elementary school field trips and understanding even then as a very young person, how learning beyond the classroom had an impact on how I understood myself, others, and events and issues in the world. This extended learning helped me to apply and integrate the knowledge and understanding from the classroom. My own fascination and gravitation toward learning from experiences continued on from those elementary school days as I sought out opportunities to go places, do new things, travel, learn a new language, talk with someone I didn't know, and basically seek out learning wherever. I brought this approach to my role as a parent, my teaching as an ESL instructor, my work developing health and literacy programs, my elected position as a school committee member, completing my doctoral work focused on integrating global citizenship learning in undergraduate education, and, eventually, my role as cooperative education faculty at Northeastern where I work directly with students in experiential learning, and with great excitement now to the writing of this book and sharing this with you.

Jon's Story:

Moving back in with your parents after you graduate from college is a humbling experience. When I attended college my goal was to ace the classes, attain the degree, get a well-paying job after graduation, and live independently. Moving back in with my parents was not exactly the vision of a successful education. Neither was the tens of thousands of dollars of student loan debt that the starting salary could scarcely cover in those initial years. Those were, however, the unintended outcomes of the liberal arts degree and limited opportunities to integrate the theory with practice. It took me a good four to five years after I graduated to understand how much my degree actually mattered to my sense of purpose, eventual career path, and personal moments of success. No one could tell me how my deep interests in anthropology, intercultural communication, citizen diplomacy, languages, writing, and travel could actually prepare me for anything professionally tangible. I had to find out on my own. No one was there to help me reflect on how to make decisions along a career path from paperboy to landscaper to librarian assistant to fast food worker to line cook to pizza maker to bookseller to digital mapping technician to regional director for high school student exchanges to graduate school career counselor to study abroad administrator to higher education academic program administrator to experiential educator/advisor/faculty member to who knows what next. The transitions came from a lot of feeling in limbo, attention to my confusions and misunderstandings, strong family and personal supports, a loving partner, lots of advice from unexpected places, more student loans, and a general ability to be adaptable, open-minded, and attentive to the changes happening around me.

When I look back on these transitions, I still see the person I was in those moments, in those jobs—sometimes carefree, mostly living paycheck to paycheck, not always strategic, but taking opportunities when they presented themselves. The seminal turning points in those career transitions came from recognizing when my interests and studies kept coming back into my life, being humble enough to know when to ask for help, asking good questions, listening attentively, deepening important relationships, and showing gratitude even when it is hard. Opportunity follows those who do these things and sometimes appears when you are not looking for it. As an educator, my hope is to be able to pay it forward by helping the readers of this book with tools, resources, and guidance on what to attend to when facing difficult transitions in their lives, professions, and education. My experiences working with students have taught me that no experience is insignificant and that spending time studying what you love is never time wasted. Understanding what skills and knowledge you develop in those studies and finding a way to transfer them to your social life or career, including your personal and professional ambitions, is oftentimes the hard part.

This book is intended to help you with the hard part. With all of this in mind, we have compiled student narratives, faculty and employer insights, research from the field, case studies, classroom simulations, and inquiry-based activities that foster experiential learning and related skill sets and perspectives to allow our readers to actively participate and engage fully as learner, worker, and citizen in the global society. Specifically, in writing this book we hope to provide possibilities for students to *look up*, to step outside of themselves and their places of familiarity, to examine and reflect upon their role in diverse environments, to offer tools for them as students to deconstruct their learning and contextualize knowledge so as to add practical value, and, overall, to foster the notion of themselves as "social scientists in the field" gaining knowledge, perspective, agency, and purpose. We would like this book to be able to reach those students who are grasping for meaning during their time in college. We would like this book to provide advice and a strategy by which to find a way to practically apply and continue to use the skills and knowledge gained in college in a way that is personally fulfilling and meaningful. Most of all, we would like for this book to help students early in college to prepare for postgraduation in order to feel more empowered and confident as they continue to be curious, and learn and grow through all their experiences beyond college and university.

In a sense, this is one of those "all the things we wish someone had told us about life and college" books, which makes it equally exciting to write. Before you read this book, we encourage you to take a moment to stop, look up from the book, and think. Think about what college can be for you. Why are you choosing college? Answer it in the context of what is it that you want from college. This is your opportunity and your chance to set your own intention and expectations. Think about these important considerations as you begin to read. We believe that the core areas defined in this book are key to developing and supporting your lifelong learning goals and the necessary personal, professional, and civic skills to thrive in our interconnected and ever-changing global society.

How This book Is Structured—Outline of Chapters and Learning Activities

This book is modeled on the process through which we prepare our students at NEU for a path of professional, social, and civic engagement through lifelong experiential learning. The chapters of the book are ordered similarly to the approach we bring to our freshman orientation and sophomore professional development classes, which are designed to prepare students for engagement in their experiential learning and professional development programs during their second through fourth/fifth years at the university. Our model is driven toward helping students to open themselves up to new experiences, integrate their in- and out-of-classroom learning experiences, and then, through reflection, better understand the connections between theory and practice. We hope that our strategies and approach will help students cultivate a set of attitudes, habits of mind, and skills that develop into a flexible and adaptable sense of self with the personal agency to actively engage with, innovate within, and positively influence new communities of practice. By interacting with and engaging in the activities throughout this book, either independently or in a classroom setting, our hope is that you will assume a sense of intentionality and ownership in your education, career, and civic engagements.

How to Read/Engage with This Book

As we are experiential education faculty members and advisors, we would like for this book to also be experiential for you. The concepts, activities, and prompts you will find while reading through this book have been designed with other cooperative education faculty at Northeastern. Our hope is that as you read the book you will take time to pause, reflect, and engage with the material from your own unique perspective. This is how this book can be practical for you and help you to make the most out of your time at your own school and institution and beyond. Many of the materials you find here will help you in the development of your professional portfolio and also to foster the mindset of a lifelong learner and active, engaged citizen.

Chapter 1: Fostering Self-Awareness

In Chapter 1, we will demonstrate the importance of self-awareness, self-authorship, and metacognition (knowing how we learn and know things), on how you can become a more engaged and successful student and leader. What we have found to be most effective for students to obtain a clarity of self and purpose through education is to take steps through reflection to become more self-aware in our social, academic, civic, and professional engagements. This requires a regular interpretation of how values, attitudes, motivations, and beliefs are applied through activities and action rather than passive "absorption of knowledge." This cataloging of experiences helps us to better interpret the shaping of our values and perspectives while also prompting a need to better understand our emotions, vulnerabilities, routines, and priorities. In addition, this process better frames how we view others and how others view us; it is the prioritization of face-to-face interactions that leads to improvement on situational awareness and more accuracy in our reflective questioning. This is the starting point for this book and for how you can best utilize and leverage your college experience for your personal and professional future beyond the institution.

Chapter 2: Engaging in Adaptive Decision-Making

In Chapter 2, we will review how we work with students in our professional development course on the job search and preparation for society and the workplace, and how we lead them through activities and exercises designed to help them examine their motivations, goals, and intended outcomes of their experiences. This balancing of short- and long-term outcomes is intended to develop an intentionality in how students contemplate the development of skills and knowledge. This balancing of goals and priorities helps students to self-evaluate and examine the difference between intuitive gut reactions and adapting to changes in circumstances with logical thought. For the purpose of this book, we frame this concept as adaptive decision making.

By reading this chapter, our hope is that you will begin a process of examining your own motivations, intuition, and choices as it relates to making life decisions that influence your growth and social, civic, or professional engagements. With this chapter we will introduce you to ways in which you can examine your intuitions, emotions, routines, influencers, and perspectives on change that shape your sense of purpose and direct your decisions and choices. We hope that through your engagement in this chapter's activities you will begin to better understand how and when to trust your gut decisions, take risks, exercise patience in relation to your emotional responses, accept the realities of your situation, and learn how to develop fault-tolerant thinking. This chapter will help you to ask the right questions to inform your decisions, and how to best-balance trade-offs when managing your internal cost–benefit analyses.

Chapter 3: Creating and Belonging to a Mentoring Community

In Chapter 3, we will move from maximizing our decision points to maximizing the relationships we create, nurture, and maintain as we navigate our life transitions. For the purpose of this book we call friends, critics, and advocates, our mentors. Mentors come in many forms, but it is essential for us to grow interpersonally, professionally, and intellectually to have these people in our lives.

This chapter will provide you with ways to understand how developing personal and professional relationships and belonging to a mentoring community can help you to better understand yourself. We will provide you with proven methods for how to effectively seek out and build trust with these individuals. It is through these mentorships that students begin to understand how to develop empathy, embrace a gracious approach to all social engagements, and build a professional and social life that can be both fulfilling and joyful.

Chapter 4: Navigating Diverse Learning Environments

In Chapter 4, you will be prompted to further examine your environments to better understand how your sense of place influences your understanding of your identity and will begin to help you reimagine all of your environments as places of learning. Throughout your college lives you will encounter numerous new, exciting and challenging environments. Our hope is that through reading this chapter you will begin to see that every environment you navigate through is a place of potential learning. It is through the transitions from one environment to another that we see students transferring skills and tacit knowledge to create imagined worlds that build spaces into places and influence how they construct their identities and worldviews. It is by navigating these new environments mindfully that you begin to better understand how you contextualize knowledge through social interactions, observation, imitation, and practice.

In our work with students, we use workplaces and new cultures as a catalyst to help students understand how to make meaning of their experiences by shadowing, listening to, and developing trust with others. For this to happen, it is important that you engage directly in new experiences with diverse groups of people actively. In this chapter, we will review how examining our assumptions helps us to develop a sense of shared responsibility to engage as stewards within all of our communities of learning and practice.

Chapter 5: Let's Talk! Boundaryless Communication

In Chapter 5, we examine the ways in which we co-construct meaning with others as our communities become globally interconnected and interactions with people across cultural, national, and organizational boundaries increase. As we traverse our lived experiences and collaborations with others, it is important that we become more self-aware of our own interpretative frameworks, assumptions, perceptions, and misperceptions. In this chapter, we explore how implicit and explicit meaning is embedded within our verbal and nonverbal communications with others and provide strategies through which we can better listen, understand, and be understood. Implicit in this is to approach all interactions as an intercultural interaction, and we will provide frames by which to explore our abilities to empathize with others by being willing to shift perspectives.

Here we will introduce you to methods by which to develop your interpersonal skill sets and communicate more effectively across boundaries. At the conclusion of the chapter, you will find techniques for improving your abilities to work effectively as a team member and enhance your professional interviewing skills. We will show you how to effectively build trust, deepen interpersonal relationships, and engage respectfully with others according to the context in which we are collaborating and communicating.

Chapter 6: Developing Agency for Ethical and Impactful Professional and Civic Engagement

Chapter 6 is the call to action. All too often, we have found in our own experiences from college and in the experiences of our students that there can be a disconnect in how what one learns in the college classroom can be applied practically to life and the world beyond college. It is our hope that by engaging with the material in the preceding chapters you will already be cultivating a sense of purpose for how you intend to make an impact in your shared experiences and communities. This chapter will ideally compel you to take those steps to translate purpose into action and develop strategies for making meaning in all of your college/university activities and learning across a lifetime.

In this chapter, we will demonstrate through our own experiences with students how you can leverage the awareness of your values, skills, and abilities to imaginatively and actively shape your communities. This chapter is designed to help you make sense of it all and shows that it is possible to both find success and meaning in your life both during and beyond college. We will show that it is through the understanding of ourselves, communities, and relationships that we will find the means and courage to make responsible, ethically informed, purposeful, and collaborative steps to positively change our society. Our hope is that this chapter will provide you with new strategies and ways of thinking that will help you along that path as a unique agent of social change.

LOOK UP-Reality Checks

At the conclusion of each chapter, you will find an activities section called "LOOK UP: Reality Check." These are example situations that highlight current issues or stories of unique developments that are impacting or changing the greater society. These "Reality Checks" are intended to make the concepts presented in each chapter relevant and experiential in nature. They are designed to prompt a change in perspective and also offer the opportunity to more deeply engage in an experience yourself. These are opportunities to look up from the book, ground yourself in your own lived experience, and find a way to more authentically experience the concepts we are presenting here.

Toolkit—Look Up, Listen Up, Join Up, Act Up

In addition, as we conclude each chapter, we will identify key takeaways along with an invitation to visit the Toolkit at the end of the book. In the Toolkit you will find resources, activities, and tools that we use with Northeastern students for personal/professional/civic development and reflection. These materials provide you with instructions on how to develop a personal and professional portfolio that will enable you to fully engage in the global workplace and society. The activities have been designed to help you be more intentional in your learning and experiences in and out of the classroom. Engage with these activities as you need them, depending on the types of experiences you are having at your place of learning.

Advising Sessions

In addition, in the Toolkit we have included "Advising Sessions" that are modeled on our own advising techniques with our students at NEU. We recommend that in order to get the most out of these sessions, you should first answer the questions posed in a substantive way yourself and then bring them to a trusted mentor, advisor, friend, and so on to discuss and open yourself to reimagine your beliefs around these concepts. We have found that it is through facilitative discussions that include agreement and critique with our students opens new pathways for learning and action. For this, it is important to find someone who will equally believe in you and be honest with you to ground your approach to your next endeavors. So get out there, be courageous, and connect with someone else whom you trust.

So get ready for an interactive experience, and we look forward to helping you look up, act up, and join up to set you on a path of engaged and mindful lifelong learning!

Works Cited

Association of American Colleges and Universities. (2007). *College learning for the new global century: A report from the national leadership council for liberal education and America's promise.* Washington, DC: Association of American Colleges and Universities.

Association for Experiential Education (2011). *What is Experiential Learning?* Retrieved from http://www.aee.org/about/whatIsEE

Aoun, J. (2017). *Robot proof—higher education in age of artificial intelligence.* Cambridge, MA: MIT Press.

Brown, B. (2017). *Braving the wilderness: The quest for true belonging and the courage to stand alone.* New York, NY: Random House.

LaMachia, J. (2017) *Integrating Global Citizenship Learning in Undergraduate Education.* https://repository.library.northeastern.edu/files/neu:cj82nr13g/fulltext.pdf

1

Fostering Self-Awareness

The Importance of – Tell Me About Yourself

You have something to say that no one else can say. Your history, your unique sensibilities, your sense of place, and your language bestow upon you a singular authority. You have your own set of life themes, habits, and ways of organizing yourself into a coherent "I." All of this individuality that is you, properly understood and clearly presented, is a tremendous gift to the world. (Pipher, 2006)

The above reference by Mary Pipher encourages individuality and authenticity in presenting ourselves. In her book, *Writing to Change the World*, Pipher emphasizes the power of words and the importance of finding our unique voice and expressing ourselves authentically in order to actively participate in and contribute to the greater society. Related to Pipher's advice, we begin this section on self-awareness with an often-asked interview question that we review with students—Tell me about yourself. At Northeastern University, we teach the Introduction to Professional Development course to students as part of their preparation for cooperative education and transitioning to the workplace. One aspect of the course deals with helping to students respond to interview questions and converse with employers. When meeting in our first advising meetings with students it might go something like this. "Nice to meet you, so why don't we start this with you telling me a little bit about yourself"; student replies, "Umm . . . so . . . what should I tell you? What would you like to know?" We reply, "Just tell me a little about yourself." What follows is typically a list of name, major, hometown, accomplishments from high school, list of previous jobs held, volunteer experiences, study abroad experiences, grade point average, a list of extracurricular activities, the languages spoken, the technical knowledge, and so on . This simple question can be tricky to address and calls upon you to be authentic and articulate, which is important information if you are applying for a job, but not if you are in a social situation. Often students opt for less of a personal narrative and more of a generalizable list of accomplishments that would look great on a resume or college application but don't always provide context, unique information, or sense of personality. The question does require a bit of navigation between understanding who you are, how others view you, and what information would be useful for your counterpart to know. How you answer this question confirms not just what you can recall about what you have done but demonstrates a relational awareness of your audience. It also in many ways makes you vulnerable to revealing too much, too little, something that would welcome judgment, or even deeper insights into your values, beliefs, and sense of self-worth.

In thinking about a balanced answer to the question of telling a bit about yourself, we can reflect on what it is that we want others to know about us. What is unique to me/my lived experience? What are my values? What is important to me? How do I want to engage with others or with my work? David Brooks (2015)

© Orianna Timsit

in his book *The Road to Character* presents an interesting way to think about these questions. Through the narratives of his book, he presents, promotes, and puts a focus on the deeper values that inform our lives. He challenges us to better balance our "resume virtues" (achieving wealth, fame, and status) with our "eulogy virtues" (kindness, humility honesty, and faithfulness). In thinking about this sentiment, what occurred to us was the importance in helping students to think both about what they wish their legacy to be—as part of their college, workplace, community, and global experiences—and what it is that they want people to remember about them—their contributions, values, participation, interactions, and way of being. In our Introduction to Professional Development course at Northeastern University, we begin by helping students assess their skills, abilities, habits of mind, internal and external motivations, as well as core values and beliefs. Our goal is not only to assist you in using this information to develop your professional resume, craft a cover letter or personal statement, and prepare for job interviews but also to provide the time and support for you to really think about who you are, what is important to you, what you hope to do, what you possess, and what you need to be able to move along your path—as a student, worker, and citizen.

For these reasons, it is not surprising that "Tell me about Yourself" is one of the most standard professional interview questions. The question helps you begin to make meaning out of your experiences, better define your inclinations, examine your social relationships and affiliations, and explore your sense of purpose. Through self-inquiry, students are encouraged to move beyond simply demonstrating a collected record of affiliations, accomplishments, and travels, toward a more expressive construction of how these experiences confirm interests, demonstrate how interpersonal relationships are nurtured, contextualize how skills were acquired, and show how personal values are put into action. In the process, you realize that your achievements alone are not evidence that you are qualified for a job, college, graduate school, or community, but that it is your ability to articulate what you learned through these achievements and relate this to others that determines your preparedness for new opportunities. What it comes down to is that "tell me about yourself" is a rapport-building opportunity and an offer from a counterpart to forge a relationship through robust dialogue, sharing of values and motivations, and mutual meaning making.

Self-awareness does not always begin with the self, but with situational awareness in regards to a relationship with another. When we teach self-awareness in this way, it is showing that personal and professional development is less about building confidence in yourself and more about building confidence in how well you understand and develop trust with others. It is moving beyond the experiences you have had to connect with the needs and experiences of other people. In most cases, answering the "Tell me about yourself" line of questioning effectively requires you to move beyond "what you did" to expressing a sense of purpose of "why you did it," "why it is important to where you are today," and "how it relates to others." A good starting point for fostering self-awareness is to move beyond the life events themselves and examine the ways we interpret those events and the relationships we create and maintain in the course of life events.

Self-Cultivation and Confrontation—Building Character and Depth

I made a huge mistake that could have affected every single employee in the office. The worst part of it was that I lied about making the mistake. Then, there came a point when I couldn't lie about it and had to be honest. I had to confront it myself. That was the most humbling experience I have ever had. Realizing that no matter what happens you still have to be forthcoming was an incredible personal and professional lesson. (Student Respondent, 2018)

This student reflection illustrates how confronting a weakness enabled the student to learn a valuable personal and professional lesson. One of the key benefits of participating in experiential learning beyond the classroom is the opportunity to cultivate not just our intellectual growth but our moral development. Part of what happens when you "put yourself out there" in diverse environments and situations is that through various challenges and situations you begin to better understand your limitations, challenges, and weaknesses. David Brooks talks about developing "intellectual humility," which he refers to as "accurate self-awareness from a distance." Brooks (2015) describes the process as "moving over the course of one's life from the adolescent's close-up view of yourself, in which you fill the whole canvas, to a landscape view in which you see, from a wider perspective, your strengths and weaknesses, your connections and dependencies, and the role you play in the larger story." He raises an interesting point in terms of how we tend to look at our lives through the external world and, therefore, see things as external achievements, such as having an impact on a person or situation, establishing a successful company, and/or doing something to better an organization/community. He states that people with a humble approach tend to their internal challenges and inner work, in addition to their external accomplishments. People with this approach, he says, acknowledge that they have certain talents but also certain weaknesses and see that to fully develop, they must deal with their individual struggles, temptations, and weaknesses. This process of self-cultivation, in which we build character and depth, is fully realized through self-confrontation, where we challenge and work through our moral failings and, as Brooks describes, "become strong in the weak places." (Brooks, 2015).

Interestingly, an interview question that often presents a challenge to students is when they are asked about their weaknesses. It is a rather odd thing to have to talk about our challenges in the context of a situation where we are trying to be the "winning candidate." But what we have seen over the years in guiding students through their co-op searches and job placements is that one of the most important aspects of finding your "right place" is authenticity. We are all human and none of us are perfect. Being able to speak of our abilities, the areas we want to improve, and both the successes and the challenges that we have had is critical because it helps us connect and find the places that will help us to develop both internally and externally. As Brooks says, there is something democratic about life viewed in this way—it doesn't matter your background, or your position, your status, or lack thereof—the most important thing is that you are willing to address the full spectrum of your growth as a human being, flaws and all. This is a great moment to stop, *look up*, and think about this opportunity to develop yourself—what are your areas of weakness? In what areas do you need further development? How could you proactively attend to these? What sort of job, community, or campus activity might offer ways for you to work on these identified areas? Addressing the combination of self-awareness and humility allows you the opportunity to truly flourish as individuals, workers, and citizens.

Clarity of Self and Purpose

My experience abroad changed me by making me aware of who I wanted to be and the type of lifestyle I eventually want in life. There are all these different ways to live in the world, and for me, going abroad really helped me to develop the idea of what I personally liked and what I didn't like apart from what a culture had told me before. (Student Respondent, 2018)

This student's reflection on how work experience abroad provided greater clarity about herself and her sense of purpose provides a great example of how you can foster self-awareness by reflecting on your learning and experiences. Self-awareness is an exceptionally important lifelong ability. As Daniel Goleman (1995) outlines in *Emotional Intelligence: Why It Can Matter More Than IQ*, self-awareness relates to "the sense of recognizing feelings and building a vocabulary for them, and seeing the links between thoughts, feelings and reactions; knowing if thoughts or feelings are ruling a decision; seeing the consequences of alternative choices; . . . recognizing your strengths and weaknesses, and seeing yourself in a positive but realistic light." It is a quality that is highly desired for those in organizational leadership positions. In a recent study by Tasha Eurich on *What Self-awareness Really Is (and how to cultivate it)*, she cites existing research, which suggests that when we see ourselves clearly, we are more confident and more creative, and we make sounder decisions, build stronger relationships, and communicate more effectively. We are better workers who get more promotions, and we are more effective leaders with more satisfied employees and more profitable companies (Eurich, 2018). Eurich and her colleagues synthesized their findings to come up with an overarching definition of self-awareness. Across the studies on self-awareness they examined, they found two main categories. The first category they cited as *internal self-awareness*, which represented how clearly we see our own values, passions, and aspirations, how we fit with our environment, how we handle reactions, and how we influences others. In addition, they found that internal self-awareness correlated with higher job and relationship satisfaction, personal and social control, as well as overall happiness. However, poor self-awareness is related to anxiety and depression.

The second category they cited, *external self-awareness*, had to do with how other people view us, in terms of the factors listed in the first category. An interesting finding from the study showed that the greater experience and power people hold, the more likely they are to overestimate their skills and abilities and refrain from seeking disconfirming evidence and questioning their assumptions. Someone who is self-aware better understands how their actions impact their employees and coworkers and can better interpret emotional responses in social situations. In addition, self-awareness has been linked to improved relationships, enhanced skill development, improved confidence, and stronger decision-making abilities. For our purposes, with our professional development class at Northeastern, it is a critical first phase of the class for the students to better understand their personal and professional values, motivations, and sensibilities.

Effective education begins with clarity of self and purpose. In cooperative education and experiential learning programs, our purpose is to prepare students for making the transition to and then actively participating in workplaces, communities, and the greater global society. Guiding students through the initial process of self-reflection and inquiry is an important foundation for continued learning and development. We begin this process by getting you to identify and articulate personal abilities, motivations, and professional interests. Students begin by reflecting backward and forward in terms of their self and the wider society—*What have I done? What can I do? What do I want to do? What needs to be done?* This process of clarifying purpose helps you to better understand your values, skills, and competencies. In addition, it provides insights by understanding the communities you have lived in and the knowledge you have gained. We then examine how this connects to what you want to study, who you want to be, and what civic activities you wish to engage in. How can you then choose experiences that will help you move in this direction, and identify tools to do so?

Through your experiences and meaning-making processes, students begin to comprehend that self-inquiry is an important step in better understanding how we learn, how we engage with others, and how these steps can lead to greater confidence and better outcomes. We all carry ideas and patterns of thought and preconceived notions about the nature of the world. Learning how to expand, transform, challenge, and ultimately reintegrate these ideas and patterns of thought through experiential learning and reflection is one cornerstone of developing self-awareness. At Northeastern University, we have mentored and observed hundreds of students as they reimagine and reconstruct their previously held habits of mind. Through this process, students are encouraged to identify, analyze, and begin to address their fears and vulnerabilities, which then allows them to move forward confidently and to reduce stress and anxiety.

The Impact of –
Self-Monitoring and Situational Awareness

Each time I travel to a new place, or walk into a new situation, I am more confident—mostly because there's not too much you can throw at me that will surprise me anymore. Traveling and living abroad has helped me gain confidence in myself, and prepared me for new situations. (Student Respondent, 2018)

Our students at Northeastern overwhelmingly cite an improvement in self-awareness and confidence as one of the top learning outcomes from their first professional co-op experiences. It is through these experiences that students frame their understanding of the context of the workplace and the expectations of the employers. It also provides a valuable opportunity for students to understand whether or not they are a good fit for a particular field of work, which helps them align their studies and career pursuits with their personal value systems and ambitions. Conversely, students without prior professional experiences often have a low level of certainty about workplace standards and expectations. This can lead to difficulties for students in matching their values and experiences to employer values and needs when preparing for their first job search and interview process. Preparing students for these new situations (job interviews, networking fairs, employer panels, etc.) is a process of helping students understand how to self-monitor. By self-monitoring we are referring to a person's ability to adapt their behaviors and articulate their values, knowledge, skills, motivations, attitudes, and beliefs for new social contexts. "High self-monitors try to fit into different social situations. Low self-monitors do not" (Twenge & Campbell, 2017).

To better understand your approach to self-monitoring, think of places where you self-present. This could be on your social media page or blog, in class with your professors, or it could be at a career networking event. On social media, where you have a potentially broad audience, how much effort do you put into controlling your online identity or personas? Do you have different types of accounts for friends versus the ones you would want your parents or future employers see? For face-to-face situations, how much attention do you put into your style of dress, your hygiene, and your nonverbal body language and facial expressions? How does this vary for friends, family, professors, potential employers, and so on? Reflecting on these kind of questions will help you to know how to be more in control of your self-presentation according to the context.

We have found that coaching improves a students' approach to self-monitoring as they address challenging and unfamiliar experiences, such as a first job interview. It can be very empowering for a student to have someone there to objectively critique them while simultaneously fostering belief in them during these critical learning moments. It is through this combination of experience and mentorship that students begin to better understand themselves, their strengths and weaknesses, and the impact of their personality and behaviors on others in a social setting. For us, this is a crucial starting point in a students' personal and professional development during their time at the university. We practice the refinement of these skills through individual and group activities on presenting themselves with an elevator pitch, crafting professional statements for LinkedIn, writing cover letters that align to specific job descriptions, and preparing for interviews (see the toolkit for specific activities and examples).

Through these activities, students gain valuable practice and awareness through self-monitoring and identifying the values, needs, and goals of their audience, employer, or counterparts. In the course of these activities, they are challenged to find specific examples of experiences and activities they have had that can demonstrate their skills and values as they relate to the needs or expectations of their target audience. By gaining practice in refining their approach to these activities they are also slowly defining what is important to them and their life goals. In addition, by being able to gauge the reactions of others to their modes of self-presentation they begin to recognize how others perceive them and their strengths and weaknesses in various social situations.

Self-Awareness and Self-Authorship

We can all think of people in our lives who seem to be in full control of their destiny, who are comfortable in their own skin, and who can articulate and defend their beliefs to others. And we can also think of (perhaps many more) people who seem to be floating through life, letting things happen to them, good or bad, and who are unsure of who they are and who they want to be. In the field of higher education, we talk about a concept called "self-authorship," which at its heart refers to the process of making intentional, informed choices about what you want to do and who you want to be. As the name suggests, self-authorship is the process of writing your own story, as opposed to having it written for you. Those who are adept at self-authorship are better able to choose and defend their values and beliefs, rather than simply inherit them from their family or environment, and they ultimately feel more ownership and pride over their identity (Magolda, 2001).

The process of becoming a better self-author begins with self-awareness and reflection around three main ideas:

1. *What is your relationship to knowledge?* How do you decide what, if anything, represents "truth"? Who do you consider experts, and how do you weigh competing information? How do you construct and evaluate your own beliefs about the world?
2. *What is your relationship to yourself?* What values guide you? Do the choices you make typically match those values? Does your internal "sense of self" match the identity you present to others?
3. *What is your relationship with others?* Do you feel that you are able to make deep, meaningful relationships with a wide range of other people? Are you able to connect with others without being overly focused on needing their approval? Do you give as much as you get from relationships, and vice versa?

These are not easy questions, and your answers will change as you move throughout different phases of your life. However, the sooner you start and the more deeply you think about those questions, the better able you will be to be an active author of your own experience and identity.

Needless to say, self-authorship is a quality that is highly linked to feelings of happiness and fulfillment with one's life (Magolda, 2008), and many schools and universities use self-authorship as a grounding theory when creating learning environments for students. We at Northeastern have developed an initiative called SAIL, or Self-Authored Integrated Learning, which is geared toward having students think more deeply about what they learn from their daily experiences—classes, co-ops, study abroad—and also conversations with mentors, co-curricular events, in the residence and dining halls, and even internal "ah-ha!" moments. SAIL then helps to make meaning of all of this data: By mapping each past experience, goal, and reflective moment with the SAIL dimensions and skills, learners can begin to see connections, themes and transference of skills across contexts that lead to greater understanding and confidence.

Thinking about past experiences in terms of transferable skills is certainly not a new or unique strategy. A quick search on the Internet for "list of transferable skills" will show that this is a well-established topic and the focus of many career and internship centers. And in surveys and research studies around the world, employers list these transferable skills, or "soft skills," as both what they are desperately seeking in new employees and what they seem to find lacking in so many new graduates.

That same search for transferable skills may also be a little bit daunting. Some of the lists include more than 80 different skills, and not all of the lists match. You could spend a very long (and ultimately unproductive) time trying to think about how you have practiced all these skills in the past, and how you want to develop them in the future. To address this problem, many of these lists identify groups and categories of skills. The Northeastern SAIL program has adopted this tactic and divided the skills into five "dimensions" that represent five key areas of human growth in development that have been identified by educators, researchers, and employers alike (Figure 1.1).

In the Intellectual Agility dimension, the focus is on the word "agility." The most common misconception is that this is the "being smart" dimension, but it is more closely related to seeing unexpected patterns, reflectively learning from experiences, and integrating past knowledge to create new ideas. Skills in this dimension include design thinking, quantitative reasoning, and entrepreneurship, among others. These skills are in high demand in the workforce, where employers are less concerned with what you have memorized and more interested in what new knowledge you can generate.

Global Mindset refers to the ability to live, work, and communicate with people from many different cultures and backgrounds, and it also describes the process of thinking about the global impact of our decisions. The component skills in this dimension include cultural agility, inclusivity, and systems thinking. Gaining experience as a global citizen is not only an intrinsically rewarding experience but also an increasingly necessary competency as global networks become more interconnected and the world ultimately becomes a smaller place.

We experience growth in the Social Consciousness and Commitment dimension by acting as advocates for positive social change in our communities. This requires the ability to articulate the intersectionalities of our own identities and to recognize how those identities interact with systemic power structures. This dimension incorporates skills such as advocacy, civic-mindedness, and conflict transformation. These skills can be enacted not only in large social change initiatives but also in the daily ways in which we interact with and strengthen our community.

Figure 1.1: SAIL Dimensions
Source: sail.northeastern.edu

The Personal and Professional Effectiveness dimension is not just about the skills required to get a job or a promotion. It refers to the ability to intentionally develop our personal and professional identities, persevere and grow through setbacks, and to build and leverage networks for interdependent benefit. Coaching and mentoring are important skills in this dimension, and we will go into much more detail on these in Chapter 3. You will change roles many times in your career, and it is likely you will have job titles that don't even exist today. In that paradigm, it is critical to have a strong personal and professional philosophy and identity to guide your overall path.

The most appreciated dimension of the SAIL framework is Well-Being, and we will talk a lot more about this important quality later in this chapter. The days of praising the "selfless martyr" are coming to an end, and there is increasingly more respect for those who are able to prioritize their own health and wellness along with their other competing responsibilities. Have you ever noticed in the airplane safety videos before take-off the flight attendants tell you to secure your own air mask before putting one on the children around you? That is a great analogy to help you remember that if you are not taking care of yourself, it is hard or impossible to do your best work for others and in the other domains of your life.

The five dimensions of the framework are a great way to think about your holistic growth around the many different transferable skills that exist. There is also a category of skills that exist across the five dimensions called Foundational Masteries. These are skills that are critical in all aspects of your life and can't be broken out into one particular category. These masteries include skills like critical thinking, integrity, empathy, and initiative. You can imagine how these skills could be leveraged in all five of the dimensions we discussed previously, and also how they are transferable across the many different contexts of your past and future experiences.

At the end of the day, you may be working from a very different set of skills from the SAIL framework, but the practice of breaking them down into meaningful categories and assessing your growth in those areas will still be immensely beneficial. The self-awareness you will gain by reflecting on your past experiences in an integrated and meaningful way will better enable you to articulate a coherent and targeted personal narrative to others, whether they be peers, colleagues, or potential employers. It also enables you to more intentionally prepare for and seek out future opportunities that are in line with their values and goals.

SAIL is a robust and unique tool at Northeastern, but you can start benefiting from its principles right now. Begin by thinking back on your past experiences and mapping them to a set of values and skills, in what you might call an "experience audit." You will start to see connections and themes popping up, some of which may surprise you. Based on that ongoing reflective exercise, start thinking about how you would tell the story of your life based on those values and skills, and not just as a chronological list of what you have done. Thinking about your past experiences in this way will prime you to be more intentional about your next experiences and choices, and what direction(s) you would like to be moving forward in.

Knowing Not Just What We Learned, but How We Learned It

This experience made me realize that no matter how afraid I am of something, that doesn't not mean that I am bad at it. I think there is such a strong connection in our minds: "I am afraid of this thinking, therefore, I will be bad at it," or the other way around. I think my second co-op proved to me that that is not true. Sometimes you just have to brace yourself and do what you don't want to do and that is how you get comfortable. It is sort of an exposure therapy. (Student Respondent, 2018)

Research has shown that organizing knowledge gained from past experiences is a foundational component of making sense of new information and arranging our future activities around functional gaps in our understanding. "Students connect what they learn to what they already know, interpreting incoming information, and even sensory perception through the lens of their existing knowledge, beliefs, and assumptions (National Research Council, 2000; Vygotsky, 1978). In fact, there is widespread agreement among researchers that students *must* connect new knowledge to previous knowledge in order to learn (Bransford & Johnson, 1972; Resnick, 1983). However, the extent to which students are able to draw on prior knowledge to *effectively* construct new knowledge depends on the nature of their prior knowledge, as well as the instructor's ability to harness it" (Ambrose, Bridges, Dipietro, Lovett, & Norman, 2010). It is therefore important to continually assess what we know and can do, in order to better understand what we do not know and cannot do. To accurately understand one's own abilities, competencies, values, and perspectives serves to make one a more effective communicator, a more confident collaborator, and more productive worker and citizen.

In addition, employees of the 21st century will continually need to flexibly adapt due to the changes in their jobs as well as the emerging "gig economy" where, rather than holding regular jobs within an organization, they will work "gigs" or short term for a defined time on a specific task (Friedman, 2014). To effectively navigate a variety of work environments, individuals will need to be conscious of their skills and competencies, articulate and adapt them to potential employers, and be more self-directed in their own development. Given these realities, it is increasingly more important for students to develop skills that enable them to self-assess their strengths and growth needs, be more intentional and self-directed in their learning, and draw connections between their learning and the "real-world" contexts they face.

As the student's quote at the beginning of this section reflects, one barrier to engaging in new experiences, or pursuing future experience, is not fully understanding how past experiences have prepared us for that transition. We see this frequently with students who have doubts on whether their prior experiences working in restaurants, ice cream stands, or retail shops have given them any skills at all that qualify them for "professional fields." It is in these moments of contemplating transition to new real-world contexts that we sometimes see students doubt their abilities or fit in unfamiliar environments. This can lead them to feel they lack the necessary skills and knowledge to provide tangible value to new work or learning environments. Sometimes termed the "imposter phenomenon," these feelings of self-doubt is seen in those who have high levels of achievement and are transitioning in some way between social roles (Twenge & Campbell, 2017). First studied by Pauline Clance and Suzanne Imes (1978), the imposter phenomenon has been shown to manifest across many different demographics: college students (Ross, Stewart, Mugge, & Fultz, 2001), marketing managers (Fried-Buchalter, 1997), medical residents (Legassie, Zibrowski, & Goldszmidt, 2008), among many others.

The "imposter phenomenon" can also involve the embodiment of social stereotypes based on race, sex, or gender when experiencing new professional or cultural environments. This can have an impact on student confidence about their future and personal well-being (Bauer-Wolf, 2017). For college students, this can show up during the first experience working in a new professional setting, starting college, or moving to a new culture. These are moments of leaving a familiar comfort zone and exercising acquired knowledge, strengths, and skills in new and novel ways. In our end of co-op student reflection meetings and assignments, we often see that through significant experiential learning opportunities students are able to reconcile initial moments of fear (like the one expressed in the student's quote at the beginning of this chapter) with a burgeoning sense of confidence in how to apply skills, knowledge, and their identity in new contexts. As our student put it, you learn and adapt through "exposure therapy" and contemplating how you learn from experiences in which you have moments of self-doubt. It is being self-aware of how you traverse these "imposter" moments that you can begin to develop strategies for building confidence, reframing self-defeating attitudes, and assuming control of your learning and personal growth.

The aforementioned SAIL Program model at Northeastern offers a framework that can be helpful in understanding how you learn and internalize what you learn in new environments. The "SA" in Northeastern's SAIL program stands for Self-Authorship, but it is the "IL" for Integrated Learning is exactly what you need to start seeing how your skills are transferable to new contexts and challenges. This is another reason that the "experience audit" we discussed earlier can be so powerful; it is a way to think not just about how your past experiences were connected by the skills you developed but also to practice articulating how you plan to use those skills in the future. Imagine if you could say to a potential employer, "One of my strongest skills is empathy. I started developing it in high school as a camp counselor, where I found I was able to really connect with kids who felt scared or left out. I was able to leverage empathy in my role as a President of the Campus Sustainability club, and it helped me to better understand the concerns the members of my group had and to win their confidence more fully. And in my most recent internship at the Sierra Club I relied on my strong empathy to connect on a personal level with potential donors and encourage them to give to the cause. I think that this skill would be a huge benefit to your organization as it works to create stronger bonds with local leaders and the broader community." It is safe to say that the interviewer would be impressed.

The Art of –
Reflection as Inquiry and Intentionality

This course has taught me things I would have never known about how to write a resume, how to do an interview well, and even what an informational interview is. In my other initial reflections I had a similar mindset, that this course was about helping me get a job for while I was in school. In my second reflection about describing my personality, work style, and ethics I was not very aware of myself as a scholar and potential co-op candidate. I was not sure the differences in myself when it came to my field of studies. But after the first reflections I began to analyze my behavior in different classes and when I was studying to understand the work ethics and style I have. Towards the end of the course my reflections and class notes became vastly different. In my reflections not only did I have a better understanding of myself but I also began to expand my interests in what I wanted to learn from my future co-op. (Student Respondent, 2018)

This student's reflection describes the inquiry process by which she came to a deeper understanding of her learning and goals. It was in considering her development intentionally and thinking through how and why she progressed that she gained key insights and a better understanding of herself and her interests. Research suggests that university students are developmentally positioned to engage in self-reflection and in critical thinking about themselves, their interests, their purpose, and their role as citizens (Braskamp & Engberg, 2011). The undergraduate years, although only one part of your lifelong development, is situated at a time when you are poised to shape and further explore intellectual frameworks and habits of mind that you will bring to your adult experience. As part of self-reflection, students examine the way they understand the responsibilities that are central to their sense of self. There are many reasons that exist for this being the appropriate developmental time to further reflect and foster self-awareness; however, two primary aspects position the higher education period as a most effective time and means for students to engage in critical inquiry and self-reflection. First, the early 20s is a developmental phase in which the you will likely question of values, upbringing, vision for oneself, and the greater society, as well as your own lived experiences as it compares to others (Braskamp & Engberg, 2011). Second, in addition to this questioning and reflection, students at college age obtain the right to vote and begin to actively question and now via their voting rights participate in the political process. As part of these activities and developments, students further develop self-awareness and ideas and opinions about work, life, and society.

Through our work over the past 10 years helping students to prepare for professional co-op experiences through resume development, refining job applications, navigating interviews and offers, and working with new employers, we have found that it is not only the activities that we engage in but also how each of these experiences shapes us that matters most. Students can often give an accounting of what they did during a particular experience, but we have found that it is much harder for students to articulate how their collective experiences impact their sense of identity, shape their attitudes, inform their values, change their beliefs, influence how they engage with others, and determine how others perceive them. The ability to answer these types of questions, though, is what we mean by self-awareness.

Intentionality and inquiry are two important aspects of engaging students in self-reflection and further developing their self-awareness. Asking students to be intentional about their reflective practice—to look for opportunities to observe, ask questions, reimagine, do something in a new/different way, think outside of previously held beliefs and constructs, let go of self-limiting notions of themselves and others—creates an openness and mindset in which thinking and habits of mind can change and grow. In a longitudinal study that followed more than 112,000 college and university students from their first through third year, activities that engaged students in modes of self-reflective inquiry enhanced their whole-person development in relation to how they make meaning of their education and their lives, how they develop a sense of purpose, and the value and belief dilemmas that they experience (Astin, Astin, & Lindholm, 2010).

In Carol Dweck's book *Mindset* (2008), she provides a practical framework and guidance for students in terms of how they think about themselves and how their thinking and level of engagement impacts their learning and development. Dweck outlines two different mindsets—fixed and growth. According to Dweck, "In a fixed mindset, people believe their basic qualities, like their intelligence or talent, are simply fixed traits. They spend their time documenting their intelligence or talent instead of developing them. Others, who believe their success is based on hard work, learning, training and doggedness are said to have a 'growth' or an 'incremental' theory of intelligence." (Dweck, 2008)

What follows is a student's reflection based on Dweck's writing on mindsets as it related to her process of applying and interviewing for co-ops:

Although by that point we had read a couple of chapters from Carol Dweck's Mindset, I recognize aspects of my early mindset that were still closer to Dweck's definition of a "fixed" mindset, one characterized by a static view of ability and a need to prove my skill and my worth to others (Dweck's Mindset, 2008, pp. 29–30). Coming into the co-op search, I viewed it as a strict competition, a zero-sum game, one in which you had to work to distinguish yourself from others to get the job. Dweck astutely sees through this mindset, explaining that people with a fixed mindset "opt for success over growth . . . success means their fixed traits are better than other people's" (p. 32). Under the surface, however, lies the fear of "being ordinary," of having the outside world confirm that you are not good enough (p. 31).

Another hallmark of the fixed mindset is a fear of failure that ultimately stems from the insecurity. I have always struggled with a fear of failure; I still remember how much it hurt to receive college rejections or to be benched in softball in favor of another teammate. In my mind, these events demonstrated my deficiencies or inadequacies: someone had evaluated my abilities and decided "not good enough." In chapter two of Mindset, Dweck offers advice on how to learn from failure in a productive, growth-oriented way. Instead of dwelling on the setback and using it to tear yourself down, Dweck advises to ask yourself, "What can I learn from that experience?" (p. 53). Simple enough advice, but it really did help me reorient how I approached interviews, job rejections, and academic performance.

This student's experience in participating in a job search highlights her process of critically looking at her mindset and thinking to address certain limitations. In so doing, she begins to realize the impact of how she was thinking about and framing her experience could have on her process and outcome. In teaching and guiding students using Dweck's mindset framework, we see it as a helpful tool that helps you to take a step back and reflect on and evaluate your thinking and approach, particularly as you enter new situations and environments, and considering your mindset and how it is affecting your decisions and actions can provide helpful new insights and direction.

Being a Social Scientist in Your Own Life

Think about a time when you were confused or offended by the actions of another person. What was your first reaction in that moment? Did you dismiss that action or assume that perhaps the person was mistaken? Did you quickly jump to blaming them or defending yourself? Perhaps the person misspoke or did not really understand what they were doing at the time. Either way what they did offended you, and you sought to interpret why they would behave in such a manner. The more we look for support of our view the more we can find it and the more we reinforce our belief that our worldview is correct.

Now, on the other hand, when you were confused or offended by the actions of another person, have you ever taken the time to stop and perhaps mindfully describe the circumstances, the unseen influences, the scope, context, and the lens through which you viewed the event? Did you take time to examine the assumptions you are making? My parents used to have a saying about assumptions that I still use to this day, "When you assume you are making an ass out of u and me." This crude and clever wordplay makes a very valid point in our time of an unyielding news cycle and expansive social exposure. When we assume things, we are typically revealing something about ourselves in that we have not taken the time to vet our sources, to examine our own role in the situation, to interpret our emotional responses, or to give space to alternative perspectives and interpretations.

In our professional development courses, when discussing experiential learning and encouraging self-reflection and reflexive thinking we often ask students to envision themselves as social scientists examining their own lives. At a basic level, a social scientist is one who researches, theorizes, and makes connections between society and human behaviors. Core to this is a methodology of correlating quantitative data with qualitative analysis of interviews or descriptive accounts in order to establish supporting evidence for theories on how the world works. We encourage students to apply this mindset to their experiences in and out of the class and to adopt a quasi-ethnographic approach to their own experiences through "participant observation" in order to better observe their own biases and actions in various new environments. Central to this is teaching students to situate themselves as learners in every environment, and to better describe, analyze, and interpret their roles, decisions, and actions in relation to their coworkers or counterparts. Through this method of self-reflection students develop alternate interpretive lenses—from outward-looking analysis and judgment to an inward-looking and mindful self-awareness—in order to attempt to better understand the perspective of those around them and the environment in which they are situated. This process not only increases students' engagement in experiential learning programs but also prompts them to adopt a notion of transference of skills and knowledge from classroom environments to all experiences.

One way we endeavor to promote this notion of "being a social scientist in your own life" is through the incorporation of observational activities that promote self-reflexivity through examination of one's own assumptions, decisions, and interpretations of events. There are several activities or ways of accomplishing this, such as Darla Deardorff's OSEE (Observe, State, Explore, and Evaluate) or Kyoung-Ah Nam's Describe–Analyze–Evaluate framework for intercultural competency development to all experiences (Berardo & Deardorff, 2012). The reflective process of auditing your past experiences for fundamental, transferable skills (through a model like the SAIL framework) and then seeking out common threads of learning and development across different areas of your life can help you to identify personal strengths you were not previously aware of and to target areas where it might be beneficial to challenge yourself more. These frameworks (and several others) are ways for students to begin to use observational strategies to help challenge their assumptions and better understand their values, attitudes, skills, cultural knowledge, motivations, and desired outcomes. The key to these methods of self-analysis and discovery is to describe what you see happening while attempting to remove your propensity for subjective judgments of your environment. Objectively describing the environment, your role, the actors in your space, and the actions you take allows for active experimentation with your interpretative lenses in relation to others. It is remarkable how difficult but uniquely empowering an experience it can be to just observe and describe a situation without incorporating your own judgment or value statements. When one separates the inclination to interpret or analyze events on the first pass, they are in fact allowing space for alternative interpretations or perspectives on an action or activity. This process will draw clear distinctions between actions and assumptions and free the observer to explore and analyze alternative approaches or provide more nuanced explanations for behaviors of counterparts.

What we have found is that when students engage in this kind of self-reflection they are often forced to get to know and embody numerous selves. There is the curious self, which has a general desire to learn through observation and listening. There is the perceiving self, which is able to robustly describe the learning environment, actors, behaviors, and actions. There is the critical self, which is evaluating and analyzing the situation in order to better understand the motivations and values of all participants in a situation. And there is the judging self, which interprets situations through an individual lens and assumptions or biases. So, as we present our models for integrating learning in and out of the classroom, an important key framework to keep in mind is engaging in experiences with the numerous selves to better understand how through our own judgments and actions we are impacting others within our learning environments.

Well-Being—A Balancing Act

The Internet has been the largest change in all aspects of society, for good and for ill. Technology should never be used for its own sake (which many of us do) but as a means to an end. That end should be improving society. The smart phone and its associated technologies and culture has put a barrier between people and direct experience with the world. We need to spend a portion of each day unplugged, directly experiencing other people, nature, and our own thoughts. (Alan Lightman, Employer Partner, Physicist, Novelist and Professor of the Practice of the Humanities at MIT, 2018)

As we conclude this chapter, we wanted to take some time to address a challenge for all of us and our abilities to foster self-awareness living in a fast-paced, technology-based, and global society where exist myriad ways in which we can be connected, plugged-in, and engaged on a constant basis. Although there are certainly many benefits that this offers to us as students, workers, and citizens, at the same time there are also many challenges to this level of activity, exposure, and access. Our employer partner, Alan Lightman, speaks to these issues in his reflection quoted previously. In a recent article in the *Washington Post* (2018), "Go Ahead, Waste Some Time—It's Good for You," he addresses these questions: "What exactly have we lost when we cannot slow down our lives and find periods of the day where we let our minds wander without purpose or goal? When we cannot find a few minutes to unplug from the grid and be alone with our thoughts?" He discusses the impact of our living an automated, frenzied, technology-driven life on our creative and inner selves, noting creative activity requires unstructured time alone and attending to our inner selves and we need to allow ourselves time to dream, explore, and question ourselves to determine what is important to us. He captures it this way: "The sunlight and soil that nourish our inner self are solitude and personal reflection." (Lightman, 2018) This certainly gives us pause (pun intended!) to consider how we can balance and manage our time so that we can fully develop both our internal and external selves that we talked about earlier in this chapter.

In an age when technological advances have made it easier than ever to connect with more people than ever before, and when our devices, apps, and social media allow us to portray our lives in words, sounds, pictures, and videos in more and more unique ways, it is easy to assume that through these various means of online social interactions we are becoming more aware of who we are, who we want to be, and how others view us. We are now more able to choose, edit, and control how others view us through our digital presence. We can carefully self-select our words in text, our best angles through snaps, and our affiliations through tweets. It is easy to assume that through this added layer of self-consciousness and control that we also become more aware of how others view us, our strengths and weaknesses, imagination and innovative potential, and interpersonal communications. But does our age of technology actually make us more self-aware, or are we, through our reliance in connecting with others through online communities, actually becoming less confident, more vulnerable, and less able to meaningfully engage and empathize with others in our day-to-day lives? As Sherry Turkle uncovers in *Reclaiming Conversation: The Power of Talk in the Digital Age*, our digital devices and our online tools for connection in fact functionally disconnect us from our lived environments. Turkle writes, "In the short term, online communication makes us feel more in charge of our time and self-presentation. If we text rather than talk, we can have each other in amounts we can control. And texting and email and posting let us present the self we want to be. We can edit and retouch" (2016). In many ways, technology is allowing us to explore multiple identities, live multifaceted lives, and retreat from our day-to-day lives. As Turkle's work points out, if modern digital technology reaches its full potential in our lives (and if we can connect to an electrical outlet or battery), then we can now multitask like never before, never feel "fully" alone, receive instant gratification and validation of our viewpoints, and never have to feel boredom. The question about all this is though is that, does this functionality improve our experiences, or does it, in the long term, hamper our personal and professional effectiveness?

We often notice with students that travel to different areas to study and/or work provides them an opportunity to reconsider the balance or lack of balance in their life. For students beginning their first professional experience, time management and balancing work and other aspects of their lives can be challenging and is an important area of learning. With students traveling globally, they are exposed to different cultural norms and values. Time is one thing that often comes up as a point of consideration and learning for students. Some struggle with cultures that are more relaxed and go at a slower pace; others embrace the opportunity to take their time and not feel rushed. One student reflected on her studies in India in prompting new habits of mind and practices—

I took a ten-day Vipassana meditation course while in India. During this course I learned a meditation technique that I can use throughout the rest of my life. I returned from India a calmer, more centered person and I hope to continue to carry these values with me as I begin my life after college. (Student Respondent, 2018)

In our advising sessions with students, we often talk about how to maintain a sense of balance and practice good self-care. As part of this we discuss the notion of "well-being." How do you define well-being? What are ways that you experience wellness? What are the elements that contribute to your well-being? As the SAIL framework was being developed and adopted at Northeastern, there was one piece of feedback that was consistent from students, faculty, staff, employers, and anyone who saw the model: They loved that Well-Being was one of the five dimensions. Employers loved it because they know how critical self-care is for maintaining happy and high-performing employees. Advisors were excited to have Well-Being listed as a major component of a university-sponsored framework, since it made it easier to initiate conversations about students' mental and emotional health. And students loved that Well-Being was a major part of the SAIL framework because it signaled the university's belief that taking care of yourself is just as critical as developing critical thinking skills, building a professional portfolio, and being engaged in the community.

The five skills embedded in SAIL's Well-Being dimension shed some light on the breadth of this topic, and how it intertwines with other aspects of your growth and development. The skill of self-care is paramount to the Well-Being dimension of SAIL; it requires the self-awareness to know when you are "running low" in the areas of physical, emotional, social health, and also the associated skill of time management to find and prioritize the time you need to address those areas. Once we have set aside the time and mental space for self-care, we often give it away as soon as another commitment or responsibility pops up. Whether it be because we have a hard time saying "no" to other people, or because we have FOMO (fear of missing out), we all have to develop a strong boundary-setting skill in order to maintain the time and space devoted to our own well-being. This also means that we have to develop self-control and regulation around our habits and behaviors; you know that your physical and mental health will suffer if you are consistently staying up too late, habitually letting yourself get frustrated on your commute, or if you don't make time for physical activity in your day; it takes self-regulation and control to not slip into bad habits and behaviors that lead us away from the self-care we need.

As you can see, focusing on your well-being is not just a matter of "getting enough sleep and eating a good breakfast." It requires the development of challenging and wide-ranging skills that impact many other areas of our lives. It has been easy in our culture to put our own needs last and to think of self-care as a luxury at best, or an indulgence at worst. However, truly focusing on your well-being is perhaps one of the most important skills you can develop, and the results will pay dividends across the many different contexts of your life.

Conclusion

In conclusion, we hope that this first chapter has reinforced the importance of self-awareness, self-authorship, and metacognition (knowing how we learn and know things), on how you can become a more engaged and successful student and leader. We encourage students to begin these processes by developing clarity of self and purpose, which will enable them to become more self-aware in their social, academic, civic, and professional engagements. We hope that the chapter provided information and a framework for you to better interpret the shaping of your values and perspectives while also prompting a need to better understand your emotions, vulnerabilities, routines, and priorities. This is the starting point for the book because we believe that fostering a sense of self-awareness is the foundation for the rest of your learning in the classroom, workplace, and greater society.

LOOK UP: Reality Check

Daniel Kish had his eyes removed due to a rare cancer at the age of 13 months. At a young age, his parents encouraged him to explore his world freely and independently and instead of feeling limited by his blindness he was able to explore his sensory experiences in a way that allowed him to develop a method for activating the visual cortex of his brain through exercising all of his senses. Through his experiences Daniel developed his own method of echolocation, similar to those used by bats, by using clicking sounds to navigate his environments. He calls this method "Flashsonar" and the sound bouncing back from his environment lights up his visual cortex to give him a mental picture through which to navigate. Using this method as a young child he was capable of riding a bike to school, playing tag with the sighted friends, and climbing trees. He credits his ability to explore the world without limitations that helped him to develop his senses and abilities. (Kish, 2017) In his 2015 TED talk Daniel explained that "It's impressions about blindness that are far more threatening to blind people than blindness itself." (Kish, 2015) He has since shared his no-limits methods with the world and is working to empower the blind community around the world.

According to Daniel, "the individual transformation, we have found, is quite easy; it's not that hard. But in order to affect individual transformation, you have to affect the system in which the individual is an element."(Kish, 2015)

Please take a moment to answer these questions:

What does Daniel's story tell you about self-awareness and how we view possible limitations in our own lives? How in your life do you make use of your full set of abilities, and in what ways do you personally view social stereotypes that may limit you in some way? In what ways do you regularly challenge your assumptions about the world?

As an activity meet with someone else to practice answering the common interview questions such as "Tell Me About Yourself," "What Is Your Greatest Strength?," and "What Is Your Greatest Weakness?" Document how you answered these and how they impact your impressions of yourself. In what ways can your weaknesses be reimagined as strengths and in what way can your confidence in your perceived strengths reveal a blind spot for areas where you need to develop personally, professionally, or academically.

Key Takeaways

- Developing a reflective mindset will assist in making meaning from your experiences
- Examining personal and professional values and motivations
- Understanding challenge and growth as fundamental elements of learning
- Integrating your learning and the concepts of self-awareness and authorship
- Balancing personal, work, and civic life for a sense of well-being

Follow-Up Activities in Toolkit—Listen Up, Look Up, Join Up, and Act Up

- Complete your **Digital Audit** of your online self
- Complete **Tell Me About Yourself** outline and exercise
- **Résumé Development** activities and template
- Tips for asking for **candid feedback**
- **Explore Your "Self"** through Others
- Complete your **Defining Moments** exercise
- Foster Self-Awareness through the **Fixed and Growth Mindset** Activity
- Practice with **Intentional Storytelling** exercise

Works Cited

Ambrose, S. A., Bridges, M. W., DiPietro, M., Lovett, M. C., & Norman, M. K. (2010). *How learning works: Seven research-based principles for smart teaching.* John Wiley & Sons.

Ambrose, S. Talgar, C. & Wankel, L. (2015) Integrated Student Learning Experience (ISLE): A Model for Personalized Education Dissolving Artificial Boundaries. Northeastern University, Boston, MA

Astin, A., Astin, H., & Lindholm, J. (2010). *Cultivating the spirit: How college can enhance students' inner lives.* Hoboken, NJ: Jossey-Bass.

Bauer-Wolf, J. (2017). *Feeling Like Imposters.* Retrieved from https://www.insidehighered.com/news/2017/04/06/study-shows-impostor-syndromes-effect-minority-students-mental-health

Berardo, K., & Deardorff, D. K. (2012). *Building cultural competence: Innovative activities and models.* Sterling, VA: Stylus.

Braskamp, L., & Engberg, M. (2011). How colleges can influence the development of a global perspective. *Liberal Education, 97*(3/4), 1–7.

Bransford, J.D. & Johnson, M.K. (1972). Contextual Prerequisites for Understanding: Some Investigations of Comprehension and Recall. *Journal of Verbal Learning and Verbal Behavior,* 11(6)717-726.

Brooks, D. (2015). *The road to character.* New York, N.Y.: Random House.

Clance, P. R., & Imes, S. A. (1978). The imposter phenomenon in high achieving women: Dynamics and therapeutic intervention. *Psychotherapy: Theory, Research & Practice, 15*(3), 241–247.

Dweck, C. S. (2008). *Mindset: The new psychology of success.* New York, NY: Ballantine Books.

Eurich, T. (2018, January 4). What self-awareness really is (and how to cultivate it). *Harvard Business Review*, p. 1.

Fried-Buchalter, S. (1997). Fear of success, fear of failure, and the impostor phenomenon among male and female marketing managers. *Sex Roles, 37*(11/12), 847–859

Friedman, G. (2014). Workers without employers: shadow corporations and the rise of the gig economy. *Review of Keynesian Economics, 2*(2), 171-188.

Goleman, D. (1995). *Emotional Intelligence: Why It Can Matter More Than IQ.* New York, NY: Bantam.

Kish, D. (2015, March). *How I Use Sonar to Navigate the World* [Video File]. Retrieved from https://www.ted.com/talks/daniel_kish_how_i_use_sonar_to_navigate_the_world?language=en#t-65168

Kish, D. (2017). Retrieved from https://www.ashoka.org/en/fellow/daniel-kish#fellow-accordion

LaMachia, J. (2017). *Integrating Global Citizenship Learning in Undergraduate Education.* https://repository.library.northeastern.edu/files/neu:cj82nr13g/fulltext.pdf

Legassie, J., Zibrowski, E. M., & Goldszmidt, M. A. (2008). Measuring resident well-being: Impostorism and burnout syndrome in residency. *Journal of General Internal Medicine, 23*(7), 1090–1094.

Lightman, A. (2018). *Go Ahead, Waste some time, it's good for you.* Washington, DC: Washington Post.

Magolda, M. B. (2001). *Making their own way: Narratives for transforming higher education to promote self-development.* Sterling, VA: Stylus.

Magolda, M. B. (2008). Three elements of self-authorship. *Journal of College Student Development, 49*(4), 269–284.

National Research Council (2000). *How People Learn: Brain, Mind, Experience, and School: Expanded edition.* National Academies Press.

Pipher, M. (2006). *Writing to change the world.* New York, NY: Riverhead Books.

Resnick, L. B. (1983). Mathematics and science learning: A new conception. *Science, 220*(4596), 477-478

Ross, S. R., Stewart, J., Mugge, M., & Fultz, B., (2001). The imposter phenomenon: Achievement dispositions and the five-factor model. *Personality and Individual Differences, 31*(8), 1347–1355.

Turkle, S. (2016). *Reclaiming Conversation: The Power Of Talk In A Digital Age.* New York, NY: Penguin Books.

Twenge, J. M., & Campbell, W. K. (2017). *Personality psychology: Understanding yourself and others.* Boston, MA: Pearson Education.

Vygotsky, L.S. (1978). *Mind In Society.* Cambridge, MA: Harvard University Press.

2

Engaging in Adaptive Decision-Making

It is currently an amazing time in our world. We are getting more global than we were; the world is becoming smaller, but at the same time we are going through lots of global and grass root problems. At this time, we need people who can understand and analyze the situation in a local context but are still using the skills they have learned from past experiences. These students need to not only have the capacity to make decisions but also be able to involve the ground people into said decision. We all need to work towards making this world a better place for the next and current generations. (Employer Respondent, International NGO, 2018)

Ryan had a choice to make. After spending 2 weeks in the Netherlands he had reached a personal crisis point, one that he had never previously encountered. Three months prior he had confidently accepted a competitive research assistant job with a prominent robotics think-tank in The Hague. This was his first experience living for longer than 3 weeks outside of the United States and his first opportunity to work in a formal research capacity. He had made a number of sacrifices in order to embark on this journey; academically, he was delaying progression in his academic studies for 6 months; financially, he had accepted this position unpaid and knew he would be depleting his savings to make it work for 6 months; and socially, he was traveling alone as a self-described introvert who had not yet made any friends his own age in the Netherlands. The position he had accepted was off to a slow start. The research team he was working with traveled frequently, and the organization was still in a process of transition from one university in eastern Holland to its current location in The Hague. Ryan felt isolated socially and culturally; thus, ill-equipped to work independently on the think-tank's research, he was worried about the financial impact of his decision and was having difficulty seeing the long-term benefits of this position. He called his advisor for help in making a choice, "Should I stay or should I go?"

What would you do if you were Ryan? How would you feel when you first encountered a difficult choice or challenge? When judging the costs and benefits of the situation would you anguish slowly over all possible options or would you go forward confidently, willing to accept the risks of any decisions you make? Ryan's situation is just one example of the many types of seminal moments or decision points we regularly encounter in our work with students as cooperative education advisors at Northeastern. In our work teaching and advising students on their professional development, we discuss with students the various personal, professional, and academic decisions they need to take during their time at the university. From making decisions on the types of jobs to apply to during their first co-op searches to managing personal reactions to difficult ethical disputes on the job and making choices on participation in different classes or experiential education offerings, students determine the costs and benefits of making choices throughout their time in college. In our advising work, we seek to help students to refine and develop their decision-making

abilities into a skill that improves with experience and reflection throughout life.

In this chapter, we will be walking you through the decision-making concepts and methods that we introduce to our students as part of our advising and instructional processes at Northeastern. We will introduce concepts to consider how the decision-making process reflects unique attitudes, mindsets, motivations, emotions, values, and beliefs. In addition, we hope that when confronted with the complicated situations like the ones Ryan experienced in the Netherlands, you will feel better equipped to consult your own inner resources and personal support systems. We will also demonstrate that approaching decisions with an open and flexible outlook will better enable you to learn something useful from the outcome.

As for Ryan, he decided to stay and work through his situation, which afforded him many learning opportunities. Perhaps most importantly, he learned about his personal resiliency and ability to accept discomfort as an opportunity to adapt and change perspectives. His experience afforded him the space to develop strengths in skill areas he previously identified as weaknesses. He additionally walked away with a more refined sense of purpose for his career and education. In the end, his story highlights how framing decision points flexibly, and as opportunities for learning and skill development, can yield unexpected positive outcomes. This chapter will encourage you, like Ryan, to question your gut reactions, consult with your mentors, and determine when the easiest and most obvious path on a decision is indeed the most beneficial.

Begin with Examining How You Make Decisions

This chapter is an invitation to *look up* for a moment and to reflect on those things influencing our problem-solving and decision-making abilities in our day-to-day life experiences. As we navigate our daily experiences, we are regularly encountering challenges, choices, and novel decision points. In addition, as our society becomes increasingly globalized and interconnected it can be easy to be overwhelmed by choice. These choices can be as simple as what detergent or deodorant to buy, or as complicated as what college or university to attend. Any decision point we face, no matter how big or small, is in essence a challenge that needs to be overcome. Adapting around challenges and honing the ability to make informed decisions is an essential benefit of experiential learning. As presented in Alice Kolb and David Kolb's research on learning styles, "Learning is a holistic process of adaptation to the world. Not just the result of cognition, learning involves the integrated functioning of the total person—thinking, feeling, perceiving, and behaving" (Kolb & Kolb, 2005). Integrating these areas occurs by actively reflecting on what was felt through an experience; drawing conclusions about what was learned through examining personal values, motivations, and beliefs; and then adapting behaviors by actively experimenting with what was learned in new settings. This adaptive experiential learning process helps to derive meaning from experiences while helping to inform decisions for future actions, and this is what we mean by adaptive decision-making.

In particular, in this chapter we will examine the following factors that influence adaptive decision making:

1. The intrinsic and extrinsic motivators that inform purposeful decisions
2. The ability to interpret and refine intuitive gut reactions
3. The impact of distractions and scarcity in our routines on how we perceive flexibility in our lives and choices
4. The influencers in support communities who advise on decisions

We will walk you through some of these considerations and decision-making methods and concepts that we teach our students at Northeastern as a part of the experiential learning curriculum. Our hope is that by working through this chapter you will better understand your decision-making thought process and become more skilled, flexible, and adaptable when making large and small decisions.

The Importance of –
Seeking Purpose: Motivations and Decision-Making

Our motivations are an important piece of what propels us to persist through life experiences. It is not easy, though, to fully grasp what motivates us toward making a particular decision. Many students we work with at Northeastern know that they want their college experience to help them find a "passion" or define their purpose, but many have trouble even defining what interests them as a starting point. Even beyond college it doesn't get easier, as Angela Duckworth, an expert on resilience, points out in her work *Grit*, "To the thirty-something on Reddit with a 'fleeting interest in everything' and 'no career direction', here's what science has to say: passion for your work is a little bit of *discovery*, followed by a lot of *development*, and then a lifetime of *deepening*" (Duckworth, 2016). This concept of development and deepening is often hard to see without first understanding what we are interested in to begin with. In addition, in the world of instant messaging, instant access, instant everything, there is not always an acceptance of being patient and allowing our experiences to ripen over time. There is not typically going to be a singular thunderbolt that strikes you with a life's purpose without first having multiple diverse experiences to either inspire you or dissuade you. What you will find over time and across experiences about your sense of purpose, however, is that there will often be many thunderbolts, rain, flooding, and, sometimes, drought.

The key to motivations and finding passions is really to take the most obvious path of just setting out to try new things while self-assessing your ambitions along the way. As one of our students frames it,

> *I think for me experiential learning is how you see yourself in relation to your ambitions, and how you tailor your life to those ambitions. Ambition is what makes experiential learning work, to begin with. Without one, you cannot have the other. Ambition is passive, and experiential learning is a facilitator of your ambitions. To me personally, experiential learning is how I made sense of my ambitions, how I organized them.* (Student Respondent, 2018)

This quote illustrates that finding direction in life begins by understanding the motivations that direct experiential decision points. Whether it is external motivation (extrinsic) like getting a good grade on an exam or landing a high-paying job, or internal motivation (intrinsic) like feeling personally fulfilled by helping another through a crisis, your motivations frame your choices for where to focus your energies for future decisions and self-direction.

Informing your decisions with a sense of self-direction, intrinsic motivation, and purpose is going to be critical in the workplaces of the future. These factors are now influencing the way organizations and businesses are structured and managed. In his book and TED Talk, *Drive: The Surprising Truth About What Motivates Us* (2009), Daniel Pink examines the various ways employers incentivize performance. His research found that traditional notions of rewarding performance with higher pay only worked in very routine, straightforward, or algorithmic-type tasks. For complex tasks that require a higher degree of creativity, Pink found that external rewards are less effective. Instead, what motivates people to perform these kind of tasks are intrinsic rewards like autonomy, mastery, and purpose. Autonomy is a person's ability to self-direct; mastery refers to feeling as though you are making progress at getting better at something; and the purpose of motive is feeling as though you are engaged in something with a meaning larger than yourself.

In 2010, the *Harvard Business Review* interviewed Daniel Pink, and he reflected on what this means for the future of professional workplaces, "I think that there are a lot of small, and not elaborate or expensive things, that individual managers can do. Kind of dial back the carrot and stick motivators, and infuse the workplace with a greater sense of autonomy, allow people to make progress, and animate what the people are doing with a greater sense of purpose" (Bell, 2010). As we adapt our expectations to the workforce, we should also shift our approach to evaluating our intrinsic motivators in all experiences. This will allow us to be more self-directed and work with a sense of purpose. Becoming more self-directed requires reflection on how to become a stronger independent learner, sharpen the abilities to think ambitiously, and continuously try new things to discover meaning and purpose in all our work, activities, and studies. Understanding your motivations will better inform decisions on where to look next.

Consulting with Your Gut

I have always been very afraid of making mistakes. Half of the reason I don't leap for opportunities or hunt for new experiences is that I am afraid of making a mistake along the way. For me, making a mistake is not just "whatever, I will do it better next time." It really shifts a way out of my senses of worth and purpose.
(Student Respondent, 2018)

As your motivations begin to help you sort out the value derived from prior experiences, it is also important to be reflective on how those prior experiences influence your intuitive reaction during decision points. This is a *look up* moment. Take the time now to think about a time when you felt the need to make a big decision quickly. Perhaps it was a time when you had a term paper due, but your friends were trying to convince you to go somewhere exciting. What propelled your decision at that moment? Was your gut reaction telling you to spend more time on the paper or did you rationalize around the circumstance? What was the outcome of the decision? What did you learn and how did it influence your previous and current behavior?

It is common in our role as cooperative education advisors at Northeastern, when advising students on decisions, to help them balance between their intuitive "gut" feelings about an opportunity and their need to be strategic, logical, and analytic. We, therefore, often play a mediating role as part cheerleader/advocate and part devil's advocate/critic when helping students to evaluate choices such as which jobs to apply to and accept. Frequently, these sessions will be with students who face the decision of choosing between the merits of two or three good job offers. Our conversations progress through a variety of factors based on everything from the skills that they will develop to their financial situation, increased access to professional networking opportunities, or feelings they have about the individual interviewing them and the office environment.

Within these conversations, inevitably, we ask, "What does your gut tell you?" Interestingly, this elicits a smile, a brightening of the eyes, a pregnant pause in the conversation, and, typically, a move toward a firmer decision. It seems to be a freeing question that allows the student to drop all logic and simply express how they feel and why the easiest path may be the most obvious. This is typically the moment to deconstruct the initial gut reaction with a reasoned set of questions about the student's emotions. What led to that feeling or tug in a particular direction? Which job would you feel most motivated to get up for in the morning? Is the reaction you are having based on the opportunity to find intrinsic rewards in the work itself? Is it based more on extrinsic benefits that could be satisfying in the short term but would perhaps neglect other long-term professional and personal benefits for growth? This advising back and forth is all aimed to uncover how that gut reaction is grounded in previous experiences, current personal value systems, and goal orientation at the time the choices are presented. As Steve Jobs said in his 2005 commencement speech at Stanford University, "You can't connect the dots looking forward; you can only connect them looking backwards. So you have to trust that the dots will somehow connect in your future. You have to trust in something—your gut, destiny, life, karma, whatever. This approach has never let me down, and it has made all the difference in my life" (Jobs, 2005). It is through examining the past that we begin to understand what our intuitions are telling us.

Refining Your Intuition

The danger of intuition is that it can unintentionally create an impulsivity or boldness in our judgments and misconceptions about a decision's possibility of success. Take for example one of our former student's dilemma:

> *In my second co-op, I made a huge mistake that could have affected every single employee in the office. The worst part was that I lied about making the mistake. Then, there came a point when I could not lie about it and I had to be honest. I had to confront it myself. That was the most humbling experience that I have ever had. I messed up badly and all I was told was "look, we get it, sometimes things happen. Even if you make a mistake, it is just better for us to know."* (Student Respondent, 2018)

In this case, the student's gut decision was to cover up the mistake, but upon reflection on this decision they reversed course.

Research has shown that intuition can be potentially detrimental when making certain kinds of decisions. Daniel Kahneman, Nobel Prize–winning Economist for his work with Amos Tversky on prospect theory and the nature of rational decision making, explained the aspects of intuition in the following way:

> *There are some conditions where you have to trust your intuition. When you are under time pressure for a decision, you need to follow intuition. My general view, though, would be that you should not take your intuitions at face value. Overconfidence is a powerful source of illusions, primarily determined by the quality and coherence of the story that you can construct, not by its validity. If people can construct a simple and coherent story, they will feel confident regardless of how well grounded it is in reality.* (Kahneman & Klein, 2010)

This points to the important piece of the phrase "trust your gut." What compulsion, emotion, or storyline are you telling yourself to trust when facing a difficult spot decision? At some point, in a decision-making process, it is helpful to pause and think about which emotions specifically are influencing your logic and strategy around what is compelling you to lean toward a particular decision.

If positive emotions are driving decisions then it can lead to a more fulfilling process toward attaining long-term goals. David DeSteno in his work *Emotional Success: The Power of Gratitude Compassion and Pride* (2018) makes the argument that "emotions exist for one purpose: to guide our decisions and behaviors efficiently toward adaptive goals" (DeSteno, 2018). He highlights how three emotions in our "emotional toolbox" (gratitude, compassion, and pride), if used effectively, can help shape our habits, reinforce positive social behaviors, improve our consideration of long-term reward over short-term gains, and increase our willingness to persevere. Instead of viewing emotions as potentially driving impulsivity and limiting self-control, DeSteno shows that emotions in fact can enhance self-control. DeSteno demonstrates that through understanding and appreciating the emotions that drive us and are most effective for the decisions we face, the better equipped we are for being more effective (professionally, personally, and socially), collaborative, and virtuous in our actions. It is, therefore, of great value, and something we frequently encourage our students to do, to always examine the emotions and intuitive impulses at the key decision points to see how they are driving choices towards short- or long-term goals.

Overwhelmed by Choice

In addition to the emotional and logical elements that construct intuitive responses, our decisions are complicated in our current age of interconnectedness by an overwhelming sense of choice. Whether it is a simple decision such as which type of cereal to buy at the grocery store, or a complicated one such as which college and university to attend, we are in a time when we can turn to online communities for recommendations and opinions on just about everything. This can require a sophisticated ability to discern between all the available choices, and whether or not our unique circumstances give us a choice at all. As Leonard Mlodinow details in his new work *Elastic: Flexible Thinking in a Time of Change* (2018), reviewing all of our options can actually lead to greater anxiety. He writes, "We all want to make good choices, but research shows that making exhaustive analyses, paradoxically, doesn't lead to more satisfaction. It tends to lead instead to regret and second-guessing. Letting go of the idea that a choice must be optimal, on the other hand, preserves mental energy and allows you to feel better if you later learn that a better choice existed " (Mlodinow, 2018). So in this chaotic and complex world where it seems like we have endless choice, it is better sometimes to mindfully exercise a process of elimination. There is also often a delusion of choice as not all of the choices are real for us in our unique circumstances.

This is a principle we see daily with our student advisees who are faced with a tough decision on whether to accept a co-op job offer or not. Our students have a large database filled with thousands of potential jobs that are opened by our employer partners. With this large set of potential job choices as the backdrop, many students will lament that the first job offer they are receiving from an employer is not their "first choice" for a job, and often their "first choice" employer has not reached out to them at all for an interview. This is the "grass is always greener on the other side of the river" mentality, which can be detrimental to making a decision on the costs and benefits of the choice we have in front of us.

In these circumstances, it is especially important for us, as advisors, to employ a bit of a reality check for a student. We do this by attempting to frame the decision on real options versus hypothetical. In this circumstance, they are making a decision on the offer of employment in front of them and not the offer as it relates to choices and circumstances with other jobs that have not happened or may never happen. This confused sense of choice can often create stress when making tough decisions, which can lead to decisions that are not optimal for the individual student's goals. The salient point here is to approach choices with a realistic sense of the limitations.

In addition, approaching our challenging choices with a growth mindset (see Chapter 1) can help reorient us toward learning opportunities. The growth mindset approach and process orientation of our experiential learning programs at Northeastern encourages students to view all experiences as potential opportunities for learning. Focusing on goals oriented toward the potential learning outcomes or skill development from an experience grants the student permission to free themselves from the fear of making a wrong decision. For example, we often invite students to speak as panelists at events around campus, and one of the most frequent things we hear is "my co-op job didn't necessarily help me figure out what I want to do in life, but it did help me to discover what I don't want to do." This is a very important concept that you, as a student, should take note of in your own experiences. Allow yourself space to explore your way of learning free from the fear of wasted time or wrong choices! We all make wrong turns now and then; what is important, though, is that we don't view those wrong turns as bad choices/decisions but instead view them as an important part of the journey. There are no set maps for your life, but each new experience offers you a chance to learn something new, consider a new perspective on life, and reconsider how the experience contributes to your purpose motive and personal growth.

The Impact of –
Limited Bandwidth

Equally important during this noisy and rapidly accelerating time is to find the time for space to patiently examine our options. It is difficult to balance the cost and benefits of our decisions when we are overwhelmed, distracted, and do not give ourselves the time to think through our choices intentionally. In the book, *Scarcity: The New Science of Having Less and How It Defines Our Lives*, Mullainathan and Shafir (2014) demonstrate how scarcity in our basic needs (time, nutrition, financial resources, etc.) can reduce our bandwidth to exercise our cognitive capacities and self-control. Their research found, among other things, that scarcity can seriously hamper our ability to focus our attention, retain information, solve problems, reason abstractly, and control impulses. It can also lead to a phenomenon that they call "tunneling," which essentially is a way for the brain to try to solve problems most efficiently.

For example, the student who is focused too much on studying to improve their GPA may be skipping meals and neglecting nutrition. Or the student too focused on a side job to limit their amount of student loan burden may not have enough time and energy bandwidth to keep up with the assignments in all of their classes. These trade-offs, caused by tunneling, can often lead a person to neglect important long-term vision in their lives, or as the popular phrase instructs, "keeps them from seeing the forest for the trees." So in other words, the scarcities that play out in daily lives will have a great impact on day-to-day decisions, interrupt a sense of balance in daily routines, and can act as a barrier to eventual success on long-term goals.

The impact of having limited bandwidth to patiently and flexibly make decisions is important to consider when attempting to maintain a work–life balance. It is hard sometimes for students who feel the need to constantly be building credentials or working toward the next best thing to slow down and appreciate the experience that builds through the environment around them. As our employer partner, Zoe Gauld-Angelucci from Roots Interns in South Africa remarked,

> *It's essential to be creative and flexible (limited budgets and things often don't exactly go as planned in Africa). . . . What I do notice often with interns is that studying sometimes seems to be really competitive. CV's of some students included double majors, numerous volunteer activities and being chairman of several organizations. I regularly hear people that struggle to say 'no' or live up to expectations or have anxiety feelings. I feel we sometimes forget it's also good to just be a student and take time to relax in your spare time (2018).*

Recognizing that flexibility and patience is important in your own life can contribute to being more aware and adaptable in new unfamiliar environments. When feeling scarce in one area, it is helpful to stop, examine your commitments, and distractions in daily routines to see where you can in fact be flexible, or cut back, so learning opportunities and long-term goals are not neglected.

Distractions and Our Influences

A growing trend we see among students when considering decisions is that decisions are increasingly weighed in comparison to the choices made by others (our influencers). In our work with students, we see this when comparing their co-op jobs and experiences with another student who seems to be having a "better" job or experience. It is a fear-of-missing-out (FOMO) phenomenon, and when viewing the success of another we often assume that we see the whole story of their experience. Often overlooked is the context of the circumstances that the individual faced when traversing the string of decisions and opportunities that led to their job or experience. By doing this, we are distracting our attention away from the possibilities our own experiences are providing because of our longing for something that may seem better on the surface. There is therefore an increasing need to understand where our attentions are focused and the influences in our lives that drive these perceptions.

Christopher Chabris and Daniel Simon's research on inattentional blindness demonstrates that we are prone to miss substantial and salient events in our environment when our attention is distracted or focused on other things. In their work, *The Invisible Gorilla: How Our Intuitions Deceive Us* (2009), Chabris and Simons show, through a number of visual experiments, that humans tend to assume that how we see the world is how it is for everyone, and this frames our sense of reality. What this leads to is a blindness to small changes in our environments and to illusions of what we saw and remembered that shape our perceptions and interpretations about the world around us. These illusions are not just limited to our visual perceptions but expand to how we view our first impressions, the confidence shown by others, and event causality. "No amount of training will enable people to notice everything around them, and despite our best intentions, we cannot readily dismiss our intuitive (and incorrect) beliefs about what captures our attention. But with knowledge and the illusion of attention, we can proactively restructure our lives so that we are less likely to be misled by the illusion" (Chabris & Simons, 2009). While these illusions cannot always be overcome, Chabris and Simons suggest that just being aware of illusions in attention, memory, and perceptions can help us to seek more information to support our perceptions and double check our understanding before making decisions.

Making this type of attentive approach difficult is the inundation of distractions in our online social environments from commercialized interests that seek to exploit human needs for connectedness with value propositions of products that will help solve their daily problems and needs. As Tim Wu outlines in *The Attention Merchants: The Epic Scramble to Get Inside Our Heads*, "Without our express consent, most of us have passively opened ourselves up to the commercial exploitation of our attention just about anywhere and anytime. If there is to be some scheme of zoning to stem this sprawl, it will need to be mostly an act of will on the part of the individual" (Wu, 2016). In addition, media vies for our attention through political slants, incomplete and sensational stories, and loud spellbinding graphics that serve to support subjective opinion and biases. In this ongoing race to expand market reach and maximize bottom lines through the endless push to reach everyone, everywhere, at any time, we are seeing a need to examine those things that influence our routines and to structure our lives in a balanced way.

We must learn to begin to withdraw from some things to attend to others, which is becoming increasingly difficult in our interconnected time. Our lived experience will, as one of the early writers on experiential learning William James (1890) philosophized, amount to what we attend to. It is through understanding what is influencing our attention and how our lives are structured that we become more clear-headed and adaptive decision makers across our changing environments and circumstances.

Change Affinity and Fault Tolerance

My experiences outside of classroom reassured me that I have an array of skills essential for my profession and am able to build upon already existing knowledge quickly, learn new things on the spot. My two co-op experiences were largely different from each other, but I consider both endeavors to be equally successful—this gives me confidence that if I choose to pursue a different career path in the future, I will not experience any significant difficulties and can easily rebrand myself in a new industry/field. (Student Respondent, 2018)

How often have you heard people say, "change isn't easy"? As we go through our lives we will notice that everyone has a perspective on change and managing life transitions. When things get hard, there are usual sentiments from our friends or family to be flexible, let things "play out," and "not to worry, it will all work out fine." How we anticipate change and adjust our approach accordingly also plays heavily into our choices and decisions. If we have a built-in aversion to these changes then every change will feel more and more difficult to endure. If on the other hand we realize that change is inevitable and develop an approach to anticipating, and even enjoying the prospect of change, then perhaps this can improve our ability to find satisfaction in each new experience or life transition. As the student's quote above illustrates, diverse experiences help to build skills that will provide confidence in managing these life choices and transitions.

In a time of accelerated change, we need to develop the skills and the ability to pause and recalculate the pace of change versus what skills or knowledge it takes for us to personally adapt to that change.

There is peril and promise in every decision about whether or not to embrace novelty. But in the recent past, as the pace of change has quickened, the calculus governing the benefits of embracing novelty has been dramatically altered. Today's society bestows rewards as never before upon those who are comfortable with change, and it may punish those who are not, for what used to be the safe terrain of stability is now often a dangerous minefield of stagnation (Mlodinow, 2018).

As our lives become increasingly complex, noisy, and potentially chaotic it is also important to understand how to cope with and accept change at an accelerated pace. The pace of this change will test not only our bandwidth and abilities to filter important information but also test our abilities to adapt. Those averse to change may struggle, and developing a perspective on embracing change will be crucial to your success and general mental well-being.

No longer are our global industries tailoring a workplace and society toward settling down, getting a good job that is reliable and consistent, and raising a family. As globalization accelerates, we will need to become more mobile, enhance our abilities that come with exploring new places, and connect with more people not like us. These new layers of complexity point to the need to be able to self-direct, adapt to new circumstances, display openness to new cultural perspectives, and be flexible in goals and expectations. In *Elastic,* Mlodinow describes the human trait of "neophilia," the attraction to novelty and change, as being one of the basic components of human temperament. Right alongside "reward dependence, harm avoidance and persistence," neophilia is a trait that is affected both by your genes and environment. It is a trait honed by experience and way-finding across diverse and challenging environments and one that influences the ability to adapt and persevere. It is through this trait that we are able to better understand how to best apply our knowledge and skills in new unfamiliar situations.

We call this, for the purpose of this book, the ability to be fault-tolerant. A fault-tolerant system is one that continues to operate even when some of its components fail to work. The key to adapting and thriving in the future world of work will be to develop this mindset of fault tolerance. This mindset is extremely important for us to accept the prospect of needing to invent and reinvent ourselves as we encounter problems and adaptively make decisions in the future. In other words, what will be required of you as a student, employee, and citizen is to develop your capacity for change by showing an openness to being shaped by every new experience while also adjusting readily to new realities brought about by change. The remainder of this chapter will be devoted to showing ways for you to become more fault-tolerant and a better adaptive decision maker.

The Art of –
Getting Good at Asking Questions

One practical approach to becoming a more adaptive decision maker is through the capacity to develop good questions. Dan Rothstein and Luz Santana in their book *Make Just One Change: Teach Students to Ask Their Own Questions* (2011) show how teaching people to ask their own questions strengthens their abilities to be self-directed independent thinkers and fosters capacities for self-advocacy, problem solving, and more effective participation in decisions with others. In this way, Rothstein and Santana demonstrate through their "Question Formulation Technique" that the simple process of constructing the right way of asking questions will improve abilities in divergent thinking (the ability to innovate and think creatively), convergent thinking (the ability to analyze and synthesize information), and metacognition (the ability to understand how we learn and think).

Question formulation is a skill we develop with students at Northeastern in our professional development course to prepare for either informational interviews or job interviews. This question development can be sloppy, humbling, and difficult work, but not taking the time to develop and refine good questions can cause our students to come across as inattentive, and unprepared. Asking the questions in the right way, on the other hand, can show someone that they you are informed, meticulous, curious, and respectful. In addition, asking good questions is an important help-seeking behavior and demonstrates the humility to acknowledge that one does not know everything.

According to the method/running rules put forth by Rothstein and Santana, *formulating good questions begins with presenting yourself with a simple but thought-provoking question focus.* A good focus is not a question itself, but an issue or topic of concern that will stimulate new ways of thinking. When it is a decision point you are crossing, it is helpful to determine the intended outcomes or motivators of the decision as your question focus. For example, if making a decision on what major to select in college, then the question focus could be, "Studies in biology prepare me for a career in medicine."

The second step of question formulation is to construct questions by first developing and asking as many questions as you can without stopping to judge, discuss, or answer any of the questions. In addition, you will begin by ensuring that the question you pose is indeed a question and not a statement and that it is written exactly as it crossed your mind the first time. For the example used above, you could ask questions such as "What other majors prepare me well?," "Do I even like biology?," "Does my college have a good reputation in biology?," and so on.

The next step is to work on improving the questions by first examining them as either open-ended or closed-ended questions. Open-ended questions prompt broad and expansive responses, and closed-ended questions prompt one word or yes/no responses. Going through this process will help you to eliminate questions that are not getting to the heart of your decision. It is then helpful to prioritize the questions on their merits by working with a group or a personal mentor.

The final step is to reflect on the whole process, the thought process that you went through, and the next steps of how the questions can prompt new projects or directions of thinking on a subject matter. Skipping any of these steps will make the process less effective for your learning and skill development (Rothstein & Santana, 2011) Good question formulation will help you to focus on your decision point while also developing an important personal and professional skill set. To close the chapter, we will demonstrate a way you can use question formulation and mindmapping to maximize the learning outcomes of your decisions. To begin the next section, try to think of a big decision point that is coming up in your life. From there follow the guidance below.

Adaptive Decision-Making, Step 1: Developing Learning Outcomes and Mindmapping

A useful starting point for informing any decision is by formulating good skills-focused learning outcomes. Developing good outcomes is a form of goal setting that is specific, measurable, attainable, result oriented, and timely (SMART; Doran, 1981). Learning outcome development is particularly useful in managing decision points before an experience, as it helps to frame the experience in terms of its intrinsic benefits to self-improvement and growth. If faced with two contrasting options for a decision then this process can help a student target motivations for each side of a decision.

Learning outcomes for our students usually begin as broad goals for an experience and are honed through a process of examining the potential activities of a future experience and extracting what a student will be able to do, in specific skill areas, once those activities are successfully accomplished. For example, if a student is accepting a job as a marketing assistant tasked with writing blogs, updating social media, and analyzing target market demographics as a member of a team, then to develop the outcome the student would need to project the set of professional and personal skills they will be able to acquire at the conclusion of the work experience. In this case, one could consult with a job description and possibly project that the student's interpersonal communication, time management, strategic thinking, or cultural agility skills could be positively developed in this position. So a learning outcome could look like, "At the end of this experience I will be able to effectively communicate the viability of various marketing outreach campaigns to our company's diverse target audiences." After the outcomes are developed, it is also helpful to apply a weight to each outcome in relation to how important the outcome is to overall long-term goals. To do this, we suggest developing either a matrix or a mindmap to effectively gauge the personal pros and cons of a decision as it relates to intended learning outcomes.

One particularly effective method of mindmapping was developed by Tony Buzan (2006). As the proclaimed "inventor of the mind map," Buzan's approach focuses on harnessing creative thinking by engaging several cortical skills in the right and left hemispheres of the brain to enhance memory, forward thinking, and learning. Buzan's method, which can be found on his website, http://www.tonybuzan.com/about/mindmapping/, focuses on generating ideas around a central focus topic using imagery, color, and key words to develop connecting themes and ideas to the central topic image.

When applied with the question formulation technique and outcome development simultaneously, this method holds great potential in generating purposeful decisions that are adaptable according to a range of creative options and potential learning paths. One way to do this is to begin your mindmap with a central decision (like choosing to study abroad junior year of college) and from that central decision begin with different colored branches related to career, people, health, wealth, and growth (or come up with your own). From those branches generate words that relate to the positive and negatives of each area in relation to potential outcomes or skills that could result from the decision. Remember here that we are not just referring to

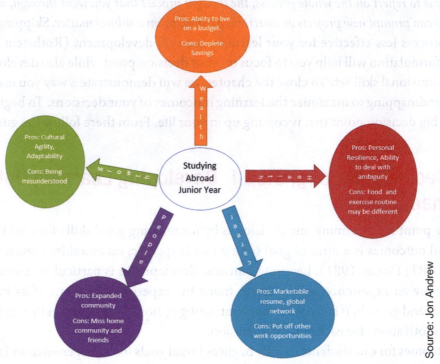

Figure 2.1: Beginning your mindmap to develop meaningful learning outcomes and decision questions

technical skills, but to skills that relate to relationship building, cultural agility, empathy development, and so on. From this mindmap (see example Figure 2.1), you can begin to develop good meaningful questions that you would have for a trusted advisor or mentor about this decision.

Adaptive Decision-Making, Step 2: Questions Formulation Through Improvisation

Generating the right questions at this point may be a bit difficult, so it perhaps can be the perfect time to meet with a peer for a session of "Yes, And." "Yes, And" is an improvisational exercise between two or more people who can generate creative ideas for solving mutual problems. Kelly Leonard and Tom Yorton's book, *Lesson from The Second City: Yes, And* (2015), demonstrates that using improvisation in the workplace and daily lives can make us more creative and collaborative. Leonard and Yorton use their experience of leading one of the most well-known improv comedy troupes to frame "Yes, And" thinking as a great alternative to "No, But" thinking. When facilitated effectively in a workplace "Yes, And" can make our environments conducive to a more inclusive, shared problem solving based on diverse perspectives. "Yes, And" is essentially a process of listening, agreeing, and building on an idea. It can also be sometimes silly, humorous, and a lot of fun.

We have facilitated "Yes, And" sessions in our professional development classes as icebreaker exercises for group work, and it is generally a great way to develop a good creative energy for problem solving. It is fairly simple; to begin, two (or more) actors decide on a central issue or theme and then for as long as they can add a new idea by beginning with the phrase, "Yes, And." You can begin with something basic like "Accepting a marketing job will give me skills in . . . communication. . . . Yes, and . . . teamwork . . . yes, and writing . . . yes, and telepathy, and so on." to generate learning outcomes. For question formulation, you could begin with, "Will accepting this job help me financially in the short and long term? Yes, and will it give me enough work–life balance? Yes, and which types of communication or writing skills will I develop most? . . . and so on." The hope is that by engaging in this sort of idea or question generation with another person will open new perspectives and ways for you to not only inform your decisions but also to think creatively on where your decisions could lead you next.

Adaptive Decision-Making, Step 3: Cost–Benefit Analysis

Once you have worked with a peer, a mentor, or a friend to generate thoughtful questions around your decision only one step remains: choosing the path you feel best aligns with your short- and long-term goals. This is often framed by our students as completing a "cost–benefit" analysis. When reviewing your list of questions take special care to attend to what closed-ended questions (those that need Yes/No answers or one-word answers) and open-ended questions (those that are more vague or need more time to think and answer) may be telling about how you are perceiving the costs versus benefits. For example, if you ask the closed-ended question, "Will this job pay well?," is it helping you to discern enough about what that good pay means to you in relation to the other factors? In contrast, if you reframe the foregoing closed-ended question as an open-ended question, it can be worded as "How will the financial benefits of the job compare to other potential benefits like commuting time, free time, autonomy, expanded professional network, skill development, and so on?" Reworking your closed-ended questions in this way can help you come to a more informed decision and better understanding of the weight of your priorities. Here, it is also important to review your questions and priorities with a trusted mentor in your life. Ideally, this person can help provide an outsider's perspective and reflect back to you what they are hearing about the priorities driving your decision. Once you make a firm decision, you will feel better, be able move forward without regrets, and develop openness to facing what comes next. After all, if you have taken the time to follow these three preceding steps, you have a pretty intentional approach to your new experience with a mindset for learning, adapting, and engaging.

Conclusion

We hope that by reading this chapter, you have a better understanding of how the mindset, motivators, sense of choice, and the influences in your life impact your adaptive decision-making abilities. Every decision is a potential point of learning, even decisions that you wish you had not made. It is through examining the factors (motivations, scarcity, and change affinity) that impact your decision-making processes will allow you to be more fault-tolerant and resilient to changes in your personal, academic, and professional environments. It is through learning to formulate and ask good questions of our mentors and those who influence our lives that we can begin to map our options when faced with tough decision points. The next chapter discusses about how to identify and utilize our mentors along the way.

LOOK UP: Reality Check

"If you can't beat it, join it." This sentiment was expressed by Elon Musk, on Joe Rogan's Podcast in September 2018, in regards to his new company Neuralink's efforts to eventually invent a "neural lace" that will serve as an interface between the human brain and the computer. This sentiment reflects Musk's contention that artificial intelligence is advancing at a currently unregulated pace that poses great risks to the future of humanity. According to Musk, Neuralink will eventually work toward developing technology to safely implant electrodes in the human brain that will enhance the ability to access knowledge at the pace of a computer, thus making humans more competitive with future machines. Yes, he is talking about developing "cyborgs" as a way for humans to remain "relevant."

While these technological advances may seem like science fiction at the moment and could be a long way off, contemplate hypothetically for a moment about what if the technology that Neuralink is working toward is already developed. If these electrodes are being implanted in humans who have the courage and financial means to do so, then it will inevitably change the way we all coexist.

Formulate your own questions around the human implications of these advancements and their impact on our society, global workplaces, and communities. Develop your own pros and cons list for this technology.

In addition, contemplate and answer the following questions before moving forward:

What impact could this technology have on how humans adapt to changes and make decisions? How could a small population of "enhanced humans" influence the future of our workplaces, industries, political leadership, and so on? How does this change the way we view education or knowledge, and our way of making decisions? How will this impact how we understand human adaptation? How can it influence how we view human ability?

Key Takeaways

- A diversity of reflective experiences can yield a better understanding of ambitions and the intrinsic motivations that propel decisions with a sense of purpose

- Examining and refining intuitive responses around decision points will help to better understand which emotions are driving those decisions

- Developing a fault-tolerant approach to decision making becomes easier with an affinity to change and a flexibility in our daily routines and expectations

- Learning to formulate good questions and learning outcomes with others can yield a stronger cost–benefit analysis around decision points

Follow-Up Activities in Toolkit—Listen Up, Look Up, Join Up, and Act Up

- Practice Adaptive Decision-Making through **Mindmapping**
- Conduct a **Strengths Interview**
- Perform a **Time Audit** Activity
- Complete a **Journey Lines** Activity
- Complete a **Choose Your Own Adventure Exercise**

Works Cited

Bell, K. (2010). What motivates us? (Interview with Daniel Pink author of Drive), *Harvard Business Review*. Retrieved from https://hbr.org/2010/02/what-motivates-us

Buzan, T. (2006). *Mind-mapping: Kick-start your creativity and transform your life.* London, UK: BBC Active.

Chabris, C. & Simons, D. (2010). *The Invisible Gorilla: How Our Intuitions Deceive Us.* New York, NY: Crown Publishers.

DeSteno, D. (2018). *Emotional Success: The Power of Gratitude Compassion and Pride.* New York, NY: Houghton Mifflin Harcourt Publishing Company.

Doran, G. T. (1981). There's a S.M.A.R.T. way to write management's goals and objectives. *Management Review, 70,* 35–36.

Duckworth, A. (2016). *Grit: The power of passion and perseverance.* New York, NY: Scribner.

James, W. (1890). *The principles of psychology, Vol. 1.* New York, NY: Dover Publications.

Jobs, S. (2005). *Stanford university commencement speech.* Palo Alto, CA: Stanford University.

Kahneman, D., & Klein, G. (2010, March). *Strategic decisions: When can you trust your gut?* Retrieved From https://www.mckinsey.com/business-functions/strategy-and-corporate-finance/our-insights/strategic-decisions-when-can-you-trust-your-gut

Kolb, A. Y., & Kolb, D. A. (2005). Learning style and learning spaces: Enhancing experiential learning in higher education. *Academy of Management Learning & Education, 4*(2), 193–212.

Leonard, K., & Yorton, T. (2015). *Lessons from the second city: Yes, and.* New York, NY: HarperCollins Publishers.

Mlodinow, L. (2018). *Elastic: Flexible thinking in a time of change.* New York, NY: Pantheon Books.

Mullainathan, S., & Shafir, E. (2014). *Scarcity: The new science of having less and how it defines our lives.* New York, NY: Picador.

Pink, D. (2009). *Drive: The Surprising Truth About What Motivates Us.* New York, NY: Riverhead Books.

Rogan, J. (Producer). (2018, September 7). *The Joe Rogan experience #1169-Elon Musk.* Retrieved from http://podcasts.joerogan.net/podcasts/elon-musk

Rothstein, D. & Santana, L. (2011). *Make Just One Change: Teach Students To Ask Their Own Questions.* Cambridge, MA: Harvard Education Press.

Wu, T. (2016). *The attention merchants: The epic scramble to get inside our heads.* New York, NY: Alfred A. Knopf.

3

Creating and Belonging to a Mentoring Community

I'm a hands-on mentor, who believes that communication and transparency are essential. I've developed that style after realizing that in order for a mentee to thrive, he or she needs guidance and feedback. They can't get to where you want them to go unless you talk to them. (Elmira Bayrasli, Foreign Policy Interrupted, 2018)

Only Connect!

E. M. Forster's *Howards End* (1910) is a novel about human connection. Margaret Schlegel, one of the two sister's central to the story, is inspired by the phrase "Only connect!" that offers two meanings. The first looks at the unity of opposing elements within each person; Margaret refers to this as the beast and the monk, the prose and the passion. The second meaning is to put the greatest energy into personal relationships. "Only connect!," the book's epigraph, emphasizes the value of personal relationships.

We would like to begin the chapter with this sentiment as it pertains to developing personal and professional relationships and creating and belonging to a mentoring community. By being purposeful in prioritizing and developing relationships, you open up a whole new area of learning and possibilities. In fact, when we ask our alumni and students about their experiences in college, most often we don't hear about a class, content area, or study; most often we hear about people they connected with or had an influence on them—faculty, alumni, advisors, friends, and peers. In research by Chambliss and Takacs (2014), who followed 100 Hamilton students through and after college to ascertain what in their undergraduate years really mattered to them, their core finding was, "Relationships shape the student experience." The "most valuable" of those relationships was found to be mentorship. In this chapter, we will focus on what it means to cultivate personal and professional relationships and to build and belong to a mentoring community. At the same time, looking at how having personal and professional relationships, as well as belonging to a mentoring community, reinforce one another and provide for deep, purposeful, and inspired learning. We will share with you examples and stories from our students, faculty, and employers on how, through experiential learning, they have observed, been motivated by, sought out, and ultimately developed relationships, which provided for opportunities to both the mentor and the mentored.

The Importance of –
Starting with You

During my first year at the University, I wanted to take advantage of everything that was happening around Boston. There was a Harvard initiative for Latin American students. I applied and I got in. It was a three-day conference and a keynote speaker was Danielle Lomes, a well-known Mexican entrepreneur. He was telling us [the participants] about his life and of course when you listen to someone so successful

© Orianna Timsit

you don't realize that they are human. From the stage, he said something along the lines of "I am going to be here during the entirety of the conference and you can approach me if you have any questions." And I decided right then that there is no way that I am going to approach him. At the last day of the conference, however, there was a social impact challenge, where participants had to create a product, an app, or a service that will tackle the problem of the informal economy in Latin America. Daniel was one of the judges and my group won the challenge. After that, he invited members of the group to join him for dinner and we immediately established a connection. He was one of the main reasons why AWEIK [an 800 people conference that was organized in Ecuador] happened. He not only encouraged me to make that long-term idea of mine a reality but helped me to organize it. (Student Respondent, 2018)

How do you respond when you meet an inspirational person? How do you identify people from whom you can learn? What would it take for you to be more comfortable with taking initiative, reaching out, and making connections? This student's story is an example of how you might be reticent or initially feel overwhelmed by the thought of reaching out to a potential mentor or person who has experience and skills that are beyond your own. Yet time and time again we hear from our students that when they take the risk to reach out and connect, it often develops into a long-term mentoring relationship or opportunity. In Pat Hedley's *Meet 100 People* she offers advice about networking and the value of proactively meeting with people in person. She notes that the first question she is asked most often when she encourages people to meet 100 people is—"How do I begin?" Her answer is, "You have to begin with you, to build an effective network, set achievable goals to establish a fulfilling career, you must first determine your strengths, weaknesses, value and ambitions, who you are and what do you want?" (Hedley, 2018, p. 33). In our previous chapter on fostering self-awareness, we introduced concepts and learning activities around how to be self-aware, reflective, and better understand your attitudes, values, and motivations. In this chapter, we will ask you to consider these aspects of self-awareness as you think about developing personal relationships, a professional network, and belonging to a mentoring community.

Investigating and Exploring—Mentors Are All Around Us

I have benefited enormously from people who have encouraged me and supported me—including scientists, writers, and social entrepreneurs. Often, it is just a single person. John McPhee encouraged me in my writing career. Veasna Chea, a Cambodian woman, inspired me with her own personal story, to begin building dormitories for female students in Cambodia. I have also mentored a number of young people myself. Mentorship takes time. It is a one-on-one proposition. You need to take a strong and continuing interest in another person. (Professor Alan Lightman, MIT Faculty, Author and Social Entrepreneur)

In J. D. Vance's recent book *Hillbilly Elegy* he tells the story of his upbringing in a poor Rust Belt town. Through many challenges, obstacles, and setbacks, Vance eventually makes his way to Yale Law School. In describing how he seemed to beat the odds, he cites his relationship with a mentor while in law school and reflects, "I didn't know how to prioritize my options, and I didn't know that there were other, better paths for me. I learned those things through my network—specifically, a very generous professor" (Vance, 2017). He goes on to detail other ways that the "social capital" he developed had helped him in numerous ways—in gaining connections and invitations to interviews at prestigious law firms, to actually being hired and joining a firm, which introduced him to an important mentor who ended up connecting him to an admired public figure who he eventually went to work with. His experience confirmed the value of developing relationships, finding mentors, and building what he calls "social capital," which he claims is all around us. "Those who tap into it and use it prosper. Those who don't are running life's race with a major handicap" (Vance, 2017).

In Robert Putnam's *Bowling Alone: America's Declining Social Capital*, he not only concurs with Vance's sentiment that those that who don't engage in social networks are at a great disadvantage but further claims that we as individuals and as a society are harmed by this lack of connection. Putnam explains "social capital" as a feature of social organizations such as networks, norms, and social trust that facilitate coordination and cooperation for mutual benefit (Putnam, 2001). In his book, he draws upon recent data, which suggest a significant decline in social networks in America and people who are increasingly disconnected from each other. For our purposes, let's proceed with Putnam's definition of social capital with a focus on relationships, mentoring, and how through experiential learning we have opportunities to counter this trend of disconnectedness by working with others for our own mutual and collective good.

Vance's is but one story of intentionally building relationships and developing and leveraging a social network. As we noted, the process starts with you and identifying who you are and what you are looking for and want to develop. The next logical step is to look to your environment with the intention of meeting people, gaining insights, and making positive connections. There are so many possibilities—coaches, facilitators, experts, employers, faculty, peers, family, and friends. Mentoring is usually thought of as someone with more experience helping someone with less experience in a particular area. For college students, mentoring can happen in a number of ways, and, according to research by Terrion and Leonard (2007), it almost always has a positive effect on the mentee. Additional evidence supports this; the Gallup–Purdue Index investigates the connection between what students do in college and how they fare later in life. It found that graduates who "strongly agree" that they had a mentor who "encouraged me to pursue my goals and dreams" were twice as likely as all others to be engaged at work and thriving on the index's measures of well-being. This made mentorship the strongest predictor of well-being out of anything that Gallup asked about (Supiano, 2018).

Mentors and mentees come in all shapes and sizes. Mentors can empower, provide resources, and help you solve problems; mentors can challenge you to make choices and decisions, can nurture and empathize, and can facilitate connections with a new network. Mentors are people who you admire, listen to and can learn from, collaborate with, and can be a source of encouragement and support. Whatever the particular role or orientation, both mentors and mentees come from the same interest and intention—making a personal connection. We see these connections from many different perspectives in our faculty and advising roles at Northeastern. There are situations where an older student provides advice and support to a younger student, an experienced supervisor/member of an organization develops and maintains a relationship with a co-op student or intern, and a faculty member mentors a student in a particular discipline or area of study; all of this happens with the intention of enhancing one another's learning and success.

Peer mentoring, in particular, was mentioned by faculty, employers, and alumnae/alumni as a mentoring relationship that was valued as part of experiential learning. Peer mentoring, which "matches mentors and mentees who are roughly equal in age, experience and power to provide task and psychosocial support" (Terrion & Leonard, 2007) is an area we see as key to our students emotional and social well-being. As part of our roles as faculty/advisors we regularly connect students to share their workplace and learning experiences. In our observations, students seem to thrive through initiating and establishing these connections. Terrion and Leonard (2007) cited that students who connect as mentors showed a stronger ability to provide psychosocial support characterized by "confirmation, emotional support, personal feedback and friendship." The authors also cite that a peer mentor "can serve as one source of support to reduce the stress experienced by a younger and less experienced student" (Terrion & Leonard, 2007). The research by Shotton, Oosahwe and Cintron (2007) listed three ways that peer mentors helped their mentees: "1) connecting students to the larger community, 2) providing support, and 3) providing guidance" (p. 94). In addition, research conducted by Fox, Stevenson, Connelly, Duff, and Dunlop (2010) confirms the academic benefit of having a mentor and demonstrates that mentees who participated in a peer-mentor program scored significantly higher in deep and strategic study methods compared to students not engaged in peer-mentoring programs. The mentees in this study scored significantly higher not only on grades but also in *how* they were studying. These "deep and strategic" methods of studying were characterized as students being "directed towards the intentional content of the learning" (Fox et al., 2010).

Now that we have introduced the benefits of developing personal and professional relationships, mentorship, and mentoring, as supported by research, hopefully you are considering joining a mentoring community, if you have not already. You might also be wondering what does it take to be a good mentor/mentee. According to a study conducted by Mee-Lee and Bush (2003), both mentors and mentees thought the most desirable characteristics of student mentors were to be "1) understanding and sympathetic, 2) accessible to students, 3) able to communicate well, 4) enthusiastic" (Mee-Lee & Bush, 2003). So as you can see mentoring isn't about what you know; it is more focused on support, encouragement, and is a process of engagement that takes time.

In order to begin investigating and exploring possibilities for developing relationships and building mentoring communities, you need to first be personally connected. We would like to take a step back here and bring in some current context to prompt your reflection. Let's begin with a challenge—notice how people are engaged/not engaged. Go anywhere these days and try to make a personal connection with someone in your periphery—whether it be walking down the street, sitting on the train or bus, spending time at a local cafe, or even visiting with friends!—What is disrupting this connection? Where are people looking? How are they engaged/disengaged? Well, if your experience is anything similar to ours and what we notice simply crossing our college campus is that the majority of folks that we pass are looking down at a technological device of choice—mobile phone, iPad, laptop, and so on. Once a seemingly easy and common exchange of eye contact, a nod, or a hello is now a rare occurrence. We would like to suggest as a first step to simply be aware of how you balance connecting person to person and face to face with your engagement with technology. What is your current experience? How might you be more aware of your daily practices to better balance connecting personally versus connecting technologically? How can "looking up" move you in the direction of fostering personal relationships and a mentoring community?

Paying It Forward: From Mentee to Mentor and Back Again

The power of the mentor got me to where I am so that I could be in a position to be a mentor to . . . every new generation that comes after me . . . sometimes it's exhausting but mostly it's just enlivening, energizing to be the person who helps these students find their way. (Faculty Respondent, 2017)

In LaMachia's research on *Integrating Global Citizenship Learning in Undergraduate Education* (2017), faculty mentoring was identified as a key factor in helping Northeastern students to leverage their experiential learning toward becoming more effective and engaged global citizens. The above quotation captures a faculty participant's enthusiasm for mentoring students to be global citizens. The consensus among program participants interviewed in the study was that faculty mentors played a key role and had significant influence on students' development as global citizens. It was through a faculty members demonstration of passion and commitment to global learning and citizenship from which students gleaned important lessons and perspectives. In fact, data from the interviews indicated that without faculty involvement in global learning programs and leading student trips abroad, participants thought the strength and momentum of global citizenship learning would be limited. Students who were interviewed reflected on the impact that faculty leaders had on their global learning and how they sought to emulate their examples. One student cited a particular faculty's example noting - the thoughtfulness with which the faculty leader went about constructing her global learning program and the intentionality with which the faculty member incorporated various perspectives on different issues. (Student Respondent, 2017).

The concept of *co-learning*, whereby faculty participants identified themselves as colleagues and co-learners with students, was cited as a valuable outcome of the mentor–mentee relationship. Co-learning was accomplished through developing teaching assistantships, incorporating students as leaders in global learning programs, and ultimately, supporting students in their career development. One faculty described a student who moved along a trajectory from her first learning program in Zambia to becoming a program partner in that country. She tells this story:

> One of my very first students [whom] I brought on a global learning experience is now my partner in Zambia. I met her as an undergraduate; she participated in my program to Mexico and was my TA for two years . . . she is now a colleague and someone I've developed a really important professional relationship with. I have other students with similar stories. At this point, I could roll into most countries, and I've got a student who has been there and doing work (Faculty Respondent, 2017).

Basically, through these stories and examples what we would like to emphasize and encourage is for you to view your learning process as moments of co-construction with your mentoring communities. We have noticed, and hopefully communicated to you through these faculty and student responses, how the experiential learning process is a way that this co-construction can occur and benefit both the mentor and the mentee.

Our co-op employer partners at Northeastern provide us with additional perspective on how mentoring relationships are helpful within their organizations for both students and supervisors. As part of the cooperative education program, students develop learning goals and objectives for their 4–6 month field experience with an employer and meet with their supervisors to review their progress. We advise our students that these meetings are great opportunities to gain insights and perspectives on their work as well as to establish trust and improve their communication skills. At the same time, we hear from our employer partners how checking in on the student's goals and progress provides them with insights and learning. One of our employers described this "give and take" process as follows:

> Mentoring is a challenging role and every student I have mentored has made an impact on me on a personal or professional level, one way or another. Usually the students' assist me by indirectly keeping me up to date on the new trends at universities and the interests of the younger generations. It is very

interesting to mentor students who are just making their first steps and trying to find their way, so I share as much advice as possible based upon my experience, and in particular, I share the things that I wish others had told me. I try to have an open door policy but it is increasingly difficult to make time, so it is also important that students take the initiative to come to me and find a time to 'pick my brain'. Regarding my own personal experience with mentors, throughout my life I have had many different people informally advise me, usually at different phases in my life, and this has worked for me (Cheryl Novak, European Public Law Organization, Athens, Greece, 2018).

The interesting thing about all of this is that students, faculty, and employers all embrace the possibility of belonging to a mentoring community and learning from and supporting one another. It is a win-win situation. In fact, the data collected from the interviews with faculty in LaMachia's (2017) study on global citizenship revealed that the majority of faculty identified mentoring as a key aspect of their role as faculty leaders and part of their learning goals and objectives within global learning programs. For students, these mentoring relationships allowed them to learn from example and have important questions answered by people whom they respected and saw as positive role models.

Being Attentive to the Random Sage

The things that stay with me are often not what this politician said to my four questions that I wrote down on a paper and later submitted for whatever. It's that one random conversation I had with a secretary at an embassy who lived under the siege of Sarajevo and told me a really casual story at lunch about it. That personal experience is one of my acute takeaways. (Student Respondent, 2017)

In addition to the structured roles of mentee and mentor embedded within educational programs, there are a myriad of opportunities to spontaneously connect with others, if you are paying attention and open. The above quotation from a student participant captures the essence of the importance of personal connection as he contrasts his two experiences. In LaMachia's study on Global Citizenship (2017), there was a general consensus among participants that personal connections to places and peoples, as well as chance encounters with others in global locations, were critical to students' learning and citizenship development. It was through global engagements that students came to distinguish their own background and experiences from others; question their assumptions; look for similarities, differences, and points of understanding; and form a greater appreciation of their individual and collective experiences. In describing these experiences, participants' emphasized being open and aware. The study underscored the importance of fostering curiosity and receptivity in meeting others. You never know when a seemingly spontaneous, random interaction will lead to a meaningful experience or relationship. The study revealed that these random encounters engendered new ways of seeing the world and students recognizing themselves as being part of a shared humanity.

LaMachia (2017) found additional benefits accrued from personal encounters with others, both ongoing interactions and chance encounters. These included helping participants to think about where they came from, what their place in the world meant, how it was interpreted by others, what kind of values and behaviors were associated with their place of origin, and how they made decisions regarding their being in the world. Interactions with others revealed participants' own cultures to have significance in the lived worlds of others; this exposed their own familiar world in the view of another person. One student noted:

We go out into the world; we have to think about who we are as global citizens. When you interact with other people and you tell them where you're from, there's a likelihood they're going to have a reaction. Thinking about how you're going to represent where you're coming from . . . is a part of it: thinking about what your impact is (Student Respondent, 2017).

Students became cognizant of how others were interpreting them and understanding them and began questioning themselves—did they fit the stereotype? Did they dispel myths about their home culture? How did they represent themselves and connect with others? These are key reflections, questions, and learning opportunities that are derived through engaging with others and are critical to one's personal, professional, and civic growth and development.

At our own university, experiential learning was greatly enhanced when it became global and students began working and studying all over the world. Students now study and work on all seven continents—even Antarctica. Why is this important? Because we live in a truly global world, indeed a complex and intercultural one, which means the chance that you will be working and learning in diverse environments is almost guaranteed. Random ideas, people, and opportunities out of your own cultural norm and traditions will present themselves and provide incredible learning and growth, if you are attentive to such possibilities. The need to engage and work with others from diverse perspectives is critical for you as learners, workers, and citizens in order to both thrive individually and to progress collectively as a society. Developing attributes of cross-cultural capability and global perspectives is important to underpin your personal, professional, and civic lives in a globally interconnected world. Such attributes are nurtured through sensitivity to the needs of others, much like what most often occurs in a mentor–mentee relationship. Former secretary of state John Kerry, in delivering the graduation speech to Northeastern 2016 graduates, offered the following challenge to graduates: "So all of us need to do much more to build relationships with partners overseas, to deliver assistance to families and communities abroad, to promote stability worldwide. Not because it is morally right; which it is: not just because it's in keeping with our national ethos; which is also true; but because our own security and prosperity demand it" (Kerry, 2016). Kerry's "call to arms" here captures the essence of this chapter and what experiential learning can provide you in terms of ways to *look up*, listen up, and act up to advance your personal connections, our shared humanity, and a civil society.

The Impact of –
Having Someone Who Believes in You

I think I have a network of people who I look up to and whom I want to emulate. Now that I have graduated and I have talked to these people I have realized how much more of an interest they have in me than I thought before. I think that is mentorship, and I don't think I ever knew how to recognize that. (Student Respondent, 2018)

Our postgraduate students often reflect back to us sentiments of appreciation and thanks for the help and advice that we gave them along the way. The phrase we hear most often is "thank you for believing in me" or "it meant so much to have someone who would believe in me no matter what the situation." We all need someone to support us and believe in us and to accurately reflect back to us, in an objective way, what we realistically can and can't do. We need someone to be a voice of support and realism to help us sort through chaos and confusion, someone who can be a sounding board, a good listener, and a critic. As we identified, mentors come in many different forms, but it is essential for us to grow interpersonally, professionally, and intellectually to have these people in our lives. Having someone in whom you can confide and go to for advice and perspective can really make a difference, and we see this with our students all the time. Take a step back, *look up*, and think about your own experience and network—who are people you *look up* to and seek to emulate? Who are people you trust and confide in? What is it that you find interesting/compelling about what they do and how they do it? How do these people model a professional practice, skill, area of knowledge, or a habit of mind that you are interested in? How could they mentor or help you to teach yourself these skills and develop in this area? Make a list or mindmap of your mentors.

When identifying a mentor who believes in you it is critical that you meet with them frequently to help them better understand your goals, abilities, tendencies and habits of learning. One of the most important aspects of our roles as faculty advisors is helping students to understand how they learn and how they can teach themselves new skills. Often times when students come into our Intro to Professional Development Course, they haven't had much professional experience. Concepts like intrinsic/extrinsic motivation and transfer of skills and workplace goals and objectives are completely new to them. In talking with employers about the future of the workplace, they emphasize the need for workers to both have the ability to teach themselves new skills and the ability to transfer existing skills across various industries. One academic faculty member interviewed also emphasized the importance of this:

> *Help students to be aware of their own learning process . . . because really good students often don't recognize the way they actually learn. This will become increasingly important as the nature of everyone's jobs will continue to change given automation, robots, artificial intelligence, etc. Again, intentionality is important as we engage students in the learning process (Faculty Respondent, 2018).*

In Barbara Fredrickson's book *Positivity*, she highlights the benefits of connecting with others and having warm and trusting relationships with other people. "Flourishing is not a solo endeavor," and it is scientifically correct to say that nobody reaches their full potential in isolation (Fredrickson, 2009). As co-op faculty and mentors, we have seen how having important people and mentors has an important impact on your learning and development. In addition, we have seen how the combination of having someone who believes in you and affirms your potential as well as helps you to understand how you learn is critical in fostering a sense of purpose and direction sense of purpose and direction in your goals and skill development. So our suggestion now is to think about who believes in you, why mentoring is important to you, and how you can pay it forward in your own life.

"Modus Operandi"—Being Upfront and Personal

Comparatively the difference between "campus-centric" universities . . . these places that are doing amazing things in academia, learning about great works and minds at the campus level, [as opposed to] universities that prioritize faculty-led global learning, you can really tell the difference . . . it's not about knowing the most recent report coming out of the Brookings Institute, but about being able to talk about on-the-ground issues with people in the location in the most concise way. (Student Respondent, 2017)

In our Intro to Professional Development Course at Northeastern University, we introduce the concept and practice of informational interviewing for exactly this purpose—to foster comfortability with, and understanding of, the benefit of face-to-face interaction. Most students have never heard of, much less organized and set up an informational interview. So, what is it exactly? An informational interview is basically a meeting that is arranged by you with someone working in a field/industry that you are interested in, and *you* as the interviewer ask questions to gain information, insights, tips, and advice about your area of interest. As part of the informational interview assignment, we have students conduct field research on organizations in their areas of interest and the kinds of work those organizations are doing. Students' initial research also includes an investigation into the jobs/career paths that exist and the people in the field, including their training, education, and background. This includes the people in the field—their training, education, background, and jobs/career paths that exist. Students are also asked to identify and document their current professional network including those they know are working and could be helpful mentors/guides as they begin their careers. Students then identify contacts whom they would be interested in interviewing to hear how they got into the field (background and experience), the reality of the field and opportunities, suggestions they have for how to prepare to get into the field, and so on. Consistently, the most difficult part of this assignment (the full assignment and guidelines can be found at the end of the book in the Toolkit section) is for students to actually make the call and take that initial step of personal connection. When we have alumni come to our classes to give their perspectives and suggestions to first-time co-op students, they most often talk about the power of informational interviewing and how these face-to-face opportunities have been useful to them in developing personal and professional relationships and progressing in their careers.

In addition to beginning to develop your professional network, there are many other benefits and advantages that students report—getting comfortable making a cold call, doing research and developing good questions, gaining insights on the reality of a given field and how to best prepare yourself, and learning associated professional skills and habits of mind such as time management, professional communication, follow-up and interview skills, just to name a few. As faculty, we notice how it seems to help students in fostering the ability to take initiative and develop an active role in figuring out what they want to do, getting more information about possibilities, and seeing the value of developing relationships with others who can guide and inform them.

In addition to informational interviewing, there are other means of connecting to people in your field of interest. We also advise and teach our students on the benefits of creating a profile on LinkedIn and using this to further develop their personal and professional networks (see full guidelines and advice on setting up a LinkedIn Account and networking in the Toolkit section at the end of the book). LinkedIn is a great way to make connections and develop and reinforce your professional network. In our work with students, we see how LinkedIn helps in setting up informational interviews, following up on these initial connections and maximizing, meeting, and connecting with folks on the job to gain further insight into a future career and skills needed. For example, we often ask upper-class students to come into our Intro to Professional Development Course and participate on a student panel to present to first-time co-op students their experiences, advice, tips, and acquired wisdom. In addition, we often connect students to talk about a particular co-op and share their insights and advice with the incoming co-op student.

In writing this chapter, a couple of things occurred to us. First, in thinking about a TA or student to speak in our classes or to tutor another student, we look to the students with whom we have developed personal relationships. These are the students who came to our office, talked with us about their thoughts and concerns, and used us as sounding boards to think through a decision. For the thousands of students with whom we have worked over the years, we have found that only a small number of students actually took the time to meet the faculty members personally. There is a certain profile to these students who *do* take the time to make this personal connection—they tend to be active and are constantly looking for ways to learn and progress with their interests, learning, and goals. They seek out opportunities to have a dialogue, in order to gain insights and perspectives, and they intentionally take the time to initiate a personal connection. They understand that it is not always what you know, but who you know and it is not always how much you know, but how much you care. This personal connection absolutely makes a difference, because we get to know these students; they are the ones whom we involve in our classes, whom we connect with others in the university and beyond to expand their networks and opportunities, whom we nominate for awards, and for whom we write letters of recommendations. We continue to support them after they leave the university by giving them contacts and supporting their graduate applications because we have gotten to know them better and have developed a relationship.

In Malcolm Gladwell's *The Tipping Point* (2000) he identifies three archetypes of people—maven, connector, and salesperson. Connectors make change by connecting with people; this is how they are oriented to the world. They are always thinking about whom they know and how they can connect themselves or people to one another. We are advocating for you to develop your "connector" self so as to benefit your learning, life opportunities, and the common good.

Challenging Assumptions—Opens Up Learning and Meaningful Relationships

A month and a half in India gave me a very deep insight about my own life. Often we are so blinded by our limited experiences or privileged positions that we forget how interconnected our world is, and how all humans, not matter where we are born, require the same necessities. My experience in India allowed me to break free from the paradigms and stereotypes surrounding poverty. We came across incredible and resilient entrepreneurs that multiplied the little that they had, and helped us see very clearly that the cause of poverty is not due to a lack of capabilities but rather, a lack of opportunities. (Student Respondent, 2018)

We all have biases and make assumptions and judgments that are based on certain experiences and ways of thinking that we have had. It is human nature to be critical, and our field of view can be limited. So, often we hear back from our students that a core area of learning came to them by realizing a certain assumption that they had and how it got challenged through their experiential learning. One faculty interviewed described students whom he sees on his global experiential learning program:

They're open to having their world rocked, 'rock my world, go for it.' I have these prejudices and preconceived notions. I dare you to shatter my myths. He comments, most of the time, they get shattered, those that are willing to accept it, say 'Wow, I really learned something new here.' (Faculty Respondent, 2017)

In thinking about developing relationships, expanding your personal and professional network, and building a community of mentors, it is critical to examine and understand that your views, knowledge, and understandings are limited and determine how you will go about expanding them. Generally, we see that when students cross cultures, which can be from hometown to college, from the college campus to studying abroad, or from classroom to workplace, the act of leaving familiar surroundings, beliefs, and experiences presents the opportunity to challenge assumptions and gain new social, emotional, and intellectual perspectives. We have observed the real benefits this learning provides as students reflect on their own culture and unpack the complexities and nuances of their own culture as they are learning about the culture of someone else. All of those previously held stereotypes start to wash away and move toward a place of cultural humility. An article in the *Journal of Counseling Psychology* that measured therapists openness to culturally diverse clients introduced the construct of *cultural humility*, defining it as "having an interpersonal stance that is other-oriented rather than self-focused, characterized by respect and lack of superiority toward an individual's cultural background and experience" (Hook et al., 2013). As one faculty respondent concurred,

> *I am a proponent of notions of cultural humility versus cultural competence. Which for me means, approaching your interactions with people from other backgrounds and other cultures with open-mindedness, recognition of power differentials and trying to diminish those in the way that you structure your relationships and the way that you engage with people, recognizing your own positionality in a society* (Faculty Respondent, 2017).

What we want to emphasize and encourage here is *looking up and out*side of yourself as you enter into new situations, meet new people, and develop new relationships and community.

Fostering a Sense of Purpose, Well-Being, and Cooperation

> *Speaking about a sense of purpose, mentorship was a profound part of my experience at Northeastern and in college in general. I think it was almost that feeling of wanting a mentor that made me a mentor. It wasn't out of the sense of arrogance or because I thought that I knew so much, it was because I learn more about myself by interacting with other people and being able to interact with people positively in a capacity where I can help them, I learned so much about myself. For me, mentorship is all about helping others to find their sense of purpose, what they want to do, what their fears are, what their hopes are. And through interacting with their personhood, I expand my own. I would not be the same person I am today without mentorship and I definitely wouldn't be as happy without mentorship.* (Student Respondent, 2018)

One of our colleagues at Northeastern, David DeSteno, a professor of psychology wrote a commentary in the *Chronicle of Higher Education* that focused on the importance of students cultivating personal relationships. In his article "We're Teaching Grit the Wrong Way" he cites research conducted by the American College Health Association, which showed that almost 54 percent of students report feeling high levels of stress, 60 percent report feeling very lonely, and more than 90 percent report feeling exhausted and overwhelmed at times (DeSteno, 2018). According to DeSteno, "all of this is taking a toll on students' well-being and the current efforts to resolve these issues which emphasize will power and executive function to achieve self-control are largely ineffective in helping these students" (DeSteno, 2018). He offers a different approach and solution to the situation—cooperation and developing strong interpersonal relationships. DeSteno states strong interpersonal relationships are necessary to thrive, and, in order to be a good partner, a person needs to be trustworthy, generous, fair, and diligent. In addition, "one needs to be willing to sacrifice immediate self-interest in order to share and invest in others. He cites emerging research, which shows feelings like gratitude, compassion, and a sense of pride in one's ability 'nudges' the mind to accept sacrifices to build relationships with others." DeSteno advocates "that it is important to you as students to know how to use your emotions as tools to achieve your goals and that focusing on feelings like gratitude, compassion and pride this contributes to your overall success." DeSteno additionally notes, "for students this approach will also help you to persevere toward long-term goals and strengthen social relationships which contribute to your learning and sense of well-being (DeSteno, 2018)."

We observe that many students who have gone out on co-op or participated in a study abroad or service learning program report back on how they have learned and been impacted by the social, emotional, and relational aspect of their experience. One student commented,

> *The true meaning of a global education and outlook is the realization that there's only one human race, that race is socially constructed. Unless we learn to act together, we're bound for total doom and self-destruction. The only way to act together is to have a common sense of purpose* (Student respondent, 2017).

It is through engaging with others, traveling to different locations with different histories and contexts, and thinking about the needs of others and the greater society that we can take advantage of opportunities to connect and cooperate toward making something better—which is affirming! We notice that when students feel in some way that they are contributing to the greater good, they feel good.

This sentiment was reflected in LaMachia's research on global citizenship (2017) in which data showed participants on global learning programs reflecting on the purpose of their experience and how it affected them as well as the people whom they encountered and with whom they worked globally. This purpose and intentionality influenced their personal values and priorities. The interviews revealed that students who identified themselves as citizens of a larger community recognized their responsibilities to that larger community. One student described her experience as part of a peer-mentoring program in Zambia:

> *The biggest thing for me was definitely that we worked with University of Zambia students, and because I was a student in Zambia, it had a different connotation than if I was a volunteer in Zambia, because I was going there with a purpose of learning and exchanging, which is different [from] going with a purpose of volunteerism. It was meaningful for me because it went back to my purpose and why I was doing this* (Student Respondent, 2017).

These characteristics that we describe are of people with a broad view and connected to what they are doing through a sense of purpose, cooperation, and well-being. They think about things beyond their own immediate community or interests, so that they may think about the impact of a particular decision they make, what food they eat, what clothes they buy, and how this might impact someone in a different part of the world. The point is that when you are committed to developing meaningful personal, professional, and civic relationships and being part of a larger mentoring community, you develop a wider and more considerate worldview that changes the way you live, work, and contribute.

The Art of –
Engaging Loving Critics—Seeking and Interpreting Honest Feedback and Critiques

> *For me, my mentors have been "critical friends"—people who are direct and don't hold back on constructive feedback. There has been sufficient trust built so I know that they have good intentions, and my best interests in mind.* (Ronnie Millar, Employer Partner, Irish International Immigration Center)

Who are the people you trust and whose opinions and feedback you value? This is the essential question as you identify people in your life who will provide valuable feedback with your best interests in mind. The process of seeking and interpreting honest feedback is not always simple. We encourage you to begin by thinking of "loving" critics or "critical friends" as our employer partner shares in his above reflection. These are your "go to" people to whom you can present questions and concerns for feedback and engage them in critiquing your performance, writing, ideas, situation, and so on. You want to choose someone who has a different perspective and can help you reflect on your own personal, work, or civic circumstance, so that you gain clarity. You are looking to engage a critic who has the capacity to formulate and ask critical questions and who has the knack for asking the questions that you have not, or could not, ask yourself. Sometimes, the truth can be hard to hear, and that is why choosing people whom you trust and whose opinion you value is important. You also want to think about the people you know who are good at attending (showing up and being present) and listening. At the same time, you need to think about your role and stance in receiving feedback that might not be easy to accept. It can be hard not to take these critiques personally, so how can you foster a sense of openness and curiosity? Viewing feedback as a constructive way to learn and improve will help you gain important information and perspective. You might want to think through how you will process and interpret feedback beforehand—would taking notes, or preparing questions/concerns in advance of the feedback session be helpful? Regardless of your strategy, being prepared and intentional will make requesting and receiving feedback more beneficial.

"Being the Mentor You Wish to See in the World"—Observing, Listening, and Empathizing

Example is the best teacher. Moral improvement occurs most reliably when the heart is warmed, when we come into contact with people we admire and love and we consciously and unconsciously bend our lives to mimic theirs. The job of the wise person is to swallow the frustration and just go on setting an example of caring and digging and diligence in their own lives. What a wise person teaches is the smallest of what they give. The totality of their life, of the way they go about it in the smallest details, is what gets transmitted. The message is the person, perfected over lifetimes of effort that was set in motion by yet another wise person now hidden from the recipient by the dim mists of time.
(Brooks, 2015)

The above quote by David Brooks in his book, *The Road to Character*, highlights the importance of developing our humanity and related traits so that we can be models of care and compassion in the world. Think of a time when you were struck by the kindness of another, when you witnessed a genuine act of compassion, when someone went out of their way to listen to something you had to say—how did you come away from this interaction? Joani reflected on this quote as it applied to her own life. Speaking for herself in these moments, she feels a sort of healthy moral challenge to her existing behaviors and thinking and reflects on how she could be more giving, helpful, and positive. She is reminded of a time when she was working on developing an ESL program in an elementary school in her hometown. The principal with whom she worked had a sign over his door that read: "No one cares how much you know, until they know how much you care." The principal himself modeled this sentiment through his actions and policies at the school. Joani was inspired by his example and as a result developed additional programs to complement her students' ESL instruction. One program sought to better integrate the students through an afterschool program where native-born students taught the ESL students how to play various games like kickball, dodgeball, and baseball, which resulted in the students playing together at recess. At the same time, Joani invited the mothers, grandmothers, and caretakers of the children to come to the school after school hours to be tutored by upper-level students. These additional programs allowed both the ESL students and their families to feel more comfortable with the language and culture, which resulted in them further integrating at the school and attending more school and community events. It truly was the principal's example and actions that inspired these initiatives on Joani's part, which served both the individual students and the collective school community. And so it goes, example is often the best teacher.

As part of belonging to a mentoring community, observing others' needs, listening and paying attention to those needs, having empathy, and providing nonjudgmental critiques or responses are required. A level of trust is important in order for sharing and discussing confidential matters that are often based in insecurity, uncertainty, fear, anxieties, and so on. One faculty member described the role his Jesuit education had on him personally and as a faculty administrator of a global program. He portrayed his own life choices and how he came to create a value-based global learning program:

> I use the principles that I learned with a Catholic education, what it means to be a good Jesuit scholar, and have created my own secular Jesuit model, which is to pursue the values of the Jesuits but do it in a non-religious capacity by engaging students in social justice through global citizenship and learning, empathy, compassion, service . . . and highly valuing education and access to education for everyone (Faculty respondent, 2017).

One of our employer partners described the importance of listening as part of the his approach to mentoring:

> I guess the lesson I'm trying to convey here is that being a good, compassionate listener is crucial, more so than I would have imagined. I know I mention the importance of listening previously, but in this situation with a mentee, there is SO MUCH on kids' plates today with school, internships, relationships, social pressures, probably a little homesickness in there, too. This connection needs to be approached holistically, covering both the professional and personal, because when you make the effort to do that you'll ultimately get a better effort back in return (Curtis Robinson, PricewaterhouseCoopers (PwC), Frankfurt, Germany, 2018).

This employer's sentiment is a wonderful example of mentorship based on observation, listening, and empathy and what is possible when a mentor approaches the experiential learning in this way. An interesting addendum to this employer's account, the student whom he mentored applied to be a teaching assistant position in Joani's Intro to Professional Development Course following her co-op experience at PWC, noting her interest and desire to mentor students and to be a source of support, helpful advice, and encouragement in their cooperative education process. What comes around, goes around!

Related to this, in LaMachia's (2017) research on global citizenship, students identified the development of empathy and cultural humility as key components of the transformative aspect of global learning, work, and citizenship. One faculty member interviewed described the importance of empathy in the following way:

> You can be globally minded and not a global citizen. If you want to focus on global citizenship, the number one thing you have to have is empathy. You have to be able to put yourself in someone else's shoes. Imagine what it's like to be a refugee. Okay, now imagine back to who you are. What can you do to help that refugee? (Faculty Respondent, 2017).

This faculty perspective emphasizes an aspect of empathy that was mentioned in multiple instances in interviews with other participants in the study—the importance of understanding what it was like to "be in the other's shoes." One student noted that a global citizen must connect with and care about other individuals, either globally or domestically, and relate through our shared humanity of similar characteristics, desires, and needs. The students interviewed as part of this study stated that it was through developing a greater sense of empathy that they came to see themselves as part of a larger world and recognize the need to challenge existing structures and limitations. Much of this mirrors what happens through a mentor–mentee relationship and community.

© Orianna Timsit

Conclusion

In conclusion, what we hope that you have gained in reading this chapter is an awareness of the importance of developing personal relationships, and how being part of a mentoring community can greatly impact your learning and experiences. It is developing this way that we believe students will be best prepared to address the guiding questions with which our university first began—what are the needs of society and how do we educate students with the knowledge, experience, and habits of mind to actively address them? By actively seeking out ways to connect personally, building supportive and reciprocal relationships, and being part of a mentoring community that is grounded in cooperation through your experiential learning, you can make progress individually while also contributing to the greater community.

LOOK UP: Reality Check

Andy Bramante left his job as a corporate scientist to become a chemistry teacher at Greenwich High School. There he has created a science research class that has gained widespread acclaim and publicity. In this class, his students work on impactful innovations that range from a fast and inexpensive Ebola test, to cures for Lyme Disease, to detection tests for pre-malignant pancreatic cancers. The accomplishments of his students have been featured in *Popular Science Magazine*, have been recognized by former president Barack Obama, and have appeared on the Steven Colbert show. In his class, Bramante acts as a mentor who facilitates access to resources with students instead of teaching in a traditional way. Students develop their own research proposals, and Bramante provides access to the classroom tools and individuals, research facilities, or companies outside of the classroom as needed along the way. Bramante lets students define their interests and learn on their own, and by treating them as adults he empowers them to see their ideas through. His model puts students in charge of their own skill and knowledge development while encouraging them to be accountable for the project outcomes they are personally invested in. He is not focused on the student project outcomes, grades, accolades, publicity, or awards but, instead, focused on the process of learning each student goes through. In his own words, "My measure of success for my students isn't what color the medal is, if there is a medal. Really, it's whether that student did learn the skills of how to think for themselves, how to think responsibly, how to be a good person, and how to articulate their ideas. You know, a lot of my kids go on to major in politics and business and these are the skills that transcends all of that" (Quiroga, 2017).

Take a Moment to Look Up and Answer These Questions

Who are the "Andy Bramantes" in your life? What is it about their mentorship that worked well for you, and why is their mentorship meaningful to you?

Looking at Bramante as an example, in what ways can mentors connect you to new communities? How can you effectively work with mentors to widen your personal and professional networks? How can you mentor others to help connect them and broaden their networks?

Draw a visual representation of your mentoring community. From this develop a networking plan and strategy for how you will expand your network and mentor others to expand their network, learn about new professional fields, and set goals for meeting five to ten new people over the next 6 months.

Key Takeaways

- Understanding and appreciating the relevance of cooperation/reciprocity for your personal, professional, and civic growth and learning

- Articulating your personal abilities, interests, and values for a variety of audiences and expand your capacity by listening to others stories, career paths, and decisions

- Considering the importance of listening and reflective practice in classroom, workplace, and community

Follow-Up Activities in Toolkit—Listen Up, Look Up, Join Up, and Act Up

- Complete a **Cultivating Relationships** Activity
- Plan, Organize and Conduct an **Informational Interview Example**
- Design a **Professional Network Map and Network Tracker**
- Create and Maintain a **LinkedIn Profile for Networking**
- Conduct the **Job Shadowing activity**
- Complete the **Past Mentors reflection**

Works Cited

Brooks, D. (2015). *The road to character*. New York, NY: Random House.

Chambliss, D. F., & Takacs, C. G. (2014). *How college works*. Cambridge, MA: Harvard University Press.

DeSteno, D. (2018). We're teaching grit the wrong way. *The Chronicle of Higher Education*. Retrieved from https://www.chronicle.come/article/We-re-Teaching-Grit-the/242854

Fox, A., Stevenson, L., Connelly, P., Duff, A., & Dunlop, A. (2010). Peer mentoring undergraduate accounting students: The influence on approaches to learning and academic performance. *Active Learning in Higher Education, 11*(2), 145–156. doi:10.1177/1469787410365650.

Forster, E. M. (1910). *Howard's End*. Edward Arnold Publishers, London, U.K.

Fredrickson, B. L. (2009). *Positivity*. New York, NY: Three Rivers Press.

Gladwell, M. (2002) The Tipping point: how little things can make a difference. Little, Brown and Company, Boston, MA

Hedley, P. (2018). *Meet 100 people—A how to guide to the career and life edge everyone is missing*. Greenwich, CT: The Path Ahead.

Hook, J. N., Davis, D. E., Owen, J., Worthington, E. L., & Utsey, S. O. (2013). Cultural humility: measuring openness to culturally diverse clients. *Journal of Counseling Psychology, 60*(3), 353–366. doi:10.1037/a0032595.

Kerry, J. (2016). *Northeastern University Commencement* [Transcript]. Retrieved from http://time.com/4321733/john-kerry-commencement-address-transcript-speech

LaMachia, J. (2017). *Integrating global citizenship learning in undergraduate education*. Retrieved from https://repository.library.northeastern.edu/files/neu:cj82nr13g/fulltext.pdf

Mee-Lee, L. & Bush, T. (2003) Student mentoring in higher education: Hong Kong Baptist University, *Mentoring & Tutoring*, 11, 263–271.

Putnam, R. D. (2001). *Bowling alone: The collapse and revival of American community*. New York, NY: Simon & Schuster.

Quiroga, E. (2017, June 9). *More than just science: An interview with Andrew Bramante*. Retrieved from https://greenwichfreepress.com/schools/more-than-just-science-an-interview-with-andrew-bramante-88884

Shotton, H., Oosahwe, E., & Cintron, R. (2007). Stories of success experiences of American Indian students in a peer-mentoring retention program. *The Review of Higher Education, 31*(1), 81–107.

Supiano, B. (2018, January 14). Relationships are central to the student experience. Can colleges engineer them? *The Chronicle of Higher Education*.

Terrion, J., & Leonard, D. (2007). A taxonomy of the characteristics of student peer mentors in higher education: Findings from a literature review. *Mentoring & Tutoring: Partnership in Learning, 15*(2), 149–164.

Vance, J. D. (2017). *Hillbilly elegy: A memoir of a family and culture in crisis* (1st ed). New York, NY: Harper, an imprint of HarperCollins Publishers.

4 Navigating Diverse Learning Environments

The Importance of –
Moving Beyond Habitual Environments of Learning

"Where Can I Buy Eggs?"—Story from Cuba

Living in Havana for the past two months, I have not only learned how to navigate the city, but also the unique situation which Cuba has been in for an extended period of time. Within a week of being at work, I had the chance to meet a leading Cuban economist who has taught at Harvard and Princeton. Before he gave a talk at our workplace, we had the chance to chat. My first question: "how do we find eggs in Cuba?" He smiled. (Student Respondent, 2018)

The above student reflection illustrates the nuances involved as you live and work in diverse learning environments. In living among diverse people and in unfamiliar places, you have opportunities to witness multiple cultural perspectives, behaviors, and values that offer a broader view through which to evaluate what is going on in the world. What we often notice in our students' stories and reflections on their global learning is how these experiences provide them with important perspectives about their own culture through the life experiences of others. By living in Cuba and experiencing life there, this student gained tremendous learning and perspective about this particular historical context and the Cuban reality. Her story shows that exposure to unfamiliar environments and circumstances force us to question what is familiar to us and the impact we have on others globally. These moments can lead to a sense of cultural humility and a shared responsibility to a global community. Experiential learning is vital to a thriving global society because it moves us beyond our own limited thinking and experiences to better understand other situations in the world.

This student's story about her work in Cuba speaks to how experiential learning exposes you to cultural worlds in which important realizations become matters to explore. As part of this student's reflection, she thought about how Cuba offered her opportunities to move beyond her own habitual ways of thinking and doing things. She reflected upon the limited connectivity in Cuba and how her constant access to information and "everything else I may so desire in America has led me to be complacent at times, if a web page takes longer than a few seconds to load, I become impatient. If I am cooking and in need of an ingredient, I can simply buy it at a nearby grocery store." She noticed how she changed her ways of thinking and doing from one of ease and expectation to one of being resourceful at work and at home. She realized a certain benefit through her lack of connectivity and felt that it allowed her to manage her time more efficiently and be less distracted. Overall, she acknowledged developing more patience and greater appreciation for what she had and changing the way that she had habitually come to think and do things. Through her experience, she learned to navigate with clarity and assuredness in her host country and also then bring the habits of mind

© Orianna Timsit

that she developed back home and continue to be more resourceful and thoughtful.

Similar to this student's experience encountering Cuba, your first encounter with college is a time that invites you to explore new ways of thinking, identities, and places that can be exciting, intimidating, and fascinating. Think of a time when you were visiting a completely foreign and new place. This can be something as simple as being lost in a new neighborhood in your own city, or your experience handling the excitement and uncertainty of encountering a completely new city or country. What do you do to get comfortable? For some it is settling into a homestay or new apartment, and for others it is immediately walking the streets of the new city to get a sense of direction. For most, it is managing a general sense of tentativeness, making connections to your new place while also feeling a lack of belonging, and, at the same time, a strong desire to connect and ground yourself. As we attempt to make sense of this new place, we compare our present conditions to our prior experiences and knowledge and begin to construct a perspective on how things work in this new environment. This process of "navigating" new experiences is what we are discussing in this chapter.

In our work at Northeastern, we have seen students react to new and/or challenging situations in many ways. For example, students coming to Boston from the West Coast sometimes lament the cold weather. They will romanticize the warm, approachable, and "friendlier" nature of their hometowns on the West Coast. We have seen students return from their 6-month co-op work experiences and make general and all-encompassing statements like "I now know what it means to work for a nonprofit, and I'll never do that again." One student we worked with even talked about how doing co-op abroad was much less of a culture shift than being at Northeastern since she had grown up in a very global school and moved multiple times. Whatever the transition or new experience may be, we encourage students to confront their initial assumptions, be curious and imaginative in how they frame and interpret their experiences, and constantly re-envision their place in the university and/or greater global society. A faculty member who leads short-term summer study programs discussed how she frames learning/goals for students:

When students are presented with this other reality, and with this other narrative, and not only presented with it, but work in collaboration with it, it changes their whole perspective and previous understanding. One of my learning goals is that students see that this is way more complicated than it looks. I'm looking for them to take that comfort with ambiguity, and comfort with complexity and apply it to their own work here (Faculty Respondent, 2017).

Managing Transitions: Navigating Spaces and Co-constructing Places

Learning in a different culture/environment is such a key factor in my conversations as far as me as an employee, or me as a researcher or me as a manager or whatever it may be. It's the ability to pull on these experiences because they're experiences that could have happened in the states, but on steroids. I had to develop really fast, working easily manipulable communication skills abroad because that's the setting

I was in. I had to be able to travel with groups of people I didn't know or traverse logistics abroad. That's much more difficult than doing it in your own language or doing it in your own country and your own culture. I had to be culturally sensitive. Something I learned very quickly versus reading McKenzie briefs here about cultural nuances. When I go to an interview now or I think about sitting in an interview the amount of times I have to stress that my skills are more potent because of the variety of environments that I have worked in. It's the difference between having colleagues in the Middle East North-African (MENA) region that you work with from New York than actually being in the MENA region. (Student Respondent, 2017)

This student's reflection illustrates the outcomes from exploring and navigating diverse learning and work environments for his personal and professional life. In our role as co-op faculty, we observe students as they maneuver through and manage multiple transitions during their college years and beyond. We also act as a guide and support as they make their way.

In thinking about navigation, consider the image of sailing a boat. There are many factors that you need to consider and attend to in order to have a safe and successful voyage—wind, tide, current, temperature, and weather. You will also have to adjust to the sudden changes that may occur, requiring reconsideration and adaption of your original plan. The navigation process calls for focused, active and engaged thinking, decision-making, and action. Experiential learning is quite similar to this example in that when you are actively engaged in a particular learning environment/situation you will have to prepare and be mindful of the elements around you in addition to being attentive to the multiple factors that will impact your experience.

At Northeastern, we see students traverse a variety of spaces and places of learning in which their navigational prowess is important. These include transitioning from home to college, from campus to studying abroad, and from classroom to a workplace co-op. According to research by Ambrose, Talgar, and Wankel (2016), in the 2014–2015 academic year, 94 percent of Northeastern undergraduates engaged in a co-op, typically 6 months in length; 35 percent participated in three or more co-ops, 41 percent participated in two co-ops, and 18 percent participated in one co-op. In addition, in that same year, 3,522 students completed 221,720 hours of community service, 900 students showcased their research at an annual research symposium, and 40 percent of graduating seniors engaged in at least one global experience. In all of these crossings, students are learning important skills that help them to maximize their learning as they manage and navigate these transitions. During this time, we have noticed certain actions and habits of mind that are consistently helpful to students—seeing learning as happening everywhere, making connections in and across learning environments, removing boundaries by identifying commonalities while concurrently being aware of areas of difference.

We offer the following questions for you to reflect upon in terms of how you prepare and engage in new environments and learning experiences. Think of a time when you were learning something in a new community or environment, that is, as a new member of an athletic team, on a study abroad experience, a service learning trip, in a workplace environment, and so on.

- What do you do that is different/the same in these various experiences?
- How to you prepare for learning in a particular environment?
- In what ways do you plan, organize, and gather materials, information, tools, and resources needed?
- How do you research, network, and seek to involve others in your new learning/practice?
- What "side trips" do you engage in to associate and maximize learning?
- Essentially, how do you intentionally prepare before, during, and after the journey?

Research supports the importance of students gaining skills and comfortability in making transitions and adjusting to diverse learning and work environments in order to navigate their way through life. In Christopher Dede's commentary, *Students Must Be Prepared to Reinvent Themselves* (2017), he cites his own career in which he has "reinvented" himself multiple times and acknowledges that students face a "future of multiple careers, not just jobs." He points out that the real issue for students "isn't which path to take, but which one to take first as a foundation for others." As part of our role as educators, we are tasked with preparing students for "unceasing reinvention to take on many roles in the workplace and for careers that do not yet exist." Dede argues that the biggest obstacle in reinventing ourselves is not learning, but unlearning. As part of unlearning and navigating diverse work environments, he encourages students to embrace active, collaborative learning and that, as part of this education, educators ensure the intellectual, emotional, and social supports that help students to continually "unlearn" old ways, as they learn new ones.

The Impact of –
Dislocation Education

My perspective has changed since I'm home. I'm more confident because I've realized that if I can manage to do these things elsewhere, I can do them at home. I can be independent. It's forced me to be more prepared. It's forced me to question more and it's forced me to think more and be more reflective. (Student Respondent, 2017)

The above student story is an example of how going beyond the classroom provides opportunities to change, enhance, and reflect on your learning and potential. As part of experiential learning, you will 'dislocate' your education, meaning that you will disrupt the normal or usual state of how you experience your education. This could be leaving the classroom to work directly in your field of study, departing from your local campus to study abroad in another part of the world, or engaging in service learning or research to understand a theoretical concept more directly. Whatever the case, as you change your focus or place of learning there will be innumerable ways that your familiar patterns of thinking and routines will be disrupted. David Kolb, an American educator and theorist on experiential learning, suggests that experience alone does not lead to learning or growth (Kolb, 2014). For this to occur, the new experience must be processed in some way that helps you to reconstruct yourself. As we have discussed previously, reflection is a key concept in experiential learning. In order to turn your experience into learning, you need to step back, recall aspects and events, and analyze and process them. Reflection is the process that serves to integrate your experience to the learning.

During their cooperative education work placements, Northeastern students respond to a series of four sets of reflection questions. Students respond to these questions online and then we (Cooperative Education Faculty) read and respond to their reflection responses. At the end of each co-op cycle, students also participate in group reflection sessions in which they unpack their experience. (See Toolkit section at end of the book for Group Reflection Guidelines and Reflection Prompts.) These reflective discussions often include where they worked; the challenges/successes they experienced; the new skills, knowledge, and habits of mind they developed; how their experience related to their academic studies; and, finally, what they learned and how they developed personally and professionally. The sessions also serve as a way for students to share among themselves information about different industries, organizations, and opportunities. The reflective discussions are robust, dynamic, and particularly helpful for students in deconstructing their learning, that is, actually discerning and articulating the particular meaning and perspective you gained through the experience.

When speaking about the importance of reflection, one colleague often emphasizes that someone can have an experience but miss the meaning. In order to find the meaning, we have found that setting aside deep, intentional, and structured time to engage students in reflection allows for true synthesis and integration of learning to occur. Keith Basso in his ethnography *Wisdom Sits in Places* (1996) discusses how the sense of belonging to a place becomes taken for granted as people establish a comfort level with that place. At a certain point, we no longer recognize the association we make between a place and our identity. Only when we feel dislocated from a place do we realize the subtle effect it has had on our lives. In our role as faculty advisors, we see the impact and learning benefit 'dislocation education' has on you as you navigate through diverse work and learning environments and how through dialogue, reflection, and community you can deconstruct your learning and take meaning from your experience. We see students gain confidence, greater clarity about what they want to study and/or areas they want to work in, and develop better understanding of themselves and their interests and potential. In addition, we find that 'dislocation education' and reflection encourage the development of skills and other benefits that are critical to acquire in order to belong and succeed in a global society. One of our employer partners noted her experience working with students in the following way:

We always see a difference in students who have worked or studied abroad versus those who do not. They're more culturally aware, can easily immerse themselves in the local culture, and they understand local problems from a different perspective in comparison to those whose first experience is with our organization. These students do not have strong biases and they are able to grasp the program without judging or adding their own previous prejudices to the situation" (Employer Respondent, International NGO, 2018)

Developing Cultural Humility and Agility

"Maybe It's Me Who's Not Getting It" . . . Story from Latin America

He was saying that the laws were unequal and they favored women more than men per se, . . . and I immediately, something came out of me and I just jumped into responding like—you don't know . . . that's not your . . . you're not a woman from Nicaragua . . . then later I actually did learn that in Nicaragua they did have some really bizarre interesting laws surrounding women. Sometimes you react badly and think "oh, they just don't get it, but it might be you who's not getting it." (Student Respondent, 2017)

The above student reflection illustrates the need to release previously held understandings and habits of mind, so as to come to a place of understanding. In this situation, she humbly reveals her judgment of a Nicaraguan coworker. Given both the increasing numbers of American students participating in global experiential learning and international students studying at American universities, it is important to consider the opportunities that mobility offers you for exposure and growth as a student, worker, and citizen. How do you take full advantage of what university and increased technology can provide for you to be engaged with others from diverse perspectives? How can you further develop your capacity to navigate across varied contexts and environments? As we have previously discussed, college campuses and the ivory tower are neither finite nor contained structures but, rather, encourage student mobility and promote learning beyond the classroom. In addition, technology today facilitates rapid circulation of information, services, and ideas that connects people all over the world and provides additional ways in which students can access new concepts and perspectives. This trend bodes well for your development as global citizens and workers. It also has positive implications for global businesses, which are reliant upon higher education to ensure the necessary preparation of students to be successful in a global world and economy. Ghose (2010) cites experiential learning as an appropriate tool and promotes it as being helpful for students in developing positive mindsets, responsibility, community involvement, power of thought, and an understanding of their abilities within the context of real-world application. One student described her experience in this way:

> *My experience completely shifted my worldview by placing me in an environment and culture completely foreign to me. It put me in the shoes of those who move by themselves or with their families to other countries and made me realize how important your mindset can be in these situations. This experience gave me a deep appreciation of other cultures, granting me an opportunity to learn about the world and the people who make up the world and really understand our basic similarities.* (Student Respondent, 2017)

In her book *Cultural Agility*, Caligiuri (2012) argues that more than ever before, organizations need a pipeline of professionals who possess "the ability to quickly, comfortably, and successfully work in cross-cultural and international environments"—a quality she calls "cultural agility." Furthermore, she describes culturally agile professionals as those who succeed in diverse contexts because of their abilities to deal with an unfamiliar set of cultural norms or multiple sets of them. She claims that their performance depends not only on the content of their jobs but also on their ability to function in the cross-cultural context of their jobs. The author also addresses the need for professionals to possess an understanding of diverse contexts/peoples with a sense of cultural humility as a highly valued competency for global professionals to possess.

There are other factors that point to the need for student mobility and cross-cultural interactions and understandings. For example, there is increasing evidence that experience in working with others from different backgrounds helps you to develop qualities like creativity, communication, collaboration, and persistence, which are critical to your future success. In the data collected in LaMachia's research on global citizenship (2017), faculty, students, and administrators reflected on issues of power and privilege and the need to develop a sense of cultural humility by paying attention to issues of equity, accessibility, and possibility. Participants in the study discussed the importance of interacting with people from other backgrounds and cultures with open-mindedness and an intention to diminish power differentials between people and recognizing their own positionality within a global society. Through your experiential learning opportunities and active engagement in the world, you can gain important tools and skills to better navigate the forces of technology and globalization and make informed personal, professional, and civic decisions.

Consulting Guides Along Your Way

> *After coming back from my first co-op, I wanted to help people who were coming from a different country because so many people had helped me out and I wouldn't be alive today if not for a lot of different people helping me out.* (Student Respondent, 2017)

Staying with the initial sailing metaphor, just as you would consult a compass or sextant as you navigate the salty seas, consulting guides as you journey in diverse environments is equally as important. During a recent group reflection that we led for students returning from their co-op workplaces, we observed a common theme among students as they shared their co-op experiences. Almost all students noted difficulty they had in asking questions of their supervisor or colleagues, particularly when they first arrived to their new position/organization. One student talked about how when she didn't know the answer to something she would avoiding asking for help and instead engage in many different ways and searches in order to try and find the answer or information. Only after exhausting all possibilities of doing this on her own, did she reluctantly ask her supervisor, who was actually only too happy to provide the information as well as additional helpful insights. She observed that her initial attempts at solving her problem were both inefficient, as it took her much longer wandering in multiple directions without background or knowledge than having a 15-minute conversation with her supervisor, as well as isolating, in that it prevented connection with her colleagues. She reflected,

> *I realized that stubbornly spending large amounts of time searching for an answer was actually unproductive and not worth avoiding the perceived 'ego cost' of asking for help. By showing a willingness to learn and take initiative by asking questions, you can quickly get answers and more efficiently figure out how to do your job.* (Student Respondent, 2018)

Asking questions and consulting others in a new environment is key to your ability to navigate and make your way. It was striking that students struggled with this to such a high degree and felt the pressure to figure it out on their own. When you think about going to a new place and/or having a new experience, it is a necessary part of your transition to *look up*, take in new surroundings and information, and find people to direct and guide you. One student participant captures their movement toward this type of approach:

> *It's not about how professional I seem. It's not about what I'm wearing. It's not about where I'm from. My university might not have any clout at all. It's really about being able to sit there and being able to communicate and being able to show interest and ask questions and express that even if it's not in your language* (Student Respondent, 2017).

The Art of –
Mindfulness Learning Through Observation

> *I gained knowledge through realizing that I do not, will not and cannot know everything. While I may be more prepared for new customs or events, there is always going to be something that I do not know about. Even cross-cultural experts have gaps in their knowledge about cultures. However, I think knowing that I don't know everything, helps me be aware of myself and be more observant to other people's words and actions.* (Student Respondent, 2018)

In support of this student's reflection on the importance of observation and sense of awareness in crossing cultures, we propose a mindful and observant approach for students to maximize their experiential learning as they navigate through diverse new experiences. We use Ellen Langer's book on *Mindfulness* (2014) in our introduction course as a guide for students preparing to go on co-op on to how to mindfully approach their learning and transition. In their article *The Elements and Benefits of Mindfulness: Deepening Learning on Co-op and Beyond* collaborators from Northeastern's Center for Advancing Teaching and Learning Through Research and Cooperative Education Faculty (Sweet, Mazor, Klionsky, Andrew, & Zaff, 2015) review some of the research on mindfulness, how it relates to student's experiences on co-op, and how being mindful and observant in an experience can assist you as you navigate through new learning and work environments. Their article focuses on sociocognitive mindfulness (adapted from Langer, 2014) and defines it as the habit of constantly taking note of new and different features, experiences, and interactions in one's environment in the present moment (Sweet et al., 2015)

In cooperative education, when teaching students about the role of mindfulness in experiential learning, we ask them to focus on the three main elements that Langer identifies: (1) a focus on the present, (2) recognition of context and perspective, and (3) critical consideration of preconceived notions, rules, and routines. In the first element, which puts a focus on being present, we encourage you to fully engage in your current situation, no matter how simple the task or situation appears. In their article, the authors translate this concept to the workplace and provide examples such as taking time to prioritize or rethink your role in the organization. In our classroom and advising sessions with students, we point out how much there is to learn simply by observing your new environment—How do people communicate? Is it a formal/informal setting? Body language? Interactions? Ways people work? Ethics? We encourage students particularly in their first few weeks while they are transitioning to their new environment to take that time to observe, to engage as a "social scientist"—by paying careful attention to dynamics, being curious, asking questions, exploring, taking notes, and reflection—basically being present, engaged, and observant.

The second element asks you to be sensitive to context and perspective and try and refrain from judgment to see your new environment and situations from a variety of viewpoints. The third element, which we have presented and discussed in previous chapters, has to do with paying attention to preconceived notions, rules, and routines. In their article, the authors share a particular example of a student on co-op where she was working in one of three units that were having communication issues. Instead of accepting the notion that only her unit had it right, she purposely sought to try and understand the language used by all three units. What she gained by employing this approach was an expanded knowledge about the industry, the ability to translate the different languages across the units, and she became recognized as a valued mediator. What we would like for you to consider and take away from this discussion on mindfulness is how this more purposeful, creative, and observant approach can impact your learning and enable you to make contributions. What we want to emphasize here is that by practicing sociocognitive mindfulness it will help you find value and meaning in all of your experiences, even those that may appear superficial to you.

Experiential Learning That Promotes Flexibility/Adaptability/Transferable Skills

People I've known who have engaged in experiential learning during college years or shortly after are more adventurous, more self-sufficient and resourceful, more enterprising, and generally more committed to making the world a better place. (Professor Alan Lightman, MIT Physicist, Writer and Founder of Harpswell Foundation)

We have found that employer partners, such as Professor Lightman, emphasize the importance of students having the ability to transfer skills, integrate learning, and develop specific soft skills. The capacity to be flexible, adaptable, and to transfer skills from one area/industry to another is key to fully participating in and contributing to the workplace and society. In Christopher Dede's recent article in *Education Week* (December 2017) he suggests that students entering the employment market focus more on developing skills that complement artificial intelligence rather than those that substitute for it, that is, creativity, empathy, and other soft skills. Dede also recommends students hone their abilities to acquire and transfer new skills. As mentioned previously, Northeastern University President Joseph Aoun articulates a similar strategy in his latest book *Robot-proof—Higher Education in the Age of Artificial Intelligence* (2017). He proposes a way to educate the next generation of college students to invent, to create, to discover, and to fill needs in society that even the most sophisticated artificial intelligence agent cannot. Employers, researchers, and educators are all in agreement that one future certainty is change. Therefore, students need to be equipped for living and working through these changes. Experiential learning helps students in developing critical skills such as fostering adaptability, cultural pliability, conflict resolution ability, and communication.

Dr. Aoun also stresses that achieving "robot-proof" mastery entails both the acquisition and integration of new skills/knowledge, and, more importantly, the ability to apply and transfer those skills to various situations. This occurs when skills and/or knowledge are learned in one context and then successfully applied to another (Aoun, 2017). He explains the process at different levels in the following way: "if the contexts are similar—say, when students take ideas they learned in a class on the Elizabethan drama and apply them to one on Restoration poetry—the transfer is *near*. The students take a theory, concept, or body of knowledge and put it to work in a new but largely familiar situation. If the contexts are largely disparate—for example, when critical thinking skills honed in a Restoration poetry seminar are used to create a public relations campaign for a marketing company—the transfer is *far*. The students are encountering an entirely novel situation but are able to step back and understand how, embedded in the context, they can use their knowledge to solve a problem" (Aoun, 2017).

We would like you to take a moment now and think about situations and ways that you have engaged in this type of application and transfer of skills. What was your process and outcome? How did it impact your learning? How did you benefit, and develop? We are suggesting and promoting the idea of thinking intentionally about how you apply and transfer tacit knowledge and skills from one context to another and the types of learning/situations that you are involved in that call for this. As we have discussed, in a fast-paced and interconnected global workplace and society, this ability to apply and transfer learning and skills is key to your successful navigation of these experiences.

Transferring Skills Across Environments—The Value of Connection and Exploration

We took traditional business consulting, which students take classes in, and we developed a version of business consulting for slum entrepreneurs. We looked at what a slum business requires versus a traditional business and then designed a consulting practice model that students use when they go into the slums in Africa and South and Central America to help entrepreneurs develop their businesses and create opportunity. (Faculty Respondent, 2017)

In the above example, a faculty member describes an experiential learning program in which a consulting model is adapted and, as a result, knowledge, skills, and opportunities are transferred across different environments. This specific situation involved students transferring classroom information and skills to a real-world experience in a global location. They applied their learning and skills by engaging in affective learning while also critically reflecting on diverse cultural contexts. It required them to reimagine an established model and utilize personal connections to develop a heightened awareness and engagement. In this way, students began to realize the value of working with others to affect change, rather than distancing themselves from social problems. This learning not only allowed them to transfer important skills and knowledge but also broadened their horizons and helped them to gain a sense of common purpose.

This ability to transfer what you learn from one context to another is important whether you are a student or faculty or professional in your field of practice. Dr. Susan Ambrose, author of *How Learning Works* (2010), emphasizes that learning is deepened when students have the opportunity to use what they have learned in new contexts. She points out that being "in the field" provides opportunities for students to transfer their knowledge, skills, perspectives, and frameworks to conditions different from those in which they originally learned. This transfer across contexts will assure that the learner "owns" the knowledge and will be able to continually use it in new contexts as they arise. This approach contrasts with traditional curricula and higher education models, in which you wait for 4 or 5 years before you actually use your knowledge and skills in authentic contexts.

In her article *10 Ways to Improve Transfer of Learning* (2017), Marianne Stenger emphasizes the importance of the ability to transfer your knowledge to new contexts and the impact this can have on your career, by simply understanding how to apply your prior knowledge to situations you may confront in a new role (Stenger, 2017). She offers tips on ways to improve transfer of learning, many of which we emphasize as part of our teaching in experiential learning. Stenger advocates thinking about how you might apply what you are learning today in your life or job to a future goal or opportunity. She also emphasizes the importance of reflection and self-articulation so that you can fully explore and then explain what you have learned and how it applies/might apply to a new situation. Just as we have identified the importance of connecting personally and our sense of belonging to a community, Stanger concurs that much of how your learning is deconstructed is through the opportunities you take to meet and discuss it with others. She cites research that shows that collaborative learning promotes engagement and benefits long-term retention. Finally, Stenger recommends establishing clear learning goals that "give you a better understanding of what you're trying to get out of your learning and how you might later transfer that knowledge and apply it in your work, personal or civic life." Finally, by setting learning goals and outcomes, you can focus your attention more specifically on what you can learn, do, and then apply to other contexts.

Developing Learning Goals and Outcomes

As part of teaching the Introduction to Professional Development Course to our students, prior to their going out on co-op, we work with them to develop learning goals and outcomes. (Refer to Toolkit for Co-op Experience Objectives and Outcomes Activity.) We do this to help you engage in thoughtful preparation for your experience and to help you mindfully develop a set of hard and soft skills that you can clearly articulate as a result of your experience and learning. The following are outcomes for students' overall experiential education at Northeastern (Ambrose et al., 2016):

1. Apply your acquired knowledge and skills in new authentic contexts
   a. Thus gaining a deeper understanding (i.e., recognize what to use, how, and when)
2. Gain new knowledge and develop new skills to successfully engage in unfamiliar tasks, activities, and so on
   a. Thus gaining the ability needed for continuous, lifelong, self-directed learning, that is, recognizing what you don't know and figuring out how to learn it or compensate for it
3. Integrate and use the deepened knowledge and skills as well as the newly gained knowledge and skills to continue to learn on your academic programs
4. Reflect on and articulate the foregoing points
   a. That is, discussing how you used your knowledge and skills, how you gained new knowledge and skills, and how "theory and practice" work together, thus developing skills of metacognition, another element of lifelong, self-directed learning

As part of our university goals related to experiential learning outcomes, we ask students to develop and review with their supervisor a list of 5–10 learning outcomes that they would like to accomplish during the time they are on co-op and also write about how they will eventually assess and measure their success on completing this outcome. We define a good learning outcome as specific, observable, and measurable. Think of skills that you hope to learn, goals you hope to accomplish, and knowledge you hope to acquire. After writing your desired outcome, think about how you will measure and assess your progress. (Full instructions on writing good learning goals, objectives, and outcomes can be found in the Toolkit at the end of the book.)

© Orianna Timsit

In our Introduction to Professional Development Course we use reflection and self-assessment to begin the process of articulating your skills and also your goals and areas that you hope to develop and gain additional experience. The process of reflecting on and articulating your abilities and aspirations for learning are key to your professional development. As we take students through the course, we practice and review the best ways to communicate their goals and experience as part of preparing themselves for a professional interview. In preparing for an interview, you will be thinking about how to answer questions about your strengths, learning, and development and how they relate to a particular position. You will need to think back to previous roles and responsibilities that you have had and how these helped you to acquire certain skills, knowledge, and competencies that relate to the position you are seeking. We began a discussion of the self-assessment process in Chapter 1 of this book. In this assessment process, you begin to connect key areas of learning and strengths, articulate these by providing examples of skills you have acquired, and clarify how these transfer to your potential new opportunity/position. (See Toolkit for Interview Preparation Case Studies and Activities.)

Conclusion

In this chapter, addressing the impact of navigating diverse learning environments we reviewed tools, narratives, mindsets, and learning activities that we hope will help you as you navigate these multiple transitions in academia, the workplace, and greater global society. We encourage you to be mindful and observant in order to thoughtfully guide your experience in new environments. In doing so, you realize how flexibility, adaptability, and transfer of skills are key to traversing different contexts. In addition, approaching your experiences this way will help you to develop learning goals and outcomes, enabling you to clearly articulate and explain your learning and aspirations while also helping you to focus on and measure your progress.

LOOK UP: Reality Check

CNN Hero and Pat Tillman Humanitarian Award winner Jake Wood and his fellow marine William McNulty founded the disaster relief NGO Team Rubicon after the devastating 2010 earthquake in Haiti. That small team of military veterans aimed to utilize their skills, honed during tours of duty in Iraq and Afghanistan, to reach disaster areas and victims in locations deemed "too dangerous" by other disaster relief organizations. Team Rubicon's mission is to solve two substantial problems: (1) inadequate and antiquated disaster relief responses and (2) reintegrating veterans effectively into civilian life. They accomplish this "By pairing the skills and experiences of military veterans with first responders, medical professionals, and technology solutions, Team Rubicon aims to provide the greatest service and impact possible" (Our Mission, 2018). Their model provides veterans with a way to continue their service while building community, purpose, and sense of worth when transitioning to civilian life. Wood and McNulty recognized that military service provides individuals with a unique set of skills, knowledge, and life purpose that transfers well to the sector of humanitarian aid. Team Rubicon started as a team of eight members and now has a growing team of over 75 employees and over 65,000 volunteers.

Look up for a moment to contemplate these questions:

What is particularly effective about Team Rubicon's approach? What challenges do you imagine they face when implementing their mission in new places and with new members?

Individually, what are the big issues or problems that are important to you and that you hope to solve? What skills are required to solve these problems, and what communities or stakeholders are important to consider?

To explore this further, develop a list of your skills and a list of your values. Think of real-world examples of how you came to know about these skills and values. How can these work toward being transferred to new settings in a way that will help you solve the problems or issues you identified that are important to you?

Key Takeaways

- Explore through specific examples the role reflection plays in the deconstruction of learning and meaning making
- Improve and foster skills in intercultural communication, cultural agility, and humility
- Gain understanding in transferring skills and understandings across workplace and cultural environments
- Set learning goals and outcomes to help you transfer learning across contexts

Follow-Up Activities in Toolkit—Listen Up, Look Up, Join Up, and Act Up

- Prepare your **Professional Reference** page
- Complete **Job Description Dissection**
- Develop your **Learning Goals and Outcomes**
- Prepare and Practice for a **Professional Interview**
- Uncover your **Transferrable Skills/Experiences**
- Do a self review with **Weekly Reflection Prompts**
- Contemplate with the **Cultural Bridge** Activity

Works Cited

Ambrose, S., Talgar, C., & Wankel, L. (2016). *Integrated Student Learning Experience (ISLE): A model for personalized education dissolving artificial boundaries.* Northeastern University, Boston, MA

Ambrose, S., Bridges, M. W., DiPietro, M., Lovett, M. C., & Norman, M. K. (2010). *How learning works.* Hoboken, NJ: John Wiley & Sons.

Aoun, J. (2017). *Robot proof- higher education in age of artificial intelligence.* Cambridge, MA: The MIT Press.

Basso, K. (1996). *Wisdom sits in places: Landscape and language among the western apache.* Albuquerque, NM: University of New Mexico Press.

Caligiuri, P. (2012) Cultural Agility: Building a Pipeline of Successful Global Professionals Jossey Bass

Dede, C. (2017). Students must be prepared to reinvent themselves. *Education Week.* Retrieved from https://www.edweek.org/ew/artiles/2017/12/13/students-must-be-prepared-to-reinvent-themselves.html

Ghose, N. (2010). Enhancing competitiveness through experiential learning: Insights into successful programming. *American Journal of Business Education,* 3(7), 1–5.

Kolb, D. (2014). *Experiential learning: Experience as the source of learning and development* (2nd ed). Hoboken, NJ: Pearson Education.

LaMachia, J. (2017). *Integrating Global Citizenship Learning in Undergraduate Education.* https://repository.library.northeastern.edu/files/neu:cj82nr13g/fulltext.pdf

Langer, E. (2014). *The power of mindful learning.* Reading, UK: Da Capo Books.

"Our Mission". (September 14, 2018). Retrieved from https://teamrubiconusa.org/mission/.

Stenger, M. (2017). *10 Ways to improve transfer of learning.* Retrieved from https:www.opencolleges.edu.au/informed/author/marianne

Sweet, M., Mazor, D., Klionsky, S., Andrew, J., & Zaff, M. (2015). *The elements and benefits of mindfulness: Deepening learning on co-op and beyond.* Northeastern University, Boston, MA

5

Let's Talk! Boundaryless Communication

To say you can speak the most broken version of a language, but if you're able to communicate exactly what you mean to another individual in whatever language you're trying to work in, then you're fluent. You're fluent in communication. That's a linguistic point of view. That sunk in immediately. If you want to work abroad and if you want to have these experiences that are really meaningful and engage with multi-levels of narratives or multi-levels of conflict, then you really have to be willing to be patient and then also communicate concisely. (Student Respondent, 2018)

The 1981 diesel Mercedes rumbled through the verdant landscape of North Germany. Jon struggled to take it all in. Sleep-deprived from his travels, he was having trouble making sense of where he was. The smell of fresh pig manure spread on the farm fields and diesel engine exhaust stung his nose. The open windows and roar of the Mercedes engine made it nearly impossible to hear his host mother starting up a conversation in German. Jon had never been to Germany and had only studied German for 1 month prior to arriving for a year abroad living on a pig farm. With every question from his host mother he smiled nervously, nodded to feign understanding, and sunk deeper into the large leather seats of the car. Eventually, his host mother gave up and turned on the radio as they rode the final 30 minutes of the journey in silence to Jon's new German home.

Have you ever had an experience where communication felt impossible? Have you ever just been completely misunderstood no matter how hard you tried to clarify your message? Our coauthor Jon's first experience with his host family in Germany illustrates just how difficult it can be to understand and to be understood. In an extreme cross-cultural situation like this, simply getting around can feel hopeless, and the inclination to give up is strong and acute. When walls and barriers to social connection are thrown up on all sides, the feeling can be so strong that emotional and physical sickness can result. Conversely, these situations present a tremendous opportunity to find great joy in the development of important relationships and skills that arise from a willingness to actively listen, laugh at yourself, and try new ways of having your message understood.

Most cross-cultural interactions are not as awkward or disorienting as being thrust into a year-long stint abroad in a foreign region, and living a life immersed in completely foreign language and culture. All interactions, however, are to some degree cross-cultural and can present boundaries in how we make sense of the world and communicate with others. Judy Brownell, in her work *Listening: Attitudes, Perspectives and Skills*, describes our perceptual differences in the following passage, "Another person's behavior or words are understandable to the extent that you can put them into a context, connect them to things with which you are familiar. In fact, people often become angry when others violate their expectations about how to behave or what to say. Predictable people tend to be better liked than unpredictable ones ..." (Brownell, 2006). Making meaning and sense through our negotiation of human relationships is complicated, but communicating

across these various relationships is an extremely vital skill in a globalized and interconnected society. It is a skill that is developed across a lifetime through experience, and nurtured by a willingness to engage with others despite occasional emotional distress, insecurity, or discomfort.

Our work within interconnected online communities and globalized workplaces are steadily increasing our daily interactions with ways of thinking and styles of communicating very different from our own. Jean Twenge in her book *iGen* (2017) presents U.S. Census data research demonstrating that those born between 1995 and 2012 in the United States are the most ethnically diverse generation in American History. In addition, as a generation that never knew the world without the Internet and with some who never knew the world without iPhones, this generation is fundamentally changing how we connect and communicate socially. Twenge's research shows that the average high schooler spends about 6 hours per day on their cellphones (2.5 hours on texting, 2 hours on the Internet, 1.5 hour on gaming, 5 hours on video chatting), and eighth graders spend about 5 hours per day on their cellphone. These trends show that technology is enabling more communication to happen with a much broader reach to more and more people from diverse cultural backgrounds. As our employer respondent from an international NGO puts it, "As society becomes more global and interconnected, students need to be prepared to engage with different cultures and people. Universities can continuously stress the importance of being open-minded and culturally aware and help their students learn different ways to cope with the various challenges that will occur" (2018). An acceleration in encounters with others across cultures will increasingly require skills to quickly process, understand, and interpret communication styles and context across cultural and social boundaries. Being misunderstood in these circumstances is uncomfortable and can cause us to retreat to the comfort of personal echo chambers that reinforce our ways of thinking while discounting alternative perspectives. Conversely, embarking on new cross-cultural experiences with a degree of anticipation, curiosity, humility, empathy, and understanding is great preparation for engagement in a global workplace and society.

The ability to communicate well across cultures requires practice and experience communicating in new collaborative cross-cultural situations. At Northeastern we see this frequently from our students who return from their first professional experiences. Frequently, these experiences require students to shift their communication styles regularly with teams that are local and global. Through these interactions we see an increased confidence in face-to-face and written communication with colleagues on multiple organizational management levels. As one student reflected,

"as for participation in experiential learning programs, my intercultural communication abilities have improved tremendously—mastering that skill is essential for my successful performance both in a classroom and at a workplace" (Student Respondent, 2018).

Whether it is a struggle with how to question a supervisor's decision, or a need to liaise with a team of colleagues in Mumbai, our students are constantly engaged in a process of interpreting their roles in the workplace and learning to communicate within and across perceived boundaries. In the previous chapter, we introduced Paula Caligiuri's (2012) studies on cultural agility to highlight skills that aid in navigating cross-cultural contexts. In the context of communicating well in those cross-cultural contexts, Caligiuri identified three competencies affecting an individual's cross-cultural interactions: (1) valuing diversity, (2) ability to form relationships, and (3) perspective taking. She writes, "Effective interactions with people from different cultures are not just the *goal* of culturally agile professionals; they are the way professionals *become* culturally agile" (2012). It is through these experiences with others who may not think or behave like us that we become more able to be at ease in any situation, develop positive interpersonal relationships, and understand situations through a variety of alternative perspectives. This chapter is on how you develop awareness and become an effective communicator throughout your personal, professional, and academic experiences.

Returning for a moment to Jon, his year in Germany was an incredibly formative experience that led to a path of studying, teaching, and writing on intercultural competency development for students. Learning the German language by being immersed into the local culture required him to regularly exercise creativity with nonverbal communication skills while maintaining a sense of humor when things didn't go smoothly. It required patience and slowly working through face-to-face conversations in order to increase his tolerance for ambiguity. In addition, these interactions required the outward expression of sincere gratitude toward those willing to help him while bearing with his mistakes, which led to personal relationships that have lasted a lifetime. He developed his language slowly by accepting that he would not always be understood and humbled himself to present children's books in front of a class of intimidating Gymnasium (high school) peers accustomed to presentations on the merits of Kafka, Goethe, and Kant. The benefits of learning from our interactions with others not like us can grossly outweigh the challenges. Our hope is that by reading this chapter you will seek to acknowledge, interpret, and deconstruct boundaries of misunderstanding that you encounter throughout your experiences when communicating with others.

The Importance of –
What We Mean by "Boundaryless Communication"

Educational institutions can help by getting their entire campuses to operate in a similarly connected manner. Campuses that fully embrace bringing technology and digital capabilities to all facets of the university community will help in this regard. And I make this statement not because it's right or even good, but because this is where we are all heading . . . to a fully connected world. I would suspect this is already taking place to some degree at many universities around the world. But more importantly than the connectivity, universities can serve as guides for their students about how to navigate it all, whether offering courses or other learning opportunities that highlight topics such as: how and when to turn it all off, how to use these tech/digital tools as smartly and responsibly as one can, that explore the social and professional implications for doing so, and perhaps most importantly, how to remain a human being when we're surrounded by, and using, technology around the clock. While these tools are cool and powerful and freeing, they also can be burdensome, frightening, stress-inducing, and possibly even weapons when abused . . . this point needs to be part of the larger discussion as well (Curtis Robinson, PricewaterhouseCoopers Frankfurt, 2018)

More and more, we see traditional boundaries in educational institutions, workplaces, and society being reimagined or altered. Traditional notions of teaching and learning that were previously confined to the halls and classrooms of schools and universities are being replaced with new educational models. These models take teaching and learning to venues outside of the classroom through direct community partnerships. In the fulfillment of these partnership programs community members become teachers, teachers become students, and students become innovative coworkers and community members. For example, at Northeastern University this community partnership model of learning was pioneered with our cooperative education program and is expanding through the Experiential Network (XN). XN is a program through which Northeastern partners with businesses and organizations to engage students and faculty on short-term project work that complements concepts being taught in the classroom. These projects can be completed in person or virtually from anywhere in the world. Through this experience, traditional notions of teacher, learner, and employer are broken down with all parties shifting from their traditional roles to innovate on the project deliverables ("Experiential Network", 2018). In this experiential learning model, institutional networks are becoming integrated for the benefit of the student, classroom, and workplace.

In addition, these boundaries between classroom and the real world are being rethought across all levels of schooling. Iowa BIG is an example of a K-12 school district in Cedar Rapids, Iowa, that reimagined traditional learning approaches by taking down existing boundaries between the public schools and the community. At Iowa BIG, students design interdisciplinary real-world projects in cooperation with a mentor from an organization or business in the community. Teachers work to incorporate academic concepts with the projects and assess students not with letter grades but metrics aligned with joy and efficacy. ("About Iowa Big", 2018) These expanded notions of how and where learning happens disrupt traditional models of education in favor of more collaborative community-based learning model.

With technology, these models can now additionally be expanded globally with classrooms of students now being able to collaborate and solve real-world problems in communities across national boundaries. NuVu studios is an innovation high school in Cambridge, Massachusetts, with a pedagogy focused on students learning exclusively through a multidisciplinary, collaborative design process. At NuVu, students work together in an open studio space to solve complex and multidimensional problems. Teachers act as coaches as students create, design, prototype, and implement their designs. Students at NuVu are actively contributing to the need for innovative solutions for real-world problems, and though much of the work is grounded locally, the studio has been expanding globally with programs running in India and Scotland ("What is NuVu", 2018). Recently, NuVu began a virtual exchange program called the "Innovating Across Boundaries Project," with U.S. students in Cambridge working with Syrian Refugee counterpart students in Turkey on collaborative coding and robotics projects. ("Press", 2018) These are the kind of programs that are boundaryless and changing how we conceptualize education, the workplace, and global society.

As we break through traditional boundaries, or previously underdeveloped collaborations between classroom and society, we are opening possibilities for solving some of the world's most intractable problems with new colleagues globally. The move to a more experiential and entrepreneurial way of collaborating across borders, institutional boundaries, and societies necessitates communicating with others effectively. This communication requires cultural sensitivity and a nuanced understanding of the varied environments and contexts in which we live and work. More specifically, working in this boundaryless context will require us to better understand our own interpretative filters through which we communicate with our peers, coworkers, and employers. Boundaryless communication requires awareness of our interpretations and the ability to competently, effectively, and inclusively engage with cross-cultural communities of practice to solve problems, cooperate, and innovate.

Throughout this chapter, we will be presenting you with intercultural communication concepts and techniques to help you prepare for experiential learning programs and seek to engage you in understanding your abilities to communicate across boundaries. In addition, we will include insights from our employer partners and students about the impact of cross-cultural experiences on the ability to be a more effective professional who can build trust through active listening and perspective shifting. Our hope is that by reading this chapter you will develop techniques and skills that will make you a more effective collaborator/communicator with your peers and colleagues across cultures and environments.

You Don't Know What You Don't Know: Deconstructing Our Interpretative Frameworks

I come from a developing country, for us the Internet connection is very poor and slow. The pace of work is very different; people take a two-hour lunch break to go to their houses and eat with their families. I have been in many situations where you come totally prepared with the American mentality of efficiency, PowerPoint-ready, suited up and you get to the meeting and nothing goes as expected. For example, when I was trying to raise money for Aweik, the CEO of the company I was pitching for, started the conversation wanting to know more about us, then the conversation moved to family and friends we had in common; by the time we finished talking about our families one hour was gone. However, in Latin America the most important is getting to know the person first, then business.
(Student Respondent 2018)

This student quote illustrates how we encounter disorienting shifts in behavioral and communicative expectations in our home country or abroad. As this student experienced, working across cultures presents communication challenges based on the cultural context, the traditional modes of communication, and where the work is being conducted. We adapt, as this student did, based on the cultural knowledge and resources we have about how to understand and be understood. When we have little cultural knowledge, we do our best to make sense of our interactions, which can lead to developing unfortunate stereotypes about the way people act in particular cultures. For example, in the student quote above, if they did not know why the CEO was asking about friends and family to begin the meeting then it is possible that this behavior could be interpreted as rude or intrusive. Conversely, if the student did not discuss family and friends then the CEO could think that the student was rude or untrustworthy for developing the business partnership. These are examples of the interpretative filters we carry from our own cultural backgrounds and experiences that we use to understand the intent and meaning in our experiences.

Take a minute to *look up* from the book to think of a cross-cultural experience you have had. This could have been a short trip abroad or to a part of your home country you had never previously visited. It could be a summer camp experience or of starting a new job for the first time. A cross-cultural experience can really be viewed as any that required you to orient yourself to a social group with a new set of expected behaviors and communicative norms. Describe your experience in as much detail as you can while thinking about what confused you. Were there words or acronyms that you did not know when you first heard them? How did you adjust to unfamiliar tasks or expectations? How did you react if you made a mistake or were misunderstood? What opinions did you form of the culture based on the behaviors you encountered?

Over the years, there have been several researchers and theorists who have created models by which to describe how one interprets cross-cultural experiences. The most common of these models describe our interpretations as developing through webs, flows, or spirals. For example, following the web analogy, envision yourself standing on a string of an expansive and infinite spider web, weaving new connections in all directions with each new passing experience and moment. Creating this interpretive web was noted by anthropologist Clifford Geertz when describing his concept of thick description in ethnography, "Believing, with Max Weber, that man is an animal suspended in webs of significance he himself has spun, I take culture to be those webs, and the analysis of it to be therefore not an experimental science in search of law but an interpretative one in search of meaning" (Geertz, 1973). Geertz's theories on cultural analysis attempts to show that there is no way to accurately describe a new cross-cultural experience without first revealing your own subjective lens or web you use to make meaning from your unique experiences. It is a useful model for viewing our social connections and communicative experiences as a process of simultaneously constructing meaning by learning from and influencing our communities.

The process of making meaning begins with situating ourselves physically, emotionally, and intellectually in our experiences and trying to navigate our own theories on the "way of things." It is also through our experiences with places and people that we begin to seek shared social and ideological consciousness by creating what Benedict Anderson called "imagined communities" (1983). These imagined places or affiliations arise out of a social need of belonging and color our assumptions, judgments, and stereotypes. It is in these times of being deeply suspended in our imagined places and communities that we are inclined to frame our beliefs as knowledge and influence the way others in our community understand our experiences and interpretations of the ways of the world. It is often a process of being stuck in a place of understanding without considering alternatives that we form stereotypes and lose our abilities to shift perspectives and better understand the actions or words of others.

Understanding our own interpretative framework is difficult in that we know how we would like to come across in our interactions but do not always understand how others experience us. It is a blind spot that really can only be fully understood by allowing ourselves to be vulnerable and seeking honest feedback from others. "The Johari Window" is a useful and simple model that can be used to better understand the interpretative lens we bring to our interpersonal relationships. Developed in 1955 by Joseph Luft and Harrington Ingham, "the Johari Window" is a heuristic exercise that prompts self-awareness in team-based settings where there is potential for conflict related to work being done in communications, team relations, and problem solving. The four quadrants of the window are (1) **Open Quadrant**—the behaviors, feelings, and motivations you have that are known to yourself and known to others; (2) **Blind Quadrant**—the behaviors, feelings, and motivations that you don't know about yourself but are known to others; (3) **Hidden Quadrant**—the behaviors, feelings, and motivations that you know about yourself but hide from others (your facade); (4) **Unknown Quadrant**—the behaviors, feelings, and motivations that you don't know about yourself, and others don't know about you (Luft & Ingham, 1955). There are multiple ways to use this model effectively, and a simple online search will lead to several methods to use it to improve your self-awareness in team-based settings.

One useful example of using the Johari Window to maximize the effectiveness of diverse teams was introduced by Claire Halversen and S. Aqeel Tirmizi in their work *Effective Multi-cultural Teams: Theory and Practice* (2008). Halversen and Tirmizi encourage using the Johari Window as a tool for team-building through self-disclosure and feedback seeking. To begin, the authors suggest brainstorming individually to self-disclose what you know about yourself that relates to the open and hidden quadrants. If you have trouble coming up with a list of attributes then it could help to brainstorm a mutually agreed upon list of descriptive adjectives, strengths, or skills you find best align with the nature of the work you are doing as a team. Halversen and Tirmizi then suggest to ask for feedback from a team member on your blind sector and brainstorm for potentiality in the unknown quadrant (see Figure 5.1). When using this tool, the authors emphasize the importance of how differences in cultural background, gender, and race could impact the power dynamics of the team and influence the willingness to self-disclose and provide feedback for this exercise. To counter these dynamics this activity requires a safe environment and permission for honesty, openness, and receptivity.

	Known to self	Not known to self
Known to Others	**Open** (self-disclose) As you probably know: One of my strengths is in . . . Two areas of deepest competency for me are . . .	**Blind spot** (ask for feedback) In the past, I've questioned the feedback I've received concerning. . . . How do you experience me, in that regard? I know that I don't know. . . . What have you observed about me that I may not know?
Not Known to Others	**Hidden** (self-disclose) While it may not be apparent, I'm . . . One thing I'm working on is . . . I'm challenged by . . .	**Unknown** (self-disclose and ask for feedback) I often wonder . . . I've never explored whether I have the ability . . . Do you think I . . .

Figure 5.1: Johari Window (Halversen & Tirmizi, 2008)

Republished with permission of Springer Science + Business Media B.V., from ***Effective Multicultural Teams: Theory and Practice*** by Claire B. Halverson and S. Aqeel Tirmizi. Copyright © 2008 Springer Science + Business Media B.V. Permission conveyed through Copyright Clearance Center, Inc.

When used effectively the Johari Window is a great tool for understanding your interpretative framework, skills, and communication style in relation to your social or professional context.

Self-awareness and Intercultural Communication: Following "The Platinum Rule"

Working in an embassy meant that I was simultaneously operating in two different cultures. I found myself in an environment that challenged my communication, flexibility, and problem-solving capabilities. Having grown up in a multiple culture household, the environment of opposing customs was familiar to me. However, this had never been applied to the work environment. In one culture, relationships were valued over business. In the other, business came first. It forced me to actively think of what type of communication to use with different people. By being the intermediary in many cases, I realized how the nuances of each language can cripple non-native speakers. In order to create a workable relationship between two parties of opposing business cultures, it was crucial to understand both sides of the same story.

The greatest skills I gained from the experience were effective communication and an ability to adapt to different situations. Although these are skills you can only gain from trial and error and constant exposure to a range of social situations, they are both indispensable in today's globalized society. I felt like I was constantly improving, and even though learning, working, and living in two cultures simultaneously can be mentally and physically exhausting, the eagerness to communicate that is evident from people who realize that you understand how they think makes it all worth it. (Student Respondent, 2018)

This reflection from one of our students demonstrates the importance of self-awareness when communicating with others across cultural boundaries. By growing up in a "multiple culture household," this student had a foundational experience to draw upon when working in a position that required straddling a communications boundary between two cultures. This self-awareness led to an increased confidence and competency development in intercultural communication.

Earlier in this book, we presented concepts and strategies around fostering self-awareness. In that chapter we demonstrated how values, motivations, attitudes, and beliefs influenced self-concept and identity through our experiences with others. We are revisiting some of that here, by contemplating how these elements of our identity are reflected in our communication styles and will frame how others interpret us. We emphasize here that communicating across cultural boundaries requires an open mind and a willingness to change perspectives. This requires a sense of self and an awareness that all interactions are cross-cultural to some degree.

As demonstrated by the Johari Window we all have strengths and blind spots in our ability to communicate effectively (verbally, nonverbally, virtually) with others, depending on the context. These strengths and blind spots are often culturally bound in the sense that we have been socialized to communicate in the ways that are understandable to our own cultural groups. Milton Bennett's work on intercultural learning models demonstrates how we use social dialogue and interactions with others to co-construct our interpretations and definitions of cultural differences or similarities. "Culture is a result of the lived experience (praxis) of participating in social action. Part of our experience is 'languaging', including languaging about our experience, which generates the explanations about our lived experience that we can call 'culture'. In other words, culture is a construction, but culture is not purely a cognitive invention. It is both the explanation and the essence of our lived social experience" (Bennett, 2012). When viewed in this constructivist paradigm, our cross-cultural encounters are engaging us in a process of defining and redefining our own cultures through meaning making in our communicative events with others. This requires a mindful and self-reflexive approach for us to learn how to be more effective intercultural communicators in these encounters.

By engaging in this intercultural learning process, Bennett argues that we can shed our ethnocentric notion that all humans are essentially interpreting reality in the same way as we do. Intercultural communication is essentially the process of first entering our communications with others in a way that acknowledges that others think, feel, and act in ways different from our own. This understanding of culture requires the ability to engage in relationships across perceived cultural differences with an understanding that the realities of our lived experiences can be different than what we were originally taught. To frame this, Bennett encourages us to rethink the traditional golden rule, "Do unto others as you would have them do unto you" with an alternative platinum rule (2013), "Do unto others as they would have you do unto them." Bennett demonstrates that the platinum rule encourages a more empathic approach by engaging with others in a way that seeks to really understand their perspective through their interpretations. It is difficult work that requires us to suspend our interpretations and really seek help and feedback from cultural mentors who understand the contextual cues better than we do.

Applying the Platinum Rule to the Job Interview

Let's consider for a moment how the platinum rule can be used for a practical purpose in your life. Think about the process of preparing for a job interview as a cross-cultural experience. Similar to when meeting a person from another country, the job interview is a venue that requires you to communicate in a way that demonstrates an understanding of the behavioral norms and expectations of a destination work culture. Every organization has its own structure, roles, language, and behavioral norms. So essentially every organization has a unique culture, and a job interview can be viewed as an authentic intercultural conversation. The first impressions you make in the interview setting go beyond your basic qualifications for the job to the communicative elements conveyed by your style of dress, body language, facial cues, tone of voice and enthusiasm.

Many of these elements that you bring to these interactions will demonstrate how well you understand the values of the destination workplace culture, and the feelings, needs, and perspectives of the interviewer. It requires practice to become a strong interviewer. Typically, those who are capable of telling their stories in a way that highlights background qualifications in alignment with the needs of the employer are most successful. It is a process of showing how you understand the perspective of the employer, by providing concrete examples of your working style and accomplishments while also building rapport by being relatable. This is the way to effectively demonstrate that you are not only appreciating the values of the organization but also are effectively anticipating their employment goals.

Take a minute now to *look up* and think about what it is like or would be like to go on your first professional job interview. What are the things that you want the interviewer to know about you apart from your job qualifications? What are the personal characteristics that you would like to come across about your work ethic, attitude, and personality? What are the things you would try to minimize? After answering these questions, reimagine them according to the perspective and needs of the employer. What are the cultures and values of the workplace you are joining? How will the employer expect you to act and communicate in the job interview? How will your skills be framed in the context of the needs of the employer? By thinking about your qualifications from the perspective of the employer you are beginning the process of relating to their needs and beginning the conversation of the job with an employer-centric lens instead of a self-centric lens.

A key to effective interviewing and intercultural communications is conducting research on the cultural context in which you are entering and then establishing trust by building rapport with your counterparts. The first impressions you communicate to your interviewer will demonstrate your ability to anticipate their needs, which has as much to do with nonverbal (eye contact, handshake, posture, etc.) communication cues as with verbal communication. In addition, conducting research on the culture, workplace values, and the needs of the workplace will help to anticipate the employer's interview line of questioning and prepare you to align your personal values and skills in the interview. In many ways when you are looking to join a new workplace or community of practice you are essentially joining a new culture with behavioral and communicative norms, and how you prepare and adapt for making your entry into that culture will determine your success. Reference the Toolkit at the end of the book for activities that can help you prepare well for navigating the interview process. The next section is about building on these communication techniques when forming and making first impressions in any new context.

The Impact of –
What Did You Say? Understanding Implicit and Explicit Styles of Communication

Living in Georgia required me to get out of my comfort zone every day and approach strangers on the street, taxi drivers, bus drivers, shopping assistants to find out the information needed. I had to overcome language (luckily, most people speak either Russian or English) and cultural barriers every day. When I look back at this experience, I realize that I became a much more self-confident and optimistic person; needless to say, that my overall interpersonal communication skills have improved dramatically. (Student respondent, 2018)

The student's quote above illustrates how being on the outside of a group can force you to do the hard work of observing, listening, and mimicking just to go about meeting daily needs. As you encounter these cross-cultural experiences you may find that there is as much to attend to related to the context in which you are living or working. You may observe obvious differences in greetings, table manners, adherence to planned meeting times, social hierarchies, and formality or informality of dress codes. Depending on your understanding of these social rules you will make first impressions with others that will shape how they communicate with you. As you become more immersed in the culture you become better at anticipating communicative customs and will adapt accordingly to demonstrate your knowledge and respect for cultural norms. Eventually, you may even begin to feel included and accepted as a member of the community as you feel more comfortable in expressing yourself verbally and nonverbally in a new social context. The more experiences you have like these the more your interpersonal skills will improve and transfer across all of your activities.

When encountering any new cultural context for the first time, it is helpful to prepare and understand that there will be differences in how verbal and nonverbal cues are used to communicate meaning. Anthropologist Edward Hall's research on high-context and low-context cultures is one helpful model that can be used to begin to understand cross-cultural relationships. In his work *Beyond Culture* (1976), Hall observes that the messages we communicate tend to regularly combine explicit and implicit meanings that relate to the situational context and background culture of those speaking. Low-context cultures tend to be more individualistic and rely on explicit or direct verbal communication. High-context cultures tend to be more community oriented and rely less on direct verbal communication and more on nonverbal and implicit social and cultural cues in conversation. For example, when applied to a professional setting, greetings in a low-context culture may suffice with a verbal "Hi, How are you?," whereas in a high-context culture there may be implicit meanings related to body language, proximity, eye contact, gift giving, and so on. Meetings in low-context cultures may seek to get right to the business objectives, whereas in high-context cultures meetings will require time to discuss family or friends before business is discussed. Our orientation to these various contexts of work and life will shape our abilities to communicate well interpersonally and collaborate respectfully across cultures.

In our work with students, we often see these various approaches to the cultural context of collaboration when encountering group work in the classroom. *Look up* from the book for a moment and think of your perspectives on group work. What is the first thing that comes to mind when you read the words "group work"? How much time do you take to get to know your members and their project strengths before just trying to accomplish the task at hand? Do you expect others will adapt to your style of work or do you actively try to understand that there are other possible approaches?

In our experiences teaching college-level classes we find that students have mixed feelings about group work. It is, however, a place where, if you are perceptive, you will be able to see observe cultural working styles. It makes for a great place to observe high- and low-context interactions and hone intercultural communication skills. For example, do you seek to control the project decisions or include all voices? How much time do you spend trying to get to know your group members personally? Your answers can show you how individualistic versus community oriented you are. Do you make spot judgments on a group member based on how vocal they are about their opinions? Your answer could demonstrate how you interpret implicit meaning around respect in social settings. In the end, the host culture working style typically dominates and impacts how the outcomes of the group project are accomplished. Your effectiveness as a functioning unit, where everyone is motivated to do their part, could hinge on your ability to pause and contemplate how to incorporate an inclusive approach. If you shift your communicative approach, or take time to understand the varied cultural communication styles of team members, then project outcomes could improve.

Mind the Gap: Empathic Listening

I think it's empathy that is probably the main part of being a global citizen, recognizing the shared humanity and that you are part of a global community. Yes, there are differences between people, but the boundaries are mainly socially constructed: states, nations. All of this is essentially made up. There's value to these things, yes, but if you don't challenge why they're there and what they're actually doing, then I don't think you can be a fully participating global citizen without challenging something and being empathetic. (Student Respondent, 2017)

When encountering behaviors that you personally feel are rude or offensive how do you react? Our reactions are typically culturally bound by what we have been taught to be proper social etiquette. Our boundaries of social etiquette can be tested when people do things that violate our personal space, move ahead of us in line, stare at us, make a confusing comment, and so on. Our body language, facial expressions, and verbal reactions to these moments of discomfort or annoyance are emotionally charged and provide feedback to others about what we feel the implicit rules of social behavior should be. These are our "it should go without saying" moments when we feel that somehow others should understand our rules of good behavior and communication.

In addition, new communications technologies are also changing our definitions of rude or offensive social behaviors. For example, from being interrupted in a conversation or presentation by someone's phone, to not making appropriate eye contact on a video chat conversation, to having to navigate around those who walk and text on the sidewalks, to improper capitalization or punctuation on a text message, and so on; we are constantly creating new cultural and social patterns around how we communicate and respond to people in person and virtually. In these moments, how often do you take a moment to ask yourself, What am I missing here? How might the other person be perceiving the norms of social behavior differently?

Those feelings of being offended or feelings of defensiveness when we offend another have the potential to occur more regularly as we have more interactions with a greater variety of people in a globalized and interconnected society. In addition, many feel that our technology is in fact emboldening us to be less compassionate when engaging with others we don't know well online, and creating what sociologist Sherry Turkle (2011) terms the "empathy gap." There is a growing fear that this lack of empathy in our online interactions and the development of emoting machines will impact our human abilities to relate, collaborate, and care for one another. In her most recent book, *Reclaiming Conversation*, Turkle (2015) conducted interviews with hundreds of business leaders and found consensus that the best way to form relationships through empathy and trust, problem-solve effectively, and close deals is through face-to-face conversations. Her research demonstrates that it is through navigating the emotional aspects of conversation that we can best determine authenticity, expose mutual discomfort with a business decision, understand implicit communications through body language, and find common ground through shared enthusiasm. Turkle documents several cases where businesses quickly lost productivity with too much reliance on texting, email, and situations when technology distracted from accomplishing business objectives in face-to-face meetings. Essentially, what these studies are showing is that with the increase of technological choices for socializing and working together there is an increased need of awareness around how we use these tools appropriately to communicate across boundaries and maximize our abilities to collaborate effectively.

Building empathy and emotional intelligence in our life and work requires a willingness to listen appreciatively and actively while responding and provide feedback non-defensively. As the student's quote at the beginning of this section illustrates, empathy requires an understanding of a shared humanity and, through that understanding, recognizing our responsibilities to our communities. This can be very difficult if embedded in a conflict or situation personally offensive or emotionally charged. Much can be learned through being willing to briefly suspend our interpretations by listening actively and appreciatively.

Active listening is a way of focusing your attention fully on listening, understanding, evaluating, and then responding to the perspectives, needs, feelings, and words of someone else. It is not waiting for your turn to talk, but giving someone else the space and time to fully express their viewpoint and then checking with them to make sure they were understood. To demonstrate that you are listening actively and appreciatively requires that you mirror back to your counterpart by restating what was communicated and acknowledging the emotions and feelings that went with it (Goleman, 2005). It is a key piece to the art of conversation, and it is used to build trust and value in the thoughts and meaning of another human being. It does require a degree of mindfulness and does not work well in all situations, but in moments of conflict or stagnation it is a vital component of ensuring that team members can get unstuck, close the gaps in understanding, and become more productive together.

Developing Skills for Communicating Across Boundaries

In my field of work, an increasing amount of work is being done online, through Skype/Webex and email. In this way, students should be trained in social media, online platforms for project cycle management, and other trainings on professionalism in the digital workplace. Moreover, it is important for students to know that while the West and parts of the Far East are very advanced technologically, there are still many places technically behind. As a result, students need to have a very broad "tool kit" of skills to be able to work across institutions and countries. (Cheryl Novak, European Public Law Organization, 2018)

We have never lived in a time when there were so many different technologies and possibilities for connection. As the quote above illustrates, there is a need for both developed technical and human skills to understand how and when these are best used. In just the past 25 years, we have gone from phone and email to texting, video chatting, emojis, and now even collaboration through augmented and virtual reality (see Microsoft Hololens) where humans appear to one another in the same space as a hologram of themselves or as an avatar. The possibilities of communicating anytime and anywhere are becoming boundless.

Studies are showing that productivity and effectiveness in the workplace are linked to how we determine which communication devices are best for our tasks, our physical proximity to one another, and how communication devices are used in our work environments. Ben Waber, MIT Researcher and President and CEO of Humanyze, used sociometric badges to compile and analyze data on human interactions in the workplace. His findings, outlined in his work *People Analytics* (2013), revealed surprising data that an employee's time away from their desk can actually make them more productive than if they spent all of their time at their desk. Waber's research reveals that "workers' most productive time occurs when they collaborate and interact with others. This means getting up and walking around, spending time in the coffee area, eating lunch with colleagues, jumping into chat sessions, and becoming heavily involved in the social life of the workplace" (Waber, 2013). To do this employees are challenged to create both a common work culture with a shared language of work and understanding of which tools can be most effective for each task. Also there is a challenge to communicate well with diverse groups of colleagues in ways that both accomplish common tasks and deepen relationships and build trust.

It is still uncertain how new communication technologies will change the way we view ourselves, relate to one another, and co-construct meaning. Needless to say, the norms of what we view as formal versus informal or professional versus unprofessional communication will change as well. This will impact how we construct our workspaces, view productivity, and collaborate. While in the past we only had to change our style of communications for phone, email, paper, and face-to-face interactions, we are now in a time when we have to be prepared to understand social norms for all new communication technologies in addition to these old standards. How proficient are you in utilizing each of these forms of communication effectively with your peers, coworkers, supervisors, and so on? How reliant are you on only one of these forms of communication over the other? Our goal here is to encourage you to examine how you communicate and interact across your communication technologies and better understand the skills you develop when adjusting your communication styles based on these modes.

What then can we learn by disconnecting one device to perfect communication in another way? Take a moment to *look up* and think about your preferred modes of communication. Think about the technologies you use and how they are: (1) contributing to your development of skills interpersonally and professionally and (2) contributing to the deepening of your relationships. We have all had experiences such as when our phone batteries died, we lost a wireless connection, or there was no service on our phones. How do you feel when these devices that keep you connected fail to work? We also have waited for replies by email, text, or social media. How do you respond when an instant response is not possible? Each of these forms of communication requires a different set of skills and style of constructing language that can have an impact on how we communicate and collaborate with others.

For example, by relying on texting to communicate you could be developing skills in communicating concisely, while also making you more aware of implicit communication cues in writing such as the tone conveyed via capitalization, punctuation, emojis, and visual media. In addition, texting allows for carefully selected visual communications that can communicate a sense of humor or emotion. It also can help you to frame your thoughts and get the communication just the way you want it before sending, which can have some advantages when seeking to resolve conflicts.

Knowing these qualities of texting, think about how they can be used most effectively for a variety of situations. Professionally, this tool can perhaps help with coordinating and logistics-oriented tasks. On the other hand, texting can distract you from the relationships in your immediate environment. It can additionally require you to be always on and available whether or not you are at home or work. In addition, as outlined earlier in the chapter, intent and tone without nonverbal communication cues can garble the intent of the messages. If you rely too heavily on texting, what is being sacrificed is the opportunity for developing communication skills in your face-to-face, phone, or more formal written communications.

Disconnection Education

In the previous chapter on "Navigating Diverse Learning Environments," we discussed the importance of mindfulness when learning in new and unfamiliar environments. We framed this as your dislocation education. Here we present you with a method of disconnection education. Disconnection education is the development of your communication skills and knowledge by becoming familiar and experimenting with a wide range of communication tools and styles. We develop these skills with our students in our professional development classes in the accomplishment of their semester-long informational interviewing assignment.

A big challenge of the informational interview is communicating to a professional in the field you are researching and have them respond positively to coordinate a conversation. One of the typical issues we work with students to resolve is what to do when no one is responding to emails or phone calls. Usually, the issues we find in these situations are (1) the student's email or call was not clear about who or what is being asked, (2) the email or call was sent to a generic organizational email on the website and does not belong to the individual they hope to interview, (3) only one email was sent and no follow-up by phone or in person was attempted, and (4) they are only targeting the individuals at the highest level of the organization. All of these issues point to a need to practice the outreach in a variety of communication modes and a need to develop communication styles that are appropriate and convincing to the intended audience of the message. In the end, the students most successful with this assignment realize that it is much harder for someone to say no to you in a face-to-face communication, so visiting the actual office location or asking someone to set up the interview in a networking event is the most effective form of communication for this task.

Challenge yourself to disconnect from your preferred method of communication for a day and try out different methods. By trying different ways of connecting and communicating you are providing yourself with a useful challenge that will change your perspectives on your role, your voice, your audience, and your skillset. This is your "Disconnection Education." By disconnecting occasionally, you find insights into which technology is most appropriate for the context or culture in which you are working. You also can find that when turning off one form of communication and using another you are changing the depth of your human connections.

The Art of –
Telling Your Story to Build Trust

For me, I think I did and the connection was quite clear. Learning how to do literature reviews, learning how to consolidate information, remedy all of that. There was this very clear overlap. Even going back to my less academic focused co-ops—communication skills. Constantly keeping your professor in the loop, learning that there is a human at the end of every situation and that sometimes just by showing your face at places and to people, you can actually get better results. I think especially in our age we like to hide behind computer screens and emails, we don't like talking to people face to face. (Student Respondent, 2018)

This chapter highlights that communicating well with counterparts across cultural and interpretative boundaries requires perspective shifting and self-awareness. Boundaryless communication is about being sensitive to the varied contexts in which we live while learning how to build trusting and effective relationships. This requires us to co-construct meaning with others across cultures and social roles. To do this, we don't only have to become good listeners but also become good at telling our own stories to others in a way that is not only convincing but also sensitive to the broad cross-cultural audiences we are encountering.

Human connections and trust are built through the communication of our stories and the sharing of authentic experiences. We see this as students gain confidence in their job search and interviewing after multiple on-the-job experiences. The most successful interviewers are the best storytellers who can weave a compelling real-world narrative that highlights how skills and knowledge are applied in workplace accomplishments. In addition, in a globalized and interconnected society, our multiple forms (virtual or in person) of connection and self-presentation provide us with multiple venues to communicate our stories. It also opens our narrative for scrutiny and interpretation through a much broader audience with multiple cultural lenses. Knowing that our future employers have access and are able to meet us informally online possibly before they ever meet us formally is intimidating. Communicating about ourselves to others both online and in person requires some consistency, self-awareness, and an ability to be authentic.

The key to becoming adept at telling your story, communicating well to audiences from a variety of cultures, and navigating interpersonal relationships is building our intercultural competence through experiential learning. It is about understanding your interpretative lens and adjusting it as you encounter new individuals and styles of communication. It is about adjusting your responses and seeking feedback when needed. It is about being open to diverse ways of making meaning and approaching each relationship with a certain humility and a willingness to see the world empathically through a different lens. We will close this chapter with a few examples of how we work on developing these communication skills with our students in their professional development courses.

The Elevator Pitch, Professional Statement, and Cover Letter

In our courses that we teach on professional development we spend a lot of time practicing communication with our students. A strong starting point for developing the communication skills is through exercises like delivering an elevator pitch or writing a professional statement or cover letter (see examples of these activities in the Toolkit at the end of the book). An elevator pitch is essentially a compelling and convincing statement that you make to another person within the amount of time it would take to go from the bottom floor to the top floor of a building on an elevator. In our class, we frame the elevator pitch as an activity in which we have one student act as the employer and another as the job candidate. The job candidate is required to deliver an introduction of themselves in 30 seconds to show how they are qualified for the job. It is a great way for students to develop skills in being concise and synthesizing relevant experiences and skills that would be of interest to the employer audience. It is also a great preparation for a networking or career fair. We usually begin by having students skim a job description and construct their back story based on the skills, values, and qualifications communicated by the employer. The activity is debriefed with a review of effective verbal and nonverbal communication techniques that students found through the activity.

Writing a cover letter or professional statement is a great complementary activity to the elevator pitch. In these activities, students are tasked with writing about their fit for a specific job description in a way that is compelling and formulaic. A good professional statement or cover letter will begin with an eye-grabbing introduction that demonstrates a coherence between the values of the job candidate and the values of the organizations/company. What follows is students using specific examples of past work activities and experiences to show but not tell they have the skills required in the qualifications of the job. This activity is great practice in telling a fluid narrative that introduces a student's past experiences relevant to the job. Again, it requires knowledge of how to frame language in a way that shows comprehension of the needs of the employer and target audience.

Constructing a Professional Website

An additional activity that can help you both refine skills in communication and make a positive impression in an online environment is the development of a professional website (see example in the Toolkit). Developing a professional website is a bit of high-stakes activity as it entails posting a creative and unique piece of work in a highly visible venue. For this activity, you are tasked with creating a compelling front page of the website with a professional photo and statement that communicates both the student's personality and professional mindset. To complete this activity, you additionally need to define your target audience and frame your language and materials included on the website to match the desires of your audience. You are also prompted to design the website in a way that facilitates an experience for the visitor to the website. The experience should lead the visitor through a narrative on every page of the website that demonstrates relevant skills and accomplishments in addition to interests and values the student could bring to a potential employer.

Improv for Improving Verbal and Nonverbal Communication

Laughter has the power to cure emotional wounds. One of the best ways to move past cultural misunderstanding is through having a sense of humor. Being able to laugh off your mistakes is a first step in admitting that you make them. Improv activities provide a space in which you can enjoy these mistakes at a low stakes with someone else. It also gives you a great way to try out verbal and nonverbal cues while really attempting to listen to someone else. Handling cross-cultural misunderstanding sometimes feels like work, why not take some time to make these difficult moments into play?

As we outlined in an earlier chapter, improv is a great way to problem-solve by seeing new and innovative choices. It is also a great way to exercise mental agility while in communication with those you are working and living with. Often viewed as an equivalent to a parlor game like charades or pictionary, improv is often seen in informal entertainment settings. Little attention is given to the skills we develop in these settings where we allow the mind to relax. There is great potential for team building and improving cross-cultural interactions by seeing the impact improvisation can have to co-construct meaning with those around us. It is a light way of making sense of the world in agreement with those around us and of feeling free to laugh at our mistakes or faux pas. When the games are over it is helpful to see how this can apply to our daily life and relationships.

One way to do this is through the facilitation of experiential activities or simulated experiences in which you create a culture that other students must navigate. There are endless improv activities out there, and a simple web search can yield many examples. Really any activity that is a simulated experience requiring a student to personally assume an unfamiliar role or communicate in a way that is unfamiliar and challenging can improve communication skills and creativity. For example, this can be done by removing some students from a classroom while others stay and create a task, communication limitations, and set of cultural parameters the students will be required to navigate when they return. For example, the task could be for the student to introduce themselves by writing their name on a board, but nothing can be communicated verbally or by pointing but only by clapping or stomping feet. This short icebreaker typically requires a student to improvise different things, judge the reactions, and adapt to the requirements of the group in the classroom.

Communicating That You Care

In the end, people still value the authenticity of face-to-face engagement and displays of sincere appreciation. At the end of every interview, we encourage students not only to send a thank you email to employers to show appreciation for the time spent but also to send personal thank you notes and letters through the mail. In a time when the pace of life and business is quick, informal, and sometimes emotionless, small authentic touches go a long way to building trust and deepening our human connections. When travelling to new places acquaint yourself with the cultural norms around gift giving. Be mindful of body language and the various interpretations of smiling and showing gratitude. Understanding that these types of gestures are culturally bound are important to showing the values of your relationship.

Conclusion

In conclusion, we hope that this chapter provided you with a foundational understanding of not only the complications that can arise from communicating across boundaries but also an understanding of how to bridge the gaps of understanding that can take place. Our hope is that this will encourage you to move forward in your relationships with a sense of curiosity for the ways others interpret our interactions. In addition, we hope that there is an appreciation that all of our interactions are intercultural, and while that can occasionally interfere with collaboration, it can serve to improve our abilities to shift perspectives and become more effective collaborators and global citizens. In the next and final chapter, we will show ways in which to use our acquired knowledge and skills to develop agency and act purposefully in a way that is ethical and impactful within our communities.

LOOK UP: Reality Check

As business and organizational models work to collaborate more globally there is increasingly a need to build a team mentality and sense of comradery among team members working remotely. A number of new technologies—Slack, Skype, WhatsApp, Google Hangouts—have been developed to help business and organizational leaders address this problem. Many have come to call these technologies the "virtual water cooler." Similar to the water cooler, kitchen, snack room spaces of the physical offices, the virtual water cooler is intended to serve as an informal space where team members can bump into each other throughout the course of the work day to discuss work- and non–work-related topics. This informal team building has been found to be important to keep employee morale high while also allowing for space for creative conversations about problems that come up. Morgan Norman, CEO of Work Simple, describes it this way, "The water cooler is an essential part of any company's culture and crucial to your employees feeling like a team, even if they aren't working on the same project together. Brainstorming sessions are important and the informal sessions around the water cooler are just as valuable" (2014). The virtual water cooler is just one example of the efforts being made to bring remote team members together in face-to-face interactions if there is no shared physical office.

Reflection Questions: What differences can you see about norms of conversation in these virtual water coolers versus the physical interactions around the water coolers in the workplace? Where would you feel more comfortable? What skills could you work on to be comfortable and productive in either setting?

Activity

Develop what you would consider to be the code of conduct or communication standards for a cross-cultural virtual water cooler setting. Consider how technology can impact our communication and interpretation of both verbal and nonverbal cues; for example, should there be standards on how emojis are used, or how are certain visual filters used? Develop your own set of communication standards for good professional behavior and cross-cultural collaboration.

Key Takeaways

- Communicating well across perceptual boundaries requires self-awareness of our interpretative cultural lenses and an appreciation and receptivity to the cultural interpretative lenses of others

- Communicating effectively requires an ability to understand the context in which we communicate, including cultural differences in implicit and explicit forms of making meaning

- In an interconnected global society, it is important to become skilled in multiple forms of communication to practice this; it is useful to sometimes disconnect from familiar or comfortable forms of communication and experience alternative styles

- Empathy and emotional intelligence are vital skills to develop for a global workplace that can be developed through authentic face-to-face conversation and through the practice of listening appreciatively and actively

Follow-Up Activities in Toolkit—Listen Up, Look Up, Join Up, and Act Up

- Explore **Perspective Taking**
- Construct your **Cover Letter**
- Complete the **Building Awareness** activity
- Design your **Professional Portfolio Website**

Works Cited

"About Iowa Big". (2018, September 14th). Retrieved from https://www.iowabig.org/?page_id=15

Anderson, B. (1983). *Imagined communities*. London and New York: Verson Press.

Bennett, M. J. (2012). Paradigmatic assumptions and a developmental approach to intercultural learning. In M. V. Berg, R. M. Paige, & K. H. Lou (Eds.), *Student learning abroad: What our students are learning, what they're not, and what we can do about it* (pp. 90–114). Sterling, VA: Stylus Publishing.

Bennett, M. J. (2013). Overcoming the golden rule: Sympathy and empathy. In *Basic concepts of intercultural communication: Paradigms, principles, and practices* (2nd ed.). Boston, MA: Intercultural Press.

Brownell, J. (2006). *Listening: Attitudes, principles and skills* (3rd ed.). Boston, MA: Pearson Education.

Caligiuri, P. (2012). *Cultural Agility: Building a Pipeline of Successful Global Professionals*. San Francisco, CA: Jossey-Bass.

"Experiential Network". (2018, September 14). Retrieved from https://www.northeastern.edu/graduate/why-northeastern/about-our-academics/experiential-network

Geertz, C. (1973). *The interpretation of cultures*. New York, NY: Basic Books.

Goleman, D. (2005). *Emotional intelligence: Why it can matter more than IQ*. New York, NY: Bantam Books.

Hall, E. T. (1976). *Beyond culture*. New York, NY: Anchor Press/Doubleday.

Halversen, C. B., & Tirmizi, S. A. (2008). *Effective multicultural teams: Theory and practice*. Berlin, Germany: Springer Science + Business Media.

Luft, J. & Ingham, H. (1955). *The Johari Window, A Graphic Model of Interpersonal Awareness*. Los Angeles, CA: UCLA.

Press. (2018, September 14) Retrieved from https://cambridge.nuvustudio.com/about/press#tab-press.url

Turkle, S. (2011). *Alone together: Why we expect more from technology and less from each other*. New York, NY: Basic Books.

Turkle, S. (2015). *Reclaiming conversation: The power of talk in a digital age*. New York, NY: Penguin Press.

Twenge, J. (2017). *iGen: Why Today's Super-Connected Kids Are Growing Up Less Rebellious, More Tolerant, Less Happy-and Completely Unprepared for Adulthood*. New York, NY: Atria Books.

"What is NuVu". (2018, September 14). Retrieved from https://cambridge.nuvustudio.com

Waber, B. (2013). *People analytics: How social sensing technology will transform business and what it tells us about the future of work*. Upper Saddle River, NJ: Pearson Education.

6

Developing Agency for Ethical and Impactful Professional and Civic Engagement

The Importance of –
Purpose in Action: Citizenship Development Through Experiential Learning

A model global citizen has a sustained philosophy and behavior over time. Individuals who are global citizens are conscious of geopolitical landscape, understanding what forces cause the socio-political and economic conditions that students are trying to address politically and economically responding to them. There are many ways that people act as global citizens, and those behaviors can wax and wane throughout your life course relative to where you are professionally and personally, but key is that you have and maintain a sustained commitment to the greater good. (Student Respondent, 2017)

The above student's reflection captures her development as a citizen in the global era and key areas of focus. Her reflection describes the level of both awareness and commitment to current conditions and situations in the world. We started this book with the chapter on self-awareness, asking you to begin the process by starting with yourself, and offered the guiding questions—*Who are you? What do you want to do? What can you do? What needs to be done?* In this chapter, we come full circle as we address ethics, agency, and social change. We will discuss what it means to develop as a global citizen, how you think ethically and critically in challenging situations, and how to act purposefully in your academic and professional careers, as well as in your community environments. Here we ask—how and what do you intend to contribute to society personally, professionally, or civically? Now is your opportunity to bring together what we have discussed and presented and what your thoughts were while reading the book up to this point so that you can dig deeper and think about how you can manifest your gifts, talents, and experiences to fully participate and contribute to society.

At Northeastern over the past 10 years, we have been directly involved in the university's efforts to strategically harness the strength of its experiential learning and entrepreneurial spirit as faculty, staff, and students move into the global era of higher education. Our challenge is to continue to address the university's founding question: *What are the needs of society and how do we prepare students to address them?* This is a challenging goal, given the changing landscape of higher education and the world in general. Related to this, issues of market forces, technology, and societal issues/concerns will continue to redefine and shape our global society and our roles as students, workers, and citizens. These changing times call for new approaches. Global concerns such as climate change, immigration, and ethnic conflicts have raised concerns about students' understanding of the need for commitment to civic engagement, social responsibility, and global citizenship. In their article, *Developing an Undergraduate Global Citizenship Program: Challenges of Definition and Assessment* (2010), Sperandio et al. discuss attempts that are being made to link these two concerns—civic engagement and skills

© Orianna Timsit

for operating in an environment of globalization. They cite the Association of American Colleges and Universities (AAC&U) focusing its efforts on global learning, social responsibility, and emphasis to develop social, civic, and global knowledge in university graduates. Given this state of concerns, flux, and redevelopment, what key strategies and areas of focus will you need to pay attention to in order to progress individually while also contributing to the greater global society?

As faculty in higher education, we recognize the role that colleges and universities can play in your development as citizens. Evidence suggests that college undergraduates are uniquely poised developmentally for citizenship learning. In their paper, Mickelson and Nkomo discuss the critical role of higher education in preparing students for their adult responsibilities as workers, parents, neighbors, and citizens. They suggest that college students are at an important developmental juncture when they leave family and familiar surroundings and begin transitioning into independent adults. Students are poised for advancement as they move to new settings where they are exposed to new ideas, perspectives, people, and historical/cultural understandings (Mickelson & Nkomo, 2010). One of our employer partners noted, "As society becomes more global and interconnected, students need to be prepared to engage with different cultures and people. Universities can continuously stress the importance of being open-minded and culturally aware and help their students learn different ways to cope with the various challenges that will occur" (Employer Respondent, International NGO, 2018). As discussed in previous chapters, you will have many opportunities to develop and broaden your perspective, in addition to gaining important insights into your sense of self, your beliefs, and your intercultural knowledge. Connecting your personal, professional, and civic learning and development is critical, as it influences your compassion for difference and your motivation to both engage in intercultural relationships and to be socially responsible.

College as the "Real World"

We see a big difference between those who have and haven't engaged in previous work or study abroad opportunities. Those who have, outstripped those who haven't in terms of level and sense of responsibility, their broader and deeper understanding of work that we do, and their sensitivity to the context(s) in which we work. If they've worked before they tend to take their work more seriously. For example, we love the Northeastern students because they are required to do 3 placements over the course of their degree, so by the time we get them (usually towards the end of the degrees), they've gained the skills necessary, but also have had the experience of working in different contexts, with different social groups, etc. (Zoë Gauld-Angelucci, Greenpop, South Africa, 2018)

Our employer partner here describes the student learning profile that we are encouraging as part of this chapter, that is, seeking to find learning everywhere and viewing the college experience itself as an opportunity to both develop academic knowledge and skills and build important personal, professional, and civic skills. It is common to hear students tell us what they want to do after college and once they are in the "real world." In this context, college is portrayed as a "non-real world," a place where you train for a life beyond graduation but where classroom activities are not directly influencing greater society. Thinking of college classes in this way can create difficulties in directly connecting skills and knowledge from classes to practical professional or field-based settings. A 2015 survey by the AAC&U found that while 59 percent of students believed that their college/university prepared them well for postgraduate careers, employers felt that only 23 percent of students were prepared in this way. One wonders if this gap exists because many students' college experiences are not structured in a way to provide sufficient exposure to the settings where the work is being conducted. The aforementioned survey also found that 67 percent of students believed that both field-specific and a broad range of knowledge and skills are necessary to achieve long-term career success. This is showing that students understand that theory and practice should be working more closely and in tandem. Both students and their instructors should be putting in efforts, starting the first day of college, to develop closer collaboration with communities, organizations, and companies. A student who was able to harness both her classroom and experiential learning during college speaks of her experience in the following way:

> *Both my workplace and classroom experiences contributed to the gradual improvement of my writing and qualitative/quantitative research skills. It is difficult to point out which of the experiences contributed to the development of those skills the most. As for participation in experiential learning programs, my intercultural communication abilities have improved tremendously—mastering that skill is essential for my successful performance both in a classroom and at a workplace.* (Student Respondent, 2018)

It is through these collaborations that classroom environments become more robust and students are empowered to develop a sense of agency through active, purposeful, and reflective integration of their knowledge and skills.

Experiential learning programs, and the cooperative education model in particular, show the benefit of these collaborative partnerships. Reviewing a research study (Collette, 2013) of 2010 Northeastern graduates showed that 50 percent of the 2010 graduates received at least one job offer from a previous cooperative education employer and 89 percent of those who are employed are working in jobs related to their major field of study. In addition, the study showed a 146 percent increase in graduates who had a global learning experience in 2010–2011, compared to 2006, and 195 percent increase in global co-op employers. An additional study by the Northeastern University Research Institute for Experiential Learning Science looked more specifically at whether any differences existed in these students' preparedness for the workplace when compared to students who are joining the workforce after graduating from an institution that does not have an experiential learning model. In this study, a survey distributed to 1,002 employers representing 25 industries revealed that 49 percent of employers perceived recent college graduates to be prepared for the workforce as opposed to 89 percent of employers of recent Northeastern graduates. Northeastern students were perceived by employers to be significantly better prepared across most skills and attributes when compared to the perceptions of employers who had not worked with the Northeastern graduate population. When these employers were asked whether recent Northeastern graduates were afforded opportunities because of their skills, attributes, and/or experiences as compared to their non-Northeastern employees, participants resoundingly responded that this was the case. Northeastern graduates, and generalizing to students at other institutions fostering experiential learning, were given higher levels of responsibility, access to jobs, leadership opportunities, diverse types of tasks, and access to opportunities that others might not have received. (Northeastern University Research Institute for Experiential Learning, n.d.)

In terms of your development as citizens, colleges and universities are places to question, explore, and challenge the status quo by actively engaging with others to promote civic ideals in creative and collaborative projects. As was noted in the previous section, historically colleges have been places where students become active civically. Many of the skills that you develop as part of going abroad to study or participating in a co-op workplace experience are transferable to your role and responsibilities as active citizens, such as initiative, responsibility, understanding a different perspective, and working with others to solve a problem or make a needed change. We encourage you to consider a holistic approach to your work, civic responsibilities, and studies and see the possibilities and connection of each of these areas rather than having a linear or segmented approach.

Education as Active and Self-Authored

I feel like I gained a lot of independence living and working abroad and it was definitely a great time in my life to do a lot of self-reflection. I realized during this experience that I could really go anywhere and do anything if I stayed focused and put my mind to it. There were definitely times that I would miss home and feel out of place, but, in retrospect, I believe many of these hardships that I had to overcome have made me a more resilient, global, engineer. (Student Respondent, 2018)

This student's reflection on how taking ownership of their education through a global learning and work experience resulted in significant self-awareness and success. As students, you will have the opportunity to transform yourself through your college experience. On one hand, many of you are conditioned to use your GPAs, professor recommendations, and the internships leading to a "good resume" in developing your self-value; in other words, using external, uncritical thinking, and authority to establish your internal sense of self. On the other hand, you can choose to open up to new and challenging experiences, then integrate all aspects of your college experience (academics, personal relationships, experiential learning, work experience, etc.) through intentional and critical reflection and thoughts to establish yourself as internally motivated and guided. Many authors in the past have described this process as "self-authorship": the capacity to define one's beliefs, identity, and social relations (Baxter Magolda, 2001; Kegan, 1994; Piaget, 1950). More recently, Baxter Magolda stated, "How collegians move from their socialization to rely on external authority toward establishing their internal authority depends on the dynamic interaction of their personal characteristics, experiences, their interpretation of those experiences, and their underlying constructions of knowledge, identity, and social relations" (Baxter Magolda, 2014).

Many students enter their first advising meetings in their freshman or sophomore years both hopeful and uncertain about their ability to "figure it all out" in 4–5 years, for example, about job, career, grad school, and so on. They often worry that their work and academic experiences will not sufficiently prepare them for meaningful postgraduate employment that is both satisfying and financially rewarding. Instead of valuing the totality of their experience, such as volunteer work and employment in restaurants, retail, or general labor, in addition to their academic records and related internships, as being meaningful and good preparation for work in a "professional" field, they discount all but their externally validated experience (GPA, professor recommendations, and "good resume" material). While focus on academics is important, if "success" in this arena is what you use to derive your internal authority, then the professional workplace will be a place where you need to seek constant feedback and direction as opposed to taking initiative. By comparison, you can choose to develop a unique internal authority that is self-governing and that will lead you to take initiative and guide yourself through college, career, and citizenship.

Feedback and merit in the workplace, however, usually functions much differently than in the classroom. There are typically no grades, and students are no longer responsible only to themselves but share responsibility for an organizational mission or vision. In the workplace, taking initiative in a way that contributes to the collective efforts of the group is valued, as is patience, listening actively, and providing one's voice to project objectives. Once "real world" experiences start complementing the classroom experiences, we see students develop an understanding of education as a holistic process of learning everywhere and applying knowledge/skills in new ways that were previously unknown or not activated. Here one of our students framed what they learned from their transitions between classroom and workplace as:

> the ability to communicate well (written and verbally), the knowledge of technical words so you can have good conversations with people no matter what their field is. The ability to work with diverse groups of people and understand the subtle cultural differences and work ethic. I developed most of these skills during classes but I truly realized how important and useful they were when I started working (Student Respondent, 2018).

As this student reflected, it is through experiences in social and work settings away from the classroom that you will activate latent skill and knowledge areas that were introduced in the classroom.

As we have been discussing throughout the book, and specifically in Chapter 1, students and alumni who engage more deeply in self-authoring their lives are significantly happier and more fulfilled than those who are waiting for life to happen to them (Baxter Magolda, 2008). The act of becoming more self-aware about your values, skills, and identity and then taking charge of your actions is the true work of being in the "real world". It can happen anywhere, every day, whether you are a student or a worker. Part of this process includes taking advantage of the skills you have developed so far, whether they be specific technical skills (i.e., coding, speaking another language, cell culture) or those transferable skills that are increasingly in demand from all industries (critical thinking, empathy, initiative, collaboration, etc.). As you develop deeper understanding of your skills and strengths, you keep getting better at articulating those skills to others and leverage those skills into a career. Eventually, you become prepared for, and facile in, handling unexpected scenarios, confident in your ability to navigate the options available to you as the author of your own life. We find that students who gain confidence in the workplace feel more empowered and competent. Exposure to new ways of thinking, alternative viewpoints, foreign cultures, and alternative perspectives allows you to break free from compartmentalized, linear thinking and begin a process of understanding that learning and growing opportunities abound everywhere. You will begin to discover ways to reimagine those things that you believe about the nature of the world, the value of your education, and your potential to contribute to society in a continuous fashion across your lifetime. With careful planning from the early years of your time at your institution of higher learning, you will be able to envision a pathway and continuity in your life beyond your institution.

Acting for Impact and Sustainability

> I will always remember one particular student, from Northeastern University, who came with their own skill set and made an enormous contribution on the ground. She was a part of the female health project and during her time with us was able to start a female health literacy project with a community who did not have faith in medical science. In Bhikamkor, when women would get sick, they would go to the temple as they believed a god had cursed them. In addition, teaching menstrual and general female health is a big taboo in the village. When she first began the project, she encountered women who did not know their own age and had six to seven pregnancies but still did not know how their body's functioned.

We decided to teach the village women about anemia and the other women's health issues. It was a very complex and sensitive project. This student showed a lot of patience and a very deep understanding of the culture during the entire project. Because of these qualities, she was able to build a very strong relationship with the community. As part of the project, our organization employed four local women from the village as the Health Outreach Workers and our intern trained them in female health literacy. It was very hard for us to find women who were allowed to leave the home and work in the village. During the entire process of finding the women and getting permission from their families, the student was incredibly patient. In addition, as this community is not educated, it was hard to train the women for the health project, but our intern managed to make very simple but still informational workshops for the ladies and train them through lots of videos, games, and flashcards. Today, our Health Outreach Workers are running this project on their own and the women of the village have started participating in the health project and getting more aware about their own health. (Employer Respondent, International NGO, 2018)

Take a moment to *look up* and consider this student story provided by our program partner. This provides a good example of a student putting together many of the concepts we have highlighted in this book. This student took initiative on a community project but not in a way that was imposing a change on the community. This example highlights how approaching a community project with humility and a sense of cultural awareness can make you a stronger communicator. This begins with a posture of learning from others that is critical to understanding the best method available to cooperatively implement a proposed solution to a community problem. This student demonstrated that a better understanding of community stakeholders and their strengths and needs can be identified by listening and patiently attending to guidance from community members and cultural mentors. This student's project was impactful and sustainable because she was able to bring the idea to the community in a way that was sensitive to their unique perspectives and interpretations. In addition, the end goal was not for the success of the student or the project; it was for the community to assume ownership of the project that required their own commitment. It is through seeking to learn from the members of our communities with a flexible, mindful, and attentive approach that lasting positive changes can be implemented. We encourage you to think of this approach, especially about how to understand your role in your own communities as you read through and consider the concepts in the next sections of this chapter.

The Impact of –
Stewardship—Developing Agency by Sharing Knowledge and Responsibility

Embracing North of Normal—Student Reflects on Developing Community in Fargo, North Dakota

I made this move for professional reasons. When I first got to Fargo all my attention was focused on hitting my numbers and 'moving up'. We live in an interconnected world where our professional and personal lives are constantly affecting one another. Even though I initially viewed Fargo as a location to jumpstart my career, I learned to accept that I exist in Fargo outside of a 40-hour work week. I was going to burn out fast if I didn't embrace 'North of Normal', which is how people refer to Fargo, this wonderfully weird community in the freezing upper Midwest. I needed to find fulfillment outside of work if I wanted to perform well in my position and stay positive about this new chapter in my life so here is what I did. (Burke, 2018)

The above reflection is an excerpt from one of our student's blogs in which she highlights how through community involvement, stewardship, and developing life skills, she embraced not only this new and different place where she was living but also a holistic approach to work and community. This student's reflection is a wonderful example of developing agency by sharing her knowledge and taking initiative and responsibility. Agency is the capacity to feel empowered to act. It is activated through developing the self-confidence that results from making meaningful connections between learning experiences. Your sense of agency is about feeling knowledgeable and skilled enough to coordinate actions with others with a purposeful intent. She goes on in her post to cite key areas of growth that she experienced through agency. She identified making meaningful long-term commitments and examples of how she actualized this. One was through mentorship in which she volunteered with two separate organizations, and both required a minimum of a 1-year commitment. Both of the volunteer positions kept her motivated to pursue excellence in the male-dominated industry of technology. As a mentor, her guiding principle was that by thriving in your current environment you can be an example of what is possible to someone else. She encourages us to think about how we might share our success with others. In addition to her volunteer work, she decided to run a marathon in Fargo as an exercise in empowerment and developing mental toughness—"it's about showing up and finishing, a metaphor for how to approach every challenge in life."

In addition to her community involvement, the student took this time as an opportunity to develop an important life skill—budgeting and saving money. She acknowledges, "I moved here without a comma in my bank account" (Burke, 2018); but by the end of her time in Fargo, she was financially independent and actively saving for the future. In addition, she took the time to explore the surrounding area, getting to know others and developing friendships. A key point of learning that she shares is the need to be patient and intentional in your actions, and she acknowledges her own learning that "it takes time to learn a new cloud solution, it takes time to change your mindset, and it takes time to earn people's trust." (Burke, 2018)

We use this student's story because it reinforces the key concepts that we are focusing on this chapter—agency, civic engagement, and personal/social responsibility. Take a moment and think about a situation that was initially overwhelming and challenging? What was your mindset? How did you choose to approach this situation? In this student's story, she initially approached the situation by putting limits on it ("I'll be here for two years, at the most") and being very goal-directed in the workplace ("hitting her numbers and moving up"). By taking a broader, more inclusive, and purposeful approach, she ignited a sense of agency that included stewardship and finding ways to contribute to the community through her volunteer work, training, running a marathon, as well as connecting with others in the community and developing enough financial responsibility to become more independent and save money. The student here discovered and developed a sense of obligation. The definition of obligation: "an act or course of action to which a person is morally or legally bound; a duty or commitment." (Merriam-Webster, 2018) This student example demonstrates her sense of being bound to the community and her own development within that community—personally, professionally, and civically. In seeing the importance of establishing herself in Fargo in all these ways, she realized certain duties and commitments that she might not have otherwise by fully "embracing North of Normal." We thought this was an interesting story and example that captured the notion of obligation and illustrates its benefits to self and others in sharing knowledge and responsibility, being a good neighbor and citizen, and finding ways to contribute to community and the greater society.

Obligation and Discovery in a Rapidly Changing World

I think everything you do in life has to have a flow and a coherence. If you learned something or an experience gave you a great insight you MUST take a step forward and do something that will bring you closer to the reality you want to live. I understand that if I was so privileged to have studied in the U.S. and have lived so many experiences, I had to go back to (my own country) and share this privilege in some way. (Student Respondent, 2018)

We introduced the concept of obligation in the previous section and will expand on that here beginning with a couple questions for you to consider. If you could change one thing about the world, what would it be? How would you go about enacting that change? Self-directed learning is essential to managing shifting expectations and priorities in a fast-paced and quickly evolving world. Being self-directed requires adapting skills, competencies, and an ethical compass to match the requirements of new developments brought on by the blistering pace of technological innovation, political chaos, and media/information distortion. As President Joseph Aoun of Northeastern University outlines in his book *Robot Proof: Higher Education in the Age of Artificial Intelligence,* "If we rebalance our approach—by helping students to acquire the content they need to understand their chosen domain of study, as well as the broader cognitive capacities they need in a highly automated professional workplace—future generations will not be abandoned to the economic dust heap. However, we need a new model of learning that enables learners to understand the highly technological world around them and that simultaneously allows them to transcend it by nurturing the mental and intellectual qualities that are unique to humans—namely, their capacity for creativity and mental flexibility" (Aoun, 2017). This is what President Aoun terms "humanics" and calls upon the leaders of higher education institutions to act now to prepare students with the skills and competencies to better understand and work alongside machines. Specifically, it is a call to foster and grow innately human sensibilities that will prepare students to adapt and navigate within an ever-changing environment across a lifetime.

To meet this call, we encourage students to hone their sense of obligation and desire for discovery early in their college careers—their obligation to themselves and financial supporters to make the most of their education, obligations to their communities to ensure that they are applying their education to improve those around them, and obligations to the future of global society. Implicit in these obligations is an invitation to discover, innovate, connect purpose to action, and creatively co-construct our communities effectively with whom we live and work. We are entering a time when machines and humans will work alongside one another to provide companionship to the elderly, infirm, or lonely, to help solve complicated health issues, to interpret facts and produce news, to make legal decisions, to transport us safely from place to place, and so on. As Thomas Friedman writes in *Thank You for Being Late: An Optimist's Guide to Thriving in the Age of Accelerations,* "The ultimate spring of human variability, of course, lies in our capacity to invent new ideas, practices and institutions. But invention also flourished best when contacts with strangers compelled different ways of thinking and doing to compete for attention, so that choice became conscious, and deliberate tinkering with older practices became easy, and indeed often inevitable" (Friedman, 2016). We are indeed navigating through a time of great discovery and invention and also a time of challenging decisions on how we best live and work with each other across communities and borders. It is this combination of ethically responsible behavior with a sense of creation and discovery that can propel action that is of benefit to our communities and society.

In considering our actions that can best benefit others, we will need to begin to look inward to understand what it is that makes us human and begin to make the hard choices about what we are willing to sacrifice. For example, are we willing to turn over our care of our elderly to artificially intelligent companion robots, or should we be taking a harder look at ourselves, our communities, and our routines to examine what exactly are we sacrificing by doing this? Are we sacrificing deeper human connections, our personal and family stories for the sake of solving greater social problems, or are there ways that we can think more constructively about how we can solve problems while also improving our ability to empathize and support our communities?

Friedman goes on to write that in our professional lives every job is being (1) *pulled apart faster*—becoming automated and valuing higher-level technical skills; (2) *pulled out faster*—more competitive globally; and (3) *pulled down faster*—becoming obsolete and recreated more frequently. To compete with these market demands, Friedman suggests, "at a minimum, our educational systems must be retooled to maximize these needed skills and attributes: strong fundamentals in writing, reading, coding, and math; creativity, critical thinking, communication, and collaboration; grit, self-motivation, and lifelong learning habits; and entrepreneurship and improvisation—at every level" (Friedman, 2016). The priorities of life are taking on new meaning, and tough choices will need to be made quickly, with each new invention, about the sacrifices we decide to make when considering technological or data-driven decisions. What we may find is that while such efficiencies can save money for the bottom line and profitability of an endeavor, they may in fact be making our lives and experiences less full and compromise our shared obligations to a larger global society by doing so. It is for this reason that what we have written here we hope will be a starting point and method through which students can begin to better understand and discern their role as a learner not just at the university but across their lifetime of experiences, communities, and affiliations on and off their campuses.

What Kind of Agent of Change Will You Be?

Action orientation is a big piece for me. They (students) want to be out there doing. There is a commitment to lifelong learning and social action that is a lifetime of social commitment to social justice. The action piece is the big distinguisher. It's good being informed and it's a piece of it, but I think the real important piece is that people are compelled to act. (Faculty Respondent, 2017)

The faculty member's comment above speaks to the importance of agency and being compelled to act and participate in making change. When thinking of someone who caused social change, who do you think of? What are their core skills and qualities? When we ask our students these questions, we often hear about successful entrepreneurs, influential politicians, and prominent civil rights leaders and activists and stand-alone individuals who led courageously, took great risks, and put a vision to action. We also hear stories about someone from a local community that started a food bank, a community member who mobilized a fundraiser for a local school, or a researcher who developed an idea to improve the durability of bridge building materials. There are many ways to influence positive change in our communities, and when understood broadly we all have the ability to become agents for change. Rarely, though, is change brought by one person alone. It requires a degree of collaboration and systems thinking.

In his work *Driving Social Change* (2011), Paul C. Light examines the prevailing wisdom around what propels social change. His work proposed that social change requires a number of complex systems working in tandem. To achieve this, he calls for "catalytic collaboration" among our social entrepreneurs—those who have visions for social breakthroughs; our social safekeepers—those who defend past social breakthroughs by maintaining, innovating, and expanding; our social explorers—those who anticipate alternatives and test vulnerable assumptions; and our social advocates—those who are activists and others who force us to question our assumptions and to refuse to accept antiquated, outdated ideas and unjust conditions. We all have a potential role to play in the creation, maintenance, and sustainability of our communities. How we bring our skills and talents to bear on common problems is a matter of understanding who we are, what we are capable of, and being open to alternative perspectives and approaches.

It is here that we attempt to synthesize many of the concepts of this book. A sense of agency to innovate in our workplaces and society is developed through human connections, the support of our communities, and collaboration. To reach this place of agency and ability to take initiative requires an ability to include others, build trust, listen to alternative perspectives, ask good questions to inform good decisions, and demonstrate gratitude toward diverse opinions through empathic feedback. It is through our collaborations and learning by doing that we develop an ability to see how various academic disciplines and systems can be leveraged successfully together. To reach this level of collaboration let us consider a systems thinking approach.

In the *Systems Thinking for Social Change* (2015), David Peter Stroh argues that developing a systems thinking orientation supports the ability to learn continuously, anticipate intended and unintended consequences of actions, see connections, and make better choices. Systems thinking can be thought of as a way of seeing connections between interdependent parts that make up a system structure. In social and workplace settings, good systems thinking can improve the impact of initiatives by considering the needs of all stakeholder groups, the interdisciplinary attributes of the system, and by seeking sustainable community-driven solutions to problems. It also highlights the need for patience and intentionality in implementing programs designed to improve a community or organization. One of our employer partners in Cape Town, South Africa, Zoë Gauld-Angelucci (Greenpop), expresses the importance of good systems thinking when discussing her new hires, "Problems arise when people assume they know everything, and then tell the people they're working with what to do. You need to acknowledge you definitely don't know all the answers, and instead work with drawing solutions with the people you're working with (who likely know their own context far better than you, and are usually quite equipped to work within their own experience). Know your limitations, understand deeply why you are working here. Work on distilling the value and help you can actually add, and whether it is needed, wanted or appropriate" (2018). This brings us to an important point: Taking action without considering the impact of that action is probably worse than taking no action at all. Civic engagement and collective social action require a degree of humility, empathy and ethics, as well as realizing that your actions will impact others.

The Art of –
Collaborative Problem Solving—Working as Part of Team

I think experiential learning forces you to make interaction the cornerstone of your life and forces you to deal with humanity in a way that you don't realize how applicable it is in the classroom. Even just doing group work. At school, no one likes doing group projects but co-op and experiential learning teach you how to be good at compromising and negotiating; being straightforward when you need to. (Student Respondent, 2018)

In today's college environment, there is more diversity than ever, and you have unprecedented access to others at the local, national, and global levels. This occurs whether you are making these connections on campus or through study abroad or international experiential work and research. Within this broad and varied landscape, you have a myriad of opportunities to talk and work with diverse individuals who represent a wide range of social, ethnic, and religious identities. According to research by Reich (2012), students need to be engaged in repeated and ongoing educational opportunities to develop the global competencies and knowledge necessary to participate as problem solvers and active and informed citizens in an interconnected world. Engaging in an ongoing manner in the wider world provides for a substantive and informative exchange of global and local perspectives and understandings. As such, you gain both intra- and interpersonal development by engaging in critical reflection of self, others, and issues in the world through these interactions.

These reflections and interactions provide a solid foundation from which you can continue to engage across cultures, socioeconomic status, and perspectives in working with others to solve societal problems and promote the 'global' common good (Braskamp & Engberg, 2011).

In research conducted by Zahabioun et al. (2013), which focused on global citizenship, the authors examined the global challenges of the 21st century, such as environmental justice, human rights, divided societies and conflicts, and public health, topics that require students to not only have an academic basis and understanding of these issues but also global experience and mindedness when they actively connect with others in the world to address these problems and concerns. Certainly, there is no shortage of major planetary challenges and social inequities that we currently face in the world—poverty, hunger, climate change, unequal distribution of wealth, terrorism, and social and political instability. At the same time, we also share opportunities for global collaboration in sciences, arts, business, economy, and international cooperation. These are all possibilities for us to engage in collaborative problem solving.

One of the key aspects of collaboratively solving problems and working effectively as part of a team is the ability to be empathetic and to listen and respond thoughtfully to others. We have addressed in other sections the risks that dependence on digital technology and automation can separate us from each other and even ourselves. Teamwork and collaboration require the ability to connect to people and culture of others, not just technology. As pointed out in previous chapters, Anthropologist Sherry Turkle in her work *Reclaiming Conversation* (2016) found that the proliferation of smartphone technology has created a cultural shift that is manifested by what she is calling "the empathy gap" in the younger generations. She has found that it is becoming increasingly difficult for people to navigate between their digital lives and day-to-day lives, to resolve complex emotions and to engage in meaningful conversations in uncontrolled and face-to-face environments. She also discusses how we are reaching a critical point from which we are now turning to machines to solve our problems and even provide companionship. "At a first, we speak through machines and forget how essential face-to-face conversation is to our relationships, our creativity, and our capacity for empathy. At a second, we take a further step and speak not just through machines but to machines. This is a turning point. When we consider conversations with machines about our most human predicaments, we face a moment of reckoning that can bring us to the end of our forgetting. It is an opportunity to reaffirm what makes us most human" (Turkle, 2016). As the line between machine and human becomes increasingly blurred we risk becoming increasingly less patient in the human interactions that are not tailored to our preferences.

As we work with students in the classroom and in advising sessions, we review their resumes and help them with language and expression of your skills and abilities. Related to this preparation and advising, something we hear consistently from our employer partners is that they look for students who can work independently, and even more importantly, who can work as part of a team. The ability to communicate well and be helpful, encouraging, supportive, and positive are just some of the attributes that we point to as important to being a valued member of a team. It is not just for your professional life that being part of a team is important. Certainly, your civic and community involvement also implies a capacity toward working collaboratively and positively with others.

Taking Initiative—Ethics in Workplace and Global Society

I believe that exposure to and a sense of understanding of different cultures is essential for developing an ability to make ethical and informed decisions. The development of interpersonal or, in other words, "people" skills such as empathy, ability to work in teams, flexibility, etc. in my opinion, however are of the greatest importance. (Student Respondent, 2018)

The above student quotation relates to both taking initiative and developing an ethical framework from which to relate to others and make decisions. In our day-to-day lives, we are continuously making decisions and choices without necessarily thinking about the ethics of what we do. Generally, we carry on and most of what we are doing seems pretty straightforward, not requiring added discernment about the impact of our particular decisions or actions. However, it is in the moments when we question, we sense friction, doubt or a level of discomfort about the right thing to do that provides a catalyst for considering our approach and ethical options. This notion of ethics and concerns about how our actions impact the wider community/society dates back to John Dewey, American philosopher, psychologist, and educational reformer whose ideas have been influential in education and social reform. In his foundational book, *The School and Society* (originally published in 1915), Dewey places emphasis on the importance of schools connecting to the issues and concerns of the wider society. He cites his attempt to identify and make connections to everyday life, so that the learner gains experience that can be applied and made useful in society.

We integrate this notion put forth by John Dewey almost 100 years ago into our cooperative education course when we introduce students to the practice of reflection and how to be mindful of ethical concerns in the workplace and community. As part of the course, we review workplace ethics case studies which involves reading the case studies and working as part of a team to come up with a solution or protocol. (See the Toolkit for Workplace Ethics Case Studies.) In class, each team presents their response to the case study; as a whole group we discuss the underlying ethical concerns, precedent, their particular thoughts and feelings and projected outcomes and, in this way, provide a model for how students can do these themselves. Our guiding questions as we discuss possible choices in these situations as we consider 'the right thing to do' are-will my decision and/or action enhance my personal integrity or detract from it? Will it enhance my professionalism or minimize it? Will it foster my being a good citizen or take away from it?

It is often the case that once students are working in their co-op placements issues arise that provide opportunities to discern a particular problem and through ethical reflection identify the appropriate action and/or solution. It is common that when we meet with students and discuss and review particular ethical issues and their decisions that we have an additional opportunity to further discuss and deconstruct their ethical experiences and learning. Our ultimate goal is to work with them in developing their sense of being well-informed as students, workers, and citizens who can think critically and ethically about issues in order to make important contributions in each of these areas. One student discussed how today's society offers particular opportunities for ethical consideration—

> I think the world is so connected now, you have a better sense of the humanity in all of us. Even if you haven't had the opportunity to travel very far you can still get instant information about anywhere in the world. I am sure that it is this interconnectedness that makes millennials lean toward businesses that are more ethical and socially responsible. For example, my parents didn't know whether the clothes they bought were made by underpaid labor in China or if the food they ate was full of toxins. Whereas our generation has access to all this information and knows that they can 'vote with their dollars' and make choices about what products to buy and what causes to support. (Student Respondent, 2018)

As our world becomes more interconnected and we are more mobile and our opportunities to work and study with others in various global locations is more prevalent it presents a good opportunity to consider why and how we are engaging. Talking with a student and faculty member who had participated in a short-term summer study abroad opportunity, both reflected on their experience. The student respondent noted-how they had met with a variety of different people, some of whom were very thoughtful and respectful, some who were less respectful and that made them question how they wanted to interact with the community.

The faculty respondent questioned this notion of respectful engagement as well and noted-one thing they were questioning and still unpacking concerned ethics and what it means to come into communities as outsiders. The faculty member stated, "What are some of the unintended consequences of the engagement that we participate in? How do you minimize risk for harm in the community? This is an ongoing challenge, to really look at the collective good of what is being done from a partnership perspective." (2018). This is a good example of how to build in ethical reasoning and reflection as part of our experiences. These are very good questions that we can all ask ourselves and continue to discern as global citizens and workers.

Dialogue and Action—Creating New Ideas, Narratives, and Possibilities

It is crucially important to be able to empathize with people, understand the other side. My home country, Russia, and Georgia have a history and a complicated relationship and trying to understand the 'the other side' was quite difficult, but not impossible while doing my co-op at the Georgian Foundation for Strategic and International Studies (GFSIS). Now, when I look at the outcome of my work experience, I am confident of my ability to succeed in the field of peacebuilding and conflict resolution—something I never considered before. (Student Respondent, 2018)

© Orianna Timsit

In the above quote and final student story in this chapter, the ability to connect and create new narratives and possibilities is the theme that she addresses and that we will conclude on. This ability to deeply understand one another's perspective in ways that build trust and allow for new ways of living, working, and progressing together is perhaps one of the most important aspects of learning in contemporary society. This student's story of being a Russian in the Republic of Georgia is an affirming example of how such trust and understanding lays the groundwork for progress. She reflected on how navigating around the city and country would have been nearly impossible if relying on GPS, as Internet connection was often poor and information on the Internet was scarce or primarily in the Georgian language that she did not understand. The lack of technology and information though turned out to be a blessing in disguise as it required her to get out of her comfort zone and, as she described, "everyday approach strangers on the street, taxi drivers, bus drivers, shopping assistants to find out the information she needed." It was through these human interactions and engagement that she and the Georgian people whom she met and interacted with came to talk, connect, and build understanding and seeing each other less as "the other" and more as human beings. The student noted that when she looks back on this experience, she realized she became a much more self-aware, confident, and optimistic person.

Even prior to her co-op work experience at GFSIS, this student was reflecting on how her experiences in and out of the classroom were helping her to better define her sense of purpose and motivations for taking action. She noted,

> As a Russian in an American classroom, I was quick to realize that Russia and the U.S. are still separated by a wall. Even the future politicians and foreign service officers lack knowledge of the other's culture and society necessary to understand the motivations behind the actions of the other state. I realized that it is that reality that makes the peace-building process nearly impossible; and I decided that it is up to people like me to narrow that gap in knowledge and understanding through dialogue and action. I decided to do that through education, meaning both literal teaching of students and education of masses through books and articles that I produce. (Student Respondent, 2018)

In discussing how her experiences out of the classroom helped her define her purpose and action, she noted how they enabled her to develop an array of skills essential for her profession and the ability to build upon existing knowledge quickly and learn new things on the spot. She also discussed how her two co-op experiences were largely different from each other and that she considered each of these endeavors to be successful, thus giving her confidence that if she chooses to pursue a different career path, she knows she can easily transfer skills and communicate and connect with people across contexts.

We end with this student story as it encapsulates personal, professional, and civic learning by "looking up"—being personally aware and connected, making meaning through experiences, engaging in dialogue and action, and having a sense of optimism by creating new possibilities that serve to better self and the greater society.

Conclusion

Agency is the capacity to feel empowered to act. It is activated through developing the self-confidence that results from making meaningful connections between learning experiences. In this final chapter, we have relayed how your sense of agency is about feeling knowledgeable and skilled enough to coordinate actions with others with a purposeful intent. In this book, we have exposed you to skill areas and methods for making the classroom experience transferable and compatible with the "real world" by being self-reflective and intentional. Through engaging with the chapters of this book, you have been reflecting on ways to develop your personal, professional, and civic skills in and out of the classroom. Our hope is that through the activities and advising sessions you are more intentionally exploring your sense of purpose in what you are studying and experiencing. This final chapter is intended to give you insights into how to engage in experiential learning opportunities in a way that is purposeful, ethical, and impactful. See LaMachia's (2017) *Visualization of Global Learning and Citizenship*, which captures key themes and findings from her study that have been presented in this chapter. The schematic provides one way for you to consider how many of the themes/concepts that we discuss in this chapter and throughout the book in general come together. Now that you've read through the chapter *look up* again and think about what your chart would look like – What areas have been key to your experience as a global learner and citizen? How would you diagram your experiential learning, growth and development? What do you see as integral to your process? How do you wish to further develop? What change will you bring to the world?

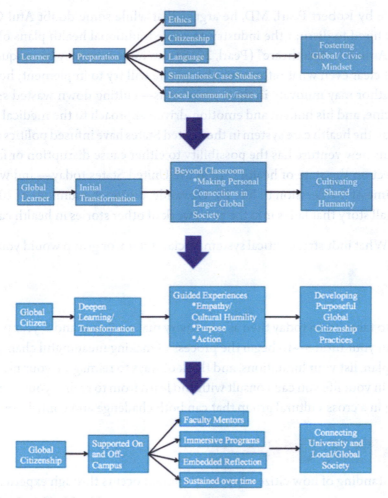

Figure 6.1: Created by Joani LaMachia

LOOK UP: Reality Check

There are times in history where a pivotal change is made—in an industry, in politics, in education, and in health care. In retrospect, it is often easier to note when this change happened, to argue the pros and cons, and to form opinions about what now is and what could have been. Leadership during these times of transition and choices by all parties involved can have lasting effects on change.

One of these systems in the United States that has been the target of much scrutiny, as it affects everyone—often in many ways—is health care. It affects the choices the U.S. citizens make in relation to jobs that they take and affects policies related to business, including for-profit, nonprofit, and government. The inequity seen and felt by many has no one origin in the complex beast that is health care, which makes any small change lead to both intended and unintended consequences and reforms on a large scale daunting at best.

Jeff Bezos, Warren Buffett, and Jamie Dimon announced in January 2018 that they would form a new nonprofit company aimed at lowering health care costs for their combined roughly 1.2 million employees and possibly one day all Americans. Subsequently, they chose to hire Dr. Atul Gawande as CEO of the nonprofit health care venture formed by Amazon, Berkshire Hathaway, and JPMorgan Chase to deliver better outcomes, satisfaction, and cost efficiency in care.

In an opinion piece by Robert Pearl, MD, he argues that while some doubt Atul Gawande to have the skills needed, he "was hired to disrupt the industry, to make traditional health plans obsolete, and to create a bold new future for American healthcare" (Pearl, 2018) and for this he may be uniquely qualified. Early in the venture, it was not clear even what reforms or changes he will try to implement; however, in Perl's opinion this doctor and author may innovate in three main areas—cutting down wasted spending, focusing on evidence-based medicine, and his human and emotion-driven approach to the medical field.

Political opinions on the health care system in the United States have infused politics nationally and locally for a long time, and this new venture has the possibility to either cause disruption or fade as other ventures have in the past. Reflect on the state of health care in the United States today—and what you know of this story—which at the time of the decision to hire Dr. Gawande, during the summer of 2018, had the potential for big change or a small story that fades into the patchwork of other stories in health care.

Reflection Question: What industry, political system, social system, or group would you choose to disrupt—if you had the chance?

Activity

If you had the choice to take action today then as an activity make a 1-year and 5-year plan on what steps you can take today—and in your future—to begin the process of making meaningful change. List your strengths in implementing this plan, list your limitations, and think of ways to reimagine your plan as it relates to those limitations. List those in your life you can consult with and learn from to realize your plan and make a strategy for how you will bring in a cross-cultural group that can both challenge and contribute to your plan.

Key Takeaways

- Gaining an understanding of how citizenship development occurs through experiential learning
- Seeing the college experience itself as "real world" learning
- Taking ownership of your education through self-authored learning
- Developing an ethical framework from which to relate to others and make decisions
- Embracing agency by sharing knowledge and responsibility

Follow-Up Activities in Toolkit—Listen Up, Look Up, Join Up, and Act Up

- Creating a personal **Code of Ethics**
- Complete **Agent of Social Change Reflection** Activity
- Develop a **Policy Memo** to Reflect on a Work Experience
- Participate in a **Purpose Mapping** activity

Works Cited

Adams, M. , & Zhou-McGovern, Y. (1990, April). Some cognitive development characteristics of social diversity education. Paper presented at the Annual Meeting of the American Education Research Association, Boston.

Association of American Colleges and Universities. (2015). *Optimistic about the future, but how well prepared? College students' views on college learning and career success* [PowerPoint Slides]. Retrieved from https://www.aacu.org/leap/public-opinion-research/2015-students

Aoun, J. 2017. *Robot proof- higher education in age of artificial intelligence.* Cambridge, MA: MIT Press.

Braskamp, L., & Engberg, M. (2011). How colleges can influence the development of a global perspective. *Liberal Education, 97*(3/4), 1–7.

Burke, M. (2018, March 1). North of Normal [Blog Post]. Retrieved from: https://www.linkedin.com/pulse/north-normal-maggie-burke/

Collette, M. (2013, May 3). Pathways to Success. Retrieved From: http://news.northeastern.edu/2013/05/03/pathways-to-success/

Dewey, J. (2001). *The School and Society & The Child and the Curriculum.* Mineola, NY: Dover Publications. (Original work published in 1915).

Fischer, K. (2011). Northeastern, once local, goes global. Chronicle of Higher Education, 20 (57), 1-20.

Friedman, T. (2016). *Thank You For Being Late: An Optimist's Guide to Thriving In The Age Of Accelerations.* New York, NY: Picador.

Kegan, R. (1994). *In over our heads: The mental demands of modern life.* Cambridge, MA: Harvard University Press.

LaMachia, J. (2017). *Integrating global citizenship learning in undergraduate education.* Retrieved from https://repository.library.northeastern.edu/files/neu:cj82nr13g/fulltext.pdf

Lavito, A. (2018, July 9). *Dr. Atul Gawande to start as CEO of Buffett, Bezos, and Dimon's healthcare venture.* Retrieved from https://www.cnbc.com/2018/07/06/dr-atul-gawande-to-start-as-ceo-buffett-bezos-dimon-health-venture.html

Light, P. (2011). *Driving social change.* Hoboken, NJ: John Wiley & Sons.

Magolda, M. B. (2001). *Making their own way: Narratives for transforming higher education to promote self-development.* Sterling, VA: Stylus.

Magolda, M, B. (2008). Three elements of self-authorship. *Journal of College Student Development, 49*(4), 269–284.

Magolda, M. B. (2014). Self-authorship. *New Directions for Higher Education, 2014*(166), 25–33. doi:10.1002/he.20092.

Mickelson, R., & Nkomo, M. (2012). Integrated schooling, life course outcomes, and social cohesion in multiethnic societies. *Review of Research in Education, 36*, 197-238. DOI:10.3102/0091732X11422667.

Northeastern University Research Institute for Experiential Learning Science. (n.d.). The Experiential Learning Advantage for Workforce Preparedness. Retrieved from: https://www.northeastern.edu/riels/impact/the-experiential-learning-advantage-for-workforce-preparedness/

Obligation. (2018). In *Merriam Webster.* Retrieved from https://www.merriam-webster.com/dictionary/obligation.

Pearl, R. (2018, June 25). *Why Atul Gawanda will soon be the most feared CEO in healthcare.* Retrieved from https://www.forbes.com/sites/robertpearl/2018/06/25/atul-gawande-ceo/#5e4614aa369b

Piaget, J. (1950). *The psychology of intelligence.* Trans. M. Piercy and D. E. Berlyne. London, UK: Routledge and Kegan Paul.

Reich, J. (2012). Global Learning as General Education for the Twenty-First Century. *Educational Research and Reviews, 2* (21), 464–473.

Sperandio, J., Grudzinski-Hall, M., & Stewart-Gambino, H. (2010). Developing an undergraduate global citizenship program: Challenges of definition and assessment. *International Journal of Teaching and Learning in Higher Education, 22*(1), 12–22.

Stroh, D. P. (2015). *Systems thinking for social change.* White River Junction, VT: Chelsea Green Publishing.

Turkle, S. (2016). *Reclaiming Conversation: The Power Of Talk In A Digital Age.* New York, NY: Penguin Books.

Zahabioun, S., Yarmohammadian, M., & Keshtiaray, N., Global Citzenship Education and Its Implications for Curriculum Goals at the Age of Globalization. *International Education Studies.* January 2013: 6 (195–206).

APPENDIX—TOOLKIT-ACTIVITIES-LOOK UP, LISTEN UP, ACT UP, JOIN UP

INTRODUCTION—TOOLKIT

Welcome to the "Toolkit" portion of this book, where you will find the following three categories of resources:

- **Activities (class and individual):** These are activities that can be used either in classroom settings or as independent activities aligned to the topic of each chapter. Some may include worksheet resources while others are prompts for you to take action.
- **Advising sessions/reflections:** These are prompts for you to consider and reflect upon. They are intended to be discussed with an instructor or mentor, depending on how you are using this book.
- **Case studies:** These student (or professional) stories are related to the content of each chapter and are based mostly within the world of co-ops and full-time employment. They typically will support, explain, challenge, and/or deepen the understanding of the topics in each chapter through a scenario based on real situations. They are intended to be used in classroom discussions or as prompts for analysis, since there is no one "right" way to understand a situation, and perspective taking is embedded in the case study process.

The activities and advising content shared come from a deep pool of experience within the Northeastern Co-op Faculty and beyond. The content comes from varied disciplines and builds upon years of determining best practices and learning what works well with students. Some of these activities will be framed for instructors, such as co-op faculty, experiential program instructors, and community leaders, to name a few. Others will speak directly to students or individual readers of this text.

Just as we discuss in the book, shifting perspectives can be helpful in many situations. This portion of the book is not excluded from the concept of perspective shifting, so while you may come across activities or prompts framed for a different purpose, use these resources in the way that best suits your needs, at this moment, for your exploration and growth.

We hope you will find these exercises and activities helpful as you explore, test, and determine your own path!

Intro for Toolkit written by Rebecca Westerling

INTRODUCTION

Advising Session

Look in: What do you hope to gain from this book? After reviewing the chapters, consider what resonates with you.

Look up: Observe what you see and hear. How do you balance your time and attention in your life—looking up (seeing, hearing, observing, participating) versus looking down (at technology or looking away from your surroundings)?

Look up: Take some time to look up and observe your surroundings. Note what you see, what you hear, and what you notice. Try to go somewhere new to you or unexpected—where there is an element of "other."

CHAPTER 1 - FOSTERING SELF-AWARENESS

Class/Activities

Explore (Look Up)

Digital Audit Exercise

© Rebecca Westerling.

While much of this book is about looking up, gaining a sense of your "digital self" by looking down can be important. Do a digital audit, of yourself, or in class do this in pairs. Put together a digital summary of yourself or your partner. Then discuss/decide how accurate this is in comparison to your perception of your "true" self. What is missing? What can't be conveyed online? What should be included in your digital footprint that you can add, and what should be removed?

Engage (Act Up)

Tell Me About Yourself

© Rebecca Westerling.

Your answer to "tell me about yourself" should feel natural, not rehearsed, and authentic. This, ironically, can often take quite a bit of practice. The goal of having a response you feel comfortable with for the "tell me about yourself" question, or "elevator pitch," is to be ready to share a bit about yourself and connect with someone in a short time.

1. **Consider your audience:** Consider who you may be connecting with and why—is it for a job where it would be good to include certain skills or interests? What would your audience find interesting, intriguing, or find common ground with? Keep this in mind as you build your response.

2. **Build your story:** This should typically be a 30- to 60-second introduction of yourself. Feel free to start with a template such as the one below:

   - Hi, my name is _____. I am a (class year)_____ at (school)_____ studying (subject[s])_____. I am very interested in (academic areas, industries, relevant topics) _____ _____. I am a part of (groups, communities, etc.) _____ _____ _____ and have previously worked in/at (previous work experience)_____ _____.

   - **If you are applying for a specific job:** I am excited to speak to you about the _____ position since it fits my interests and skills, including _____ _____ _____

   - **If you are networking:** I am excited to meet you and would love to hear about _____ (your involvement with x organization, your interest in x topic, etc.)

3. **Practice!** Practice so that it feels natural, but not to the point where it feels rehearsed. Improvise, mix things up, and get comfortable presenting yourself. If you can tell your story to yourself in the mirror and be charming, you are much more likely to feel comfortable doing so both spontaneously when you are networking and in a job interview setting.

4. **Relax!** Have fun connecting with others.

Prepare (Listen Up)

Résumé Writing and Template

© Jonathan Andrew.

Developing a good résumé is a great exercise in developing professional and personal self-awareness. Framing your prior experiences, skills, and accomplishments to a variety of employer audiences is a skill that takes practice and refinement. The key to good resume writing is developing the ability to anticipate the needs of your target employer. This involves four key steps.

1. **Polish formatting:** Utilizing a résumé format that is visually pleasing and facilitates the employer's ability to find the information they view as most important for the position. This includes ensuring that that the relevant information appears on the one-page resume in a place the employer expects to find it and making sure that there is good visual balance on the page between white space and important specifics and accomplishments that will draw the eye of the reader. When formatting your résumé it helps to begin the process with a completely unformatted document and formatting it methodically using the formatting tools available in a program like Microsoft Word.

2. **Tailor content to the jobs:** Provide content that is concise, uses active language, avoids redundancies, includes specifics, and features a diverse set of skills relevant to the position. Résumés should be tailored to the skills and qualifications detailed in the job descriptions and provide specifics and a record of accomplishments throughout. This includes relevant quantifiable information that will appear in your bullet points as relevant statistics and numbers.

3. **Find a team of editors:** Writing a good résumé takes time, patience, and multiple rounds of edits. Get as many eyes on your résumé as possible before you submit it to an employer. Seek critical feedback from career service professionals and professionals in the field you seek to enter. Résumé format and content will differ according to your field of practice, and the best way to know the standards of your chosen field is to consult with those who hire people in those fields. Your peers and family are great as extra pairs of eyes to help you with proofreading a résumé, but the language and way to infer skills from a résumé are best evaluated by someone who works or views résumés every day.

4. **Tailor your résumé to fit the screening and recruiting process:** Determine if the first pass of your résumé will be made by a human or a machine. Often when submitting résumés to an online jobs database or portal, the first pass will be made by a machine that searches for the frequency of keywords (taken from the job description) on your résumé. For these sorts of portals, it is important to have the actual skills sought in the résumé appear in multiple places on your résumé. On the other hand, if you are handing a résumé to another human it often helps to have language that does not always directly state that you have skills but infers a particular skill set by the active verbs you use, and inferring skills with authentic examples of previous workplace activities and accomplishments. In addition, small touches like printing your résumé on résumé paper adds a special touch and attention that will make you memorable and often be viewed positively by the employer.

One final point is that your resume should stand out for the right reasons and not the wrong reasons. The right reasons include a clean, polished look and a well-constructed and concise outline of relevant skills and experiences for the job. The wrong reasons is a résumé that attempts to be flashy with large fonts, colors, strange types of scripts, or template formats that do not help the employer find the information they need or would view as most relevant to the job they are hiring for. First impressions matter, and the way you present yourself through your résumé to a future employer will demonstrate your professional awareness of their hiring needs, process, and unique expectations.

The following is an example of a well-formatted and structured résumé that we use with our students at Northeastern. In addition, please find a résumé editing checklist to help with the editing process. Find the format that works well for your target professional field and remember to follow the principles of good résumé construction outlined previously.

ANDRE BRIGHAM

39 Forsyth St., Boston, MA 02115
617-373-3456, brigham.a@husky.neu.edu

EDUCATION

Northeastern University   **Boston, MA**
Candidate: Bachelor of Arts in International Affairs and Economics   *GPA: 3.35*
Expected Graduation: *May 2019*
Relevant Coursework: Macroeconomics, Microeconomics, Statistics, Introduction to Computer Science, Microeconomic and Macroeconomic Theory, International Relations, Globalization
Extracurricular Activities, Leadership and Awards: Spring 2014 Dean's List, University Honors Program, Econ Society President, International Affairs Society Treasurer

Dialogue of Civilizations Program-Social Entrepreneurship Field Study   **South Africa**
Summer Semester Abroad   *July-August 2015*

EXPERIENCE

Northeastern University, International Affairs Program   **Boston, MA**
Office Assistant   *September-December 2016*
- Coordinated strategic website marketing project to increase student engagement 20%
- Oversaw research and administrative duties for 15 staff, faculty and director
- Managed office coverage for program administrator and director on 500+ student program
- Performed routine clerical tasks such as faxing, photocopying, filing, processing incoming and outgoing mail, maintaining paper supplies for printers and fax machines for 20 person office

Burmese Refugee Assistance Program   **Copenhagen, Denmark/Chiang Mai, Thailand**
Volunteer Team Leader/Fundraising Coordinator   *May-July 2016*
- Engaged in 3 week field study July 2010 near Chiang Mai, Thailand to assess needs of over 50 Burmese refugees living in temporary villages
- Coordinated with local non-profit, "Life Development Center", to develop 3 sustainability programs related to construction of fish pond and landslide barriers
- Led strategic communication efforts in Denmark including presenting to over 100 investors, schools, and community about program to raise awareness and publicity
- Organized fundraisers including benefit concerts, school fairs, and social events and jointly raised over $7,000 USD

Social Change through Peace Games   **Boston, MA**
Community Brigade   *January-May 2016*
- Created a safe classroom environment for 15 elementary aged students through taking initiative on utilization of group discussion and games
- Performed community outreach to members of the Boston Community and local YMCA and boosted engagement by 70%
- Strategized with YMCA board on targeted social media initiatives with $10,000 budget

Newfound 4-H Camp   **Newfound, NH**
Camp Counselor   *June-September 2015*
- Facilitated group and crafting activities for 15 elementary aged campers
- Led groups on 3 mile hikes twice a week with focus on environmental education
- Created curriculum and instructed craft classes for 20 campers 3 times a week
- Analyzed camp strategic marketing social media to increase viewership by 20%

SKILLS

Computer: Advanced MS Word, PowerPoint; Skilled in MS Excel; Familiar with MS Access
Language: Advanced French, Beginning Spanish

Name on resume:_____   Name of Reviewer_____

Resume Checklist

1. **First Read the Resume in 10 seconds or less and record your first impressions; write a list of things that you noticed or that stood out to you at first glance:**

2. **Next take a longer look and go through this checklist step by step while making edits to your partners resume.**

Appearance/formatting:

☐ Resume is one page in length

☐ Resume can easily be scanned, read and understood

☐ Resume looks balanced on the page (margins are the appropriate size) and attractive to the reader.

☐ The sections are correct with correct contact information, sections: education, experience, skills and interests.

☐ Bolding, italics, indentations, bulleting and underlining is used consistently throughout the resume.

☐ Dates, job title, and location of specific jobs are consistent throughout resume

☐ Education and Experiences are listed in reverse chronological order under each category, beginning with the most recent.

☐ There are at least two bullets listed in all bulleted sections.

☐ Punctuation is used consistently.

☐ Abbreviations are correct (example: Massachusetts should be MA and not M.A. or MA. or Mass)

☐ Name is same size as section headings and clear for the reader.

☐ Education and Experiences are listed in Reverse chronological order (most recent come first).

☐ Dates are written in consistent format; either abbreviations (Jan., Feb., Mar. etc.) or fully written (January, February, March etc.)

☐ Dates are written in the proper format; Jan.-May 2010 and not Jan. 2010-May 2010

Content:

☐   Includes Current Address, Phone Number, and Email Address.

☐   Major, Year of Graduation and GPA (if over 3.0) are listed under Education Section

☐   Relevant Courses, Activities, Leadership and Honors are included as subsections in "Education" (if helpful)

☐   Every bullet begins with an active verb: Job descriptions do not begin with "Responsibilities included..." or "Duties consisted of..."

☐   Active verbs are not repeated in bullets for the same job.

☐   Job responsibilities reflect applicable skills as well as specific duties.

☐   Jobs are described with most important responsibilities first.

☐   Unnecessary articles such as "the", "a" and "an" are removed

☐   Verb tenses are consistent throughout the resume and each job description.

☐   No use of pronouns such as "I","my", "their" or "them" etc.

☐   Job bullet points are well edited and grammatically correct.

☐   Computer skills and language skills are listed, with proficiency level.

☐   Bullets feature accomplishments and include quantifiable information wherever applicable.

☐   Only jobs and experiences that can highlight relevant working skills are included in the "Experiences" section.

☐   Study abroad experiences are in the appropriate place in the "Education" section.

3. **Please give some feedback on what you observed to be the most prominent skills and strengths of the resume. Also give comments on where you thought there could be more detail.**

Explore (Look Up)

Defining Moments Exercise

© Melissa Peikin and the CCIS Co-op Team, and Rebecca Westerling.

The following exercise is one that can be done after reading Chapter 1, with special notice taken to Dweck's mindset. In class, I ask students to submit their reflection, and I respond to each one. If you are doing this independently, complete the reflection, then spend additional time considering how you can use it for growth in the future, or take the time to discuss with a trusted friend or mentor

Defining moments reflection: Is there something in your recent past job search experience that you think measures you? Your answers during an interview? The technical assessment? Not being called in for an interview? Focus on that thing. Feel all the emotions that go with it. Now put it in a growth-mindset perspective. Look honestly at your role in it, but understand that it doesn't define your intelligence or personality. Instead, ask yourself, "What did I (or can I) learn from that experience? How can I use it as a basis for growth moving forward?"

Notes for Instructors: Instructor then responds to each reflection. Many common themes surrounded: not getting called in for interviews, not answering interview questions well, not receiving an offer from a company, and

comparing themselves to others. Most reflections focused on not letting this one instance define them, and listed things they can do to improve their attitude and skillsets going forward.

This exercise evolved from at first asking students what defined them in the past (not necessarily on the job search). A few topics that students listed were SAT scores, grades in general, and a Fundamentals of Computer Science class that some students who traditionally do well in school or failed or received a low grade. We decided to focus primarily on the job search since that is a focus of our class, but this assignment can be adapted to many different experiences.

Prepare (Listen Up)

Tips for Asking for Candid Feedback!

© Rebecca Westerling.

You can often learn a lot about yourself by asking to hear from other people and getting to see yourself through their eyes, but how you do this can be a challenge. Below are some tips to steer you in the right direction. Review these and determine how you may want to proceed—knowing yourself and the person/people you are asking.

- **Best practices**
  - Be prepared to learn some great things about yourself, and know you may learn some things that surprise you or are disappointing. Take time to think through this before asking, because your request for honesty should open the door for truly honest feedback.
  - Be creative in thinking through who you might ask. Consider a colleague you interacted with quite a bit but didn't know well—they may have a lot of insight to share and not hesitate pointing out some areas you can improve as well as surprising new strengths you didn't know you had.
    Be mindful of how you ask for the feedback, and giving people enough time to think through your request. Some people may do better with a conversation in person, others may prefer email, and others may appreciate you framing what you are asking ahead of time and talking through their thoughts in person or on the phone. In person is often helpful, when possible, since it can be a conversation, but be appreciative. Thank the person for their time and thoughtfulness.
- **How do I actually ask?**
  - Start by framing what you are asking for.
    - I want to learn, from other people's perspectives, what they believe my strengths are, but I am also particularly interested in areas I can improve. Would you be able to share your thoughts with me on this?
    - I realize you may have some thoughts now, or may want some time to think about it—so let me know if you want to chat now or later.
  - Ask for specifics, if possible.
    - Can you give an example of a time I could have been more effective? Can you give an example of a time I was particularly effective?
    - Are there skills that you think I should build if I want to be more effective in the xyz role, or to be successful in the xyz field? Are there certain skills I have that make me particularly effective in the xyz role, or to be successful in the xyz field?
- **What do I do with what I learned?**
  - Use the feedback to build your strengths. You may have had strengths you were aware of shared, or you may have discovered some things that others perceive as a strength that you hadn't considered. Build on these strengths.

- Use the feedback to focus on improving your weaknesses. They may have reinforced areas you know you need to improve, or you may have discovered new areas where you could build skills. Use this information to learn and grow.
- Use the feedback to be more aware of how you are perceived by others, both positively and negatively, and consider how you can be proactive in shaping other people's perceptions of you.
- Consider that the person you asked was giving you their personal opinion, and consider the context.
- Set goals based on what you learned.

Engage (Act Up)

Intentional Storytelling Exercise

© Rebecca Westerling and Sally Conant.

Marketing your experience! This exercise is designed to help you tell your story in an intentional way. You are in charge of framing your story, and telling a compelling story to your audience, whether it is colleagues in a job, interviewers in a job search process, or friends and classmates. Taking the time to frame your story, and be intentional about what you include, can help you tell a more compelling story.

For instance, while having international experiences is a great thing to have on your résumé, it is not these international experiences that are the top hiring criteria for employers considering interns or co-op students. The top three criteria, according to a CERI study, are enthusiasm, fit, and that students are hardworking. The challenge is how to show these skills—or others—through your past experiences. This exercise is framed within international experiences; however, you can substitute any focus area that makes sense for your story—such as leadership opportunities, past internships, club involvement, or personal stories.

Pick your audience: To whom are you telling your story? An interviewer, a colleague who you are sharing past experience with, a classmate, and so on.

What skills do you want to highlight? Consider some of the skills employers typically seek, such as the ones outlined below:

- Analytical Skills
- Computer Skills
- Cultural Awareness
- Decision-Making Skills
- Detail Orientation
- Enthusiasm
- Flexibility
- Hardworking

- High-Quality Work
- High Quantity of Work
- Independence
- Initiative
- Interpersonal Skills
- Leadership
- Maturity
- Motivation

- Problem-Solving Skills
- Quantitative Skills
- Professionalism
- Relevant Work Experience
- Teamwork
- Verbal Communication
- Work Ethic
- Written Communication

Look at examples of stories to build ideas. What do you find compelling? What is not helpful or convincing? In our exercises with students, we use quotes from *The Global Journal*, Northeastern University's student–run International Affairs publication—both from the Instagram account and from full articles. Other places you can look for ideas:

- TED Talks: How do others capture their story in a short amount of time? What are the elements of a good story?
- Online publications or other student publications

- Editorials where opinions are argued
- LinkedIn profiles, Blog entries, Twitter, Instagram, and so on.

After reviewing the stories, consider the following:

- Why is the story compelling?
- What are they trying to say?
- How could this tie to a future job, career path, or graduate school goal?

Create Your Intentional Story

- **Step 1: Brainstorm Your Skills:** In your story, you will be highlighting three skills, with an overarching theme. Your story can focus on a theme—such as skills you developed during your time abroad, through leadership opportunities, past internships, club involvement, or personal stories.
  - Use the template to choose the three skills you wish to highlight, and brainstorm an example of how you used or developed this skill.
- **Step 2: Map Out Your "Intentional Story":** Use the "Map out your 'intentional' story" template to add an introduction, talk through your skills in a narrative way, and wrap it up with a closing thought.
- **Step 3: Practice!** Practice telling your story. The first time, or perhaps the first five times it may not flow easily. You may discover that in your storytelling approach you want to switch the order of how you highlight skills. You may find that you have a different way of framing the first 'tell me about yourself' introduction portion that fits your style. Figure out how to tell your story in a compelling way. Below are a few possible introductions:
  - "I love organizing the world into data that explains why things happen."
  - "Much of why I am prepared for this job and would thrive comes from my experiences of being an outsider."
  - "The challenges I felt, personally, as a child growing up in my neighborhood and within my family have sparked my passion for policy and implementing policy within government. Let me tell you how."

Once you have practiced, you should be prepared to use this story, or variations of it, in interviews, in conversation with colleague, or in any number of other settings!

Example: Leyla Latypova

Leyla Latypova, a graduate of Northeastern, did the "intentional storytelling" exercise and was able to create an amazing story. An outline of how she did the brainstorming exercise, how she "mapped her story," and her finished "story" are outlined as follows.

- **Step 1: Brainstorm Your Skills**
  - Framework for Leyla—her framework was international experiences and her target audience was potential employers.
  - Skill 1—Intercultural communication
    - Example—work at the United Nations observer organization International Anti-Corruption Academy in Laxenburg, Austria. I shared a small room with five people, a Russian, a Bolivian, an Indian, an Italian, and an Argentinian.
  - Skill 2—Flexibility—time
    - Example—I was transitioning from my study abroad at Sciences Po in Paris, where everyone runs on time, to an internship in Tbilisi, Georgia—where "on time" is an hour or so late.

- Skill 3—Empathy
  - Example—Working in a policy research in Georgia as a Russian national was challenging considering a very complex relationship between two countries.
- **Step 2—Map Out Your "Intentional Story"** (notes)
  - Introduce yourself: Leyla, senior at Northeastern, majoring in International Affairs and Political Science. I always need to have a plan, and my original plan was to build a career at the UN.
  - Skill 1—I developed intercultural communication skills while sharing an office room with people of five different nationalities at the International Anti-Corruption Academy.
  - Skill 2—I developed the ability to be flexible after my experiences in Austria (where "on time" means 5 minutes early) and then in Georgia (where "on time" means 2 hour late).
  - Skill 3—I developed empathy during my time in Georgia, I had to learn to understand the perspective of the local citizens as a Russian national, while our countries have had a very complicated relationship for the past decade.
  - Wrap up—Current plan is a career at the intersection of political science and journalism but my plans can change and that's ok!
- **Step 3: Practice!**—Here is Leyla's finished "intentional story."

"So, my name is Leyla Latypova, and I'm a senior here at Northeastern, majoring in International Relations and Political Science, and I'm one of those people who needs to have a plan! Four years ago, when I came to Northeastern, my plan was to work at the United Nations, and you can even see the evidence in one of those banners on the Northeastern campus. You can find me and that's exactly what it says.

My first experience abroad was at the UN observer organization, International Anti-Corruption Academy, in Laxenburg, Austria. There, I shared an office—a tiny room—with people of five different nationalities, a Russian, a Bolivian, an Indian, an Italian, and an Argentinian. Believe me that was the best lesson in intercultural communication that I could possibly have—from differences in work ethics to the shared struggle of navigating our second language, English. However, on my last day of work, I realized I no longer had a plan. After spending one semester at the organization—working alongside some of the best minds in the field and creating groundbreaking research—I suddenly realized that the UN was not a place for me to be.

Then, I studied abroad at Sciences Po in Paris. At the time, the French felt like quite a transition from timely Austrians. My next experience, however, was in Georgia, a tiny country in the Caucasus; with a slow pace of life, a love for good food, and long conversations; Georgians consider being one hour late to a meeting as rather arriving early.

Georgia was a challenging experience. I am a Russian national, and I had to learn to understand people with which my country has been at odds for the past decade. I had to see through the animosity and build bridges to the hearts and minds of people from different walks of life. Georgia taught me empathy.

Today, after all of the global experiences, my plan is to pursue a career on the intersection of political science and journalism. No more UN dreaming. But, you know, my plan might change at any time. And my experiences abroad have taught me—that's totally ok."

Worksheets:

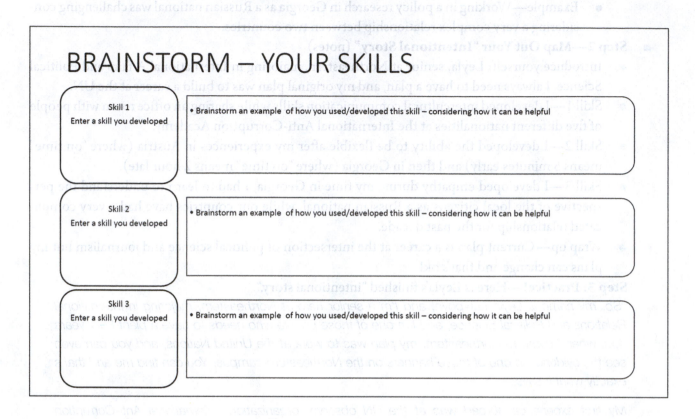

Collegiate Employment Research Institute (CERI) Study mentioned above: http://www.ceri.msu.edu/wp-content/uploads/2017/10/Recruiting-Trends-2017-Brief-5-Internships-Co-ops.pdf

Prepare (Listen Up)

Action Verb Brainstorm

© Rebecca Westerling.

In pairs take time to review a list of action verbs for résumé writing. First, circle 10 words of action verbs you think you would like to do in your next job. Next, consider when you may have used these skills/done this action in the past and write a phrase for each. Then, continue to do this for as many of the words on the sheet that you can in the span of 10 minutes. This allows you to build your résumé/interview stories/awareness of your skills in a different way than staring at a blank screen.

Resume Writing

Action Verbs

COMMUNICATIONS

acted as liaison	corresponded	instructed	negotiated	referred
advised	counseled	interpreted	notified	sold
advocated	demonstrated	interviewed	presented	trained
arbitrated	displayed	lectured	promoted	translated
authored	edited	marketed	publicized	wrote
commented	guided	mediated	published	recommended
consulted	informed	moderated		

ADMINISTRATION

administered	determined	implemented	ordered	regulated
appointed	directed	initiated	organized	represented
arranged	dispatched	instituted	overhauled	revamped
completed	dispensed	issued	oversaw	reviewed
conducted	distributed	launched	prescribed	routed
consolidated	eliminated	led	presided	supervised
contracted	executed	managed	provided	supplied
controlled	founded	motivated	recruited	terminated
contributed	governed	obtained	rectified	
delegated	headed	offered	referred	

PLANNING & DEVELOPMENT

broadened	developed	drafted	initiated	planned
created	devised	estimated	invented	prepared
designed	discovered	improved	modified	produced
				proposed

ANALYSIS

amplified	computed	evaluated	identified	solved
analyzed	detected	examined	investigated	studied
calculated	diagnosed	forecasted	programmed	systemized
compiled	differentiated	formulated	researched	tested

FINANCIAL/RECORDS MANAGEMENT

audited	collected	invested	minimized	recorded
allocated	condensed	inventoried	monitored	scheduled
balanced	documented	listed	processed	tallied
catalogued	expedited	logged	procured	traced
charted	guaranteed	maximized	purchased	updated
classified				

MANUAL

assembled	delivered	modernized	repaired	rewired
built	installed	navigated	replaced	trimmed
constructed	maintained	operated	restored	

GENERAL

accomplished	contributed	increased	provided	strengthened
achieved	delivered	initiated	served	transformed
expanded	originated	serviced	performed	completed

©**Northeastern Employee Engagement and Career Design**

Prepare (Listen Up)

Explore your "self" through others' accounts of you. Ask three to five people to share with you what they see as your key attributes—your strengths, areas where you could improve, specific skills and aptitudes, and what they think makes you "you" from their interactions with them.

Preparing Your Résumé with SAIL

© Dave Merry and Northeastern University.

The following is an exercise using the SAIL framework to develop your résumé.

Preparing your Resume with SAIL

Northeastern University
Self-Authored Integrated Learning

The SAIL Dimensions

Intellectual Agility
Developing the ability to use knowledge, behaviors, skills, and experiences flexibly in new and unique situations to innovatively contribute to your field.

Well-Being
Developing the knowledge, skills and behaviors necessary to live a balanced and fulfilling life.

Personal & Professional Effectiveness
Developing the confidence, skills, behaviors and values to effectively discern life goals, form relationships and shape your personal and professional identities to achieve fulfillment.

Global Mindset
Developing knowledge, skills and behaviors to live, work and communicate with people whose background, experience and perspectives are different from your own, as well as considering the global impact of your decisions.

Social Consciousness & Commitment
Developing the confidence, skills and values to effectively recognize the needs of individuals, communities, and societies and make a commitment to constructively engage in social action.

Skills and Foundational Masteries
(See attached reference sheet for definitions)

Intellectual Agility
- Aesthetic Appreciation
- Computational Thinking
- Design Thinking
- Entrepreneurship
- Information Literacy
- Integrative Thinking
- Quantitative Reasoning
- Strategic Thinking
- Systems Thinking

Global Mindset
- Cultural Agility
- Inclusivity/Inclusive Action
- Systems Thinking

Social Consciousness & Commitment
- Advocacy
- Civic-Mindedness
- Conflict Resolution/Transformation
- Inclusivity/Inclusive Action
- Networking
- Systems Thinking

Personal & Professional Effectiveness
- Coaching/Mentoring
- Conflict Resolution/Transformation
- Financial Literacy
- Negotiation
- Networking
- Organization
- Planning
- Strategic Thinking
- Time Management

Well-Being
- Aesthetic Appreciation
- Boundary Setting
- Self-Care
- Self-Control
- Time Management

Foundational Masteries

Intrapersonal Skills
- Help Seeking
- Independence/Autonomy
- Initiative
- Perseverance/Resiliency
- Resourcefulness
- Self-Efficacy/Confidence

Interpersonal Skills
- Collaboration/Teamwork
- Communication
- Empathy
- Leadership

Attributes
- Comfort with Ambiguity
- Humility
- Integrity
- Mindfulness
- Open-Mindedness

Strategic Toolkit
- Creative Thinking/Innovation
- Critical Thinking
- Decision-Making
- Ethical Reasoning
- Inquiry & Analysis
- Problem Solving

Unpacking Your Past Experiences

In the grid below. list 10 experiences that you might list in your resume. These can be paid jobs. volunteer experiences, projects, leadership opportunities, or other experiences that you have participated in. While it is great if some of these items relate to your intended co-ops, it is absolutely ok if you don't have any direct experience in that field yet.

The second page of this PDF list the dimensions and skills you will be using in this grid.

Experience	On a scale of 0-5, how relevant was each dimension to this experience? (0 = Not at All, 5 = Central)					What are 3-5 skills you either used or gained as a result of this experience? (Can be any of the Skills or Foundational Masteries)
	IA	GM	SCC	PPE	WB	

Totals   _____   _____   _____   _____   _____

<u>**Some questions to consider:**</u>

Which of the five dimensions were you strongest in? How might that be an asset for an employer?

Which dimension(s) did you have less experience in? How might knowing that impact the types of jobs you may be looking for?

Did you see any themes emerging about the types of skills you used in your different experiences? If so, how might you leverage those skills in the workplace? If not, how might your diverse set of skills be an asset in your co-op?

As you begin or edit your resume, in what ways might you highlight some of the skills you associated with each of the experiences above?

How might you use this information to help target your resume for specific employers? To write cover letters? To better prepare for interviews?

How might you use this information to write cover letters?

How might you use this information to better prepare for interviews?

Look Back (Look In)

Images of the Future

© Emily Planz and Northeastern Employer Engagement and Career Design.

This exercise encourages students to imagine the vision they have for their life in a visual way. It can be done in a classroom (as outlined here), or individually with a mentor/mentee. This activity is often used for students early in their college career to discuss values in decision making.

Preparation: Gather images. For this activity, you can either compile images ahead of time for the class to use or provide magazines, photos, and other images from which students can find images they wish to use. If you use magazines, consider having a wide array of magazines that cover professional organizations, as well as hobby, current events, music, and other magazines to allow for a full array of options for students.

Activity

- **Set up:** An array of images are arranged on a table. The pictures can be everything from a newborn baby, classroom, or people laughing to DNA, sparks from electrical equipment, or a sailboat. Or, a wide range of magazines and other images are provided for each group of students.
- **Choose:** Students are prompted to pick out an image that "Best represents the vision they have for their life."
- **Discuss:** Students do a think-pair-share activity using a worksheet that helps them prepare for the year ahead. We use the images to primarily discuss values in decision making and to begin a light discussion with first-year students.
  - How does your choice of images speak to your values?
  - How does this image, and what it means for your vision of your own life, help frame the decisions you will make in the coming year?
- **Worksheet:** As a final step, students may outline their vision of their college journey, starting with the images discussed above, which may help them consider their journey during the coming months and years.

My College Journey...

Reflect · Explore · Connect

What are 3 characteristics about your picture that represent the vision you have for your life:

1)
2)
3)

Who am I? What are 5 words that describe me:

What am I curious about? What do I want to learn:

What do I want to accomplish while at college:

Personal Goal

Academic Goal

Career Goal

REFLECT, EXPLORE, CONNECT
~Suggested Next Steps~

REFLECT

Keep a Journal: Use the questions on the worksheet as prompts to get started; think about the activities you enjoy; the academic subjects that interest you.

Take assessments on these sites:

MassCIS: The Career Cluster Inventory, Interest Profiler; Skills, Informal Assessments. Log in using the city "Boston" and zip code "02115 or 02116" or any other city/zip code combination. www.masscis.intocareers.org

America's Career InfoNet: https://www.careeronestop.org/Toolkit/toolkit.aspx

Interests Assessment
O*Net on Line: Choose Tell Us What You Like To Do https://www.mynextmove.org/

EXPLORE

Your University Resources:

Utilize the resources at your college or university if you are currently part of an academic program.

On Line Resources:

MassCIS: Log in using the city "Boston" and zip code "02115 or 02116" or any other city/zip code combination. www.masscis.intocareers.org

America's Career InfoNet: Review industry profiles; fastest growing fields; and tools and technology required by field.
https://www.careeronestop.org/Toolkit/Careers/Occupations/occupation-profile.aspx

O*Net on Line: http://onetonline.org

Occupational Outlook Handbook: http://www.bls.gov/ooh/

Riley Guide Career Research Center: Use the A to Z index to find websites related to your field of interest. https://www.myperfectresume.com/how-to/career-resources/atoz/

If time permits before the end of the summer, do a brief internship

CONNECT

Talk with family, friends, neighbors, current supervisor and co-workers about their majors and careers

Create a LinkedIn Profile

Request a job shadow with a local professional in your field of interest

Activity developed by the Northeastern University Department of Employer Engagement and Career Design

Northeastern University
Employer Engagement and Career Design

Look Back (Look In)

Irrational Beliefs Exercise

©Jon Andrew

React to each of these statements as True/False. Consider how you could reframe each of these:

- I am the sum of my activities.
- What I study has to relate directly to what I do professionally.
- I have to be nearly perfect for people to value me.
- I learn because others teach me about things.
- There is one best way of doing things.
- I can fully control how others perceive me (social media, digital branding, etc.).
- I haven't done anything important in my life and I have no skills.
- I'm not as interesting or employable as someone with more experience than me.
- Showing emotions or asking for help is a weakness.
- Our weaknesses define us.
- My life in the "real world" begins after I graduate from college.
- Once I graduate I need to have it all figured out on my own.
- I have to know and seem in control of what I am doing at all times.
- I am not good at managing my time

Advising Session

Look in: What makes you YOU? Without comparing yourself to others (not an easy thing to do)—what are the essential components to who you are? Your values? Your strengths? Your interests? Your passions? Keep these in mind as you go through this book.

Look up: Observe a culture/group/setting that is new to you. Consider what is novel about the space, how people interact, implicit and explicit expectations, and what you see, hear, smell, even feel, and/or taste. Tune in to minor details.

Join up: What groups are you a part of? What are your interests/passions/curiosities? Are there groups that would allow you to pursue these further that you are not a part of? Take the chance to join, get involved, and take action.

Write your "legacy" virtues: If you were to look back at your life (or class, job, etc.), what would you want to be known for? What personal characteristics? What values? What accomplishments? What relationships? (© Rebecca Westerling)

Daydream! Let your mind go free—if you could do anything you wanted, without limits, what would it be? Take the time to daydream. If I could do anything I would . . . free write—don't stop for 10 minutes!

Recommendation for yourself: Consider a trusted colleague, teammate, or teacher. Create a letter of recommendation you imagine they might write on your behalf. Be honest. If you're not used to touting your virtues, allow yourself to do so. If you're typically quite confident, consider what they may notice about you that you don't think of first and foremost.

Fostering self-awareness: *Mindset* (© **Sarah Klionsky.**)—In her book, *Mindset*, the new psychology of success, Dweck writes that "in a fixed mindset, both positive and negative labels can mess with your mind. When you're given a positive label, you're afraid of losing it, and when you're hit with a negative label, you're afraid of deserving it" (*Mindset*, p. 75). For instance, if you are labeled as a "math whiz" and do poorly on a math test, you may lose the label, so you may avoid taking challenging math classes. If you are labeled as someone who "can't do" math, you may feel like you shouldn't even attempt a challenging math course. Write about a label that you have been given, either by yourself or by someone else? How did it affect your behavior?

Animal characteristics! (© **Rebecca Westerling.**) Write a list of positive adjectives you could use to describe a coworker, boss, or employee. Then, make a list of three animals with some of these characteristics, and then write as many adjectives about each of the three animals as possible. Now, which animal are you most like?

> *Notes: The goal of this exercise is to make creative connections and also to make you (or your students) step backwards from interview questions such as "If you were an animal, what animal would you be?" While this seems fun, on the surface, if you are able to highlight three of your top qualities and tie them to the animal you choose, suddenly your response in the interview is much more substantive and tells the interviewer a lot about you.*

Letter of recommendation: (© **Rebecca Westerling.**) Think of someone who knows you well and you have worked with in the past. Write a recommendation letter for yourself, in their words. Be sure to use specific examples of qualities you have, accomplishments of yours, and reasons why they would recommend someone would hire you for a co-op or internship.

Leadership (© **Rebecca Westerling.**): Write a story about when you were a leader (at work, in class, in a volunteer organization or club, anywhere). Reflect on some of the following questions:

- Why do you think you chose this incident? Did your actions fit your values?
- Who else was involved in this story, and what other perceptions of the situation might they have?
- What type of leadership did you embody (participatory, autocratic, etc.)?

CASE STUDIES

Mindset Case Study—Tayler (© **Rebecca Westerling.**): Tayler arrived to their job ready to impress everyone. They had done two internships before, taken three classes on financial systems, and knew they would be able to hit the ground running. By the end of the first week, Tayler was frustrated with the level of work and number of projects given by the three managers working with their co-op role. One assigned only data entry, which could be done by 10 a.m., another just assigned reading that Tayler already knew the content of besides some of the company-specific jargon, and the third was too busy for a conversation. Tayler was frustrated with how the co-op had started and wrote an email to the three managers outlining their frustrations. What should Tayler do next to get the most out of their co-op? What should they be aware of as they take the next step?

Case Study—Talia (Copyright © Emily Planz. Reprinted by permission.): Talia, a freshman, first used her on-campus career development center as an attendee of a Trek, which was a site visit to a local company. She thought she wanted to go to Med School at this time. Through her first co-op, she recognized that the clinical scene was not for her, but knew she liked health care and thought it was important to help people. At this time, she was still unsure of what "helping people" meant to her. Through a variety of conversations supported by self-assessments, she began to recognize her skill in administration and leadership roles in her clubs and activities. Talia found that she enjoyed planning programs for her fraternity, delegating tasks, and working with deadlines to accomplish a goal. During a short-term study abroad experience, she recognized that she was not equipped to help support people in third world countries, and her public health class confirmed she had conflicting values with this line of work. Finally, she landed an internship doing data analysis for a health care provider, and in this role she continued to learn from the health care industry and was excited by learning new things. This internship also helped her to see that even though she enjoyed working alone, she is contributing to a team and to something bigger. What can you learn from the actions Talia took and the path she ended up following?

Permission given by student (Talia)

CHAPTER 2 - ENGAGING IN ADAPTIVE DECISION MAKING

Class/Activities

Explore (Look Up)

Adaptive Decision Making

© Jonathan Andrew.

Adaptive Decision-Making Activity—Step 1: Mindmapping

- **Mindmapping exercise**
  - Use an upcoming decision point as the central theme of your mindmap. Develop five spokes from that central decision that focuses on the impact that decision could have on your career, health, finances, the important people in your life, and your personal growth. Write this out with a different color for each spoke. From those spokes map out branches for skills or knowledge based learning outcomes or key events that your decision could lead to.

    On the mind map try to add a weight to each of the branches and build a list of questions and cost–benefit analysis from there to see what are the biggest factors influencing your decision. What does this exercise tell you about the values you are approaching this decision with and what is motivating you now?

- **Use Yes And.. for developing questions around your learning outcomes.**
  "Yes, and" Exercise: As you prepare for your next big decision—what co-op to accept, what major to pursue, which skill to develop most during your next opportunity—practice the "Yes, and" thinking with a partner. Begin with the outcomes on one of your most heavily weighted spokes and think of questions you have about the outcome and how it will help you in the future. At the end of that question your partner should pick up by saying "Yes and…" another question. Keep this going as long as you can. Afterwards write down a list of the most memorable or any new questions you and your partner generated around that outcome. Use this activity to generate ideas, open new perspectives, and find ways for you to inform your decisions, as well as consider where your decisions could lead you next.

- **Your Cost–Benefit Analysis**
  Now that you have a list of questions, categorize them as closed or open ended questions. What questions are most important to you, in terms of values, opportunities, and aspects of the experience you are making the decision around. Consider what you have learned from step 1 and 2 of this process, and list the costs and benefits of your most important or salient outcomes. What does this tell you about your final decision?. If you have more than three options, compare three to start, and remove one—with the confidence that you have two that you prefer more—then move on to consider additional options.

Engage (Act Up and Join Up)

Strengths Interview

© Esther C. Chewning.

This exercise is used in the co-op preparation course; however, it can be adapted for use throughout a job search process or as a part of self-exploration. In addition, this can be assigned as part of a course, or done independently with a coach, or on your own for self-reflection.

Understanding your strengths from the perspective of others is valuable, since on co-op you will join a team and work environment with new colleagues.

Invest 30–60 minutes and have a conversation with a friend or family member about what strengths they believe that you possess. Ask them to share at least three strengths and provide specific examples of how they have witnessed you use these strengths. You should not prompt the person you are interviewing with suggestions of what strengths that you feel you possess; rather, allow them to deeply consider your question and reflect on it.

After completing your interview, summarize what you learned in a typed one-paragraph synopsis of your strengths interview. Please include your first and last names.

Strengths Identified and Examples

1. _____
   _____
   _____
   _____
   _____

2. _____
   _____
   _____
   _____
   _____

3. _____
   _____
   _____
   _____
   _____

Student example: Strengths Interview Can be retyped/adapted if used:

Strengths Interview

I interviewed my sister. The first thing she said was that I am strong-willed and then she changed her wording to say **I'm eager to resolve conflicts.** *I was surprised by how many examples she had. She emphasized I'm quick to stand up for myself or get others to stand up for themselves. My sister was getting taken advantage of by her landlord. I wrote an email for her outlining a fair resolution. The landlord agreed. I always perceived this type of situation as my sister needing to be absurdly nice. Oftentimes I get phone calls from her asking me how to tell someone something she doesn't want to tell them. My response is usually to avoid mentioning most of the concerns my sister is worried about and simply tell the person the pertinent information. The second strength my sister said was that* **I'm organized.** *I can tell someone, almost to the inch,* *exactly where some item of mine is. Most recently, I guided my sister to find a map from several years ago of the town where she studied abroad that I kept as a souvenir. The third strength she said was that **I'm a good communicator**. I'm a scuba diving instructor and my sister has watched me teach one of my classes. My sister said I was good at facilitating a lot of involvement and subtly bringing mistakes to student's attention. I love diving and I want my students to learn to love it too. When students mess up it's important to avoid killing their confidence, but at the same time make sure they understand how to stay safe.*

Look Back (Look In)

Journey Lines Activity

© Emily Planz.

This activity allows you to look at past experiences and consider how you can use the highs and lows of life to adapt, grow, or pivot. You can use these past experiences to inform future decisions.

Outcome: A visual depiction of significant positive and negative events that occurred during a specific period of time.

Activity

- Brainstorm and write a list of 10 significant events in your life– both highs and lows
  - Think about a time that you took a risk, tried something new, overcame a challenge, achieved a goal, and faced unexpected events or outcomes
  - Rank these events from 1 to 10
  - Draw the grid and plot your points and label each event
  - Connect the points to create your journey line
  - Look for prevailing themes/beliefs/values that you developed as a result of those experiences or that you referred back to during those experiences

Look Back (Look In)

Character Strengths

© Rebecca Westerling and Esther C. Chewning.

This exercise is used in the co-op preparation course; however, it can be adapted for use throughout a job search process or as a part of self-exploration. In addition, this can be assigned as part of a course or done independently with a coach or on your own for self-reflection.

What are your strengths?
Choose one strength that you feel that you possess and answer these questions:

    FIRST—Individually—quiet reflection
- *What is one way you have used this strength in the past month?*
- *How could this strength help you achieve a goal that you have?*
- *Think of a time when you could have used more of this strength. How would you have used it?*

    SECOND—As a group discussion
- *What is one way you have used this strength in the past month?*
- *How could this strength help you achieve a goal that you have?*
- *Think of a time when you could have used more of this strength. How would you have used it?*

Engage (Act Up and Join Up)

Choose Your Own Adventure Exercise

© Rebecca Westerling.

What social/civic issues are important to you? What can you do and what do you want to do? What could make a difference? Keep in mind that small decisions can lead to big impact. Design a diagram where you map out many possibilities, starting with one decision, and branch from there. Consider how many great opportunities you "could" have if you made different choices. Consider the results after doing this for 5 to 10 minutes. Reflect on what you're most excited about with what you outlined as well as on how many possibilities you designed that could be very exciting to you. Recognize that by making choices you are sometimes giving up other opportunities, but if you are not going to make any choice, you won't move forward either.

Look Back (Look In)

Time Audit

© Rebecca Westerling.

Do a cost–benefit analysis on your time and how it is spent:

1. Map out how you spend each hour of a typical day for just one day/a week.
2. Tally your time spent on things such as reading, working out, connecting with friends in person, talking on the phone, working, social media, texting, mentoring, studying, and so on.
3. Consider your priorities and what you would "like" to do in a week.
4. Create a new map of your time—allocating time to what you value most—and try shifting your day/week ahead

Advising Session

Look in: What influences your decisions—look inside to determine what shapes why you make the decisions you do. Consider your internal pressure and goals, motivators—intrinsic and extrinsic—parents, friends, and family. Don't forget to factor in your feelings and emotions that shape your decisions as well.

Build a fault-tolerant system (© Jonathan Andrew.): Explore how to build your own fault-tolerant system through asking the right questions, examining your values and beliefs, and exhibiting healthy skepticism to received information while appreciating alternative options and viewpoints.

Think back to a past seminal decision you made. What choices did you struggle with at the time? What helped you to make the choice? After you made the choice what happened to you emotionally? What opportunities did that choice provide? Did you have any regrets? What does this teach you about tough choices you face in the future?

Create an initial pros and cons list of that decision.

Consider whether you would approach this decision, or one similar to it, in the same way in the future given the insights you now have.

Gratefulness reflection (© Rebecca Westerling.): What are you grateful for? Think about your current situation (job, classes, friends, communities). Much of what we do to plan is focused on where we will go next; however, knowing what we are grateful for now can help us make wise decisions in the future.

Interviewing nightmares! (© **Rebecca Westerling.**): Write a story about an interview from the perspective of the interviewer. You are interviewing Nathan at Northeastern, a third-year student who is interested in working with your company. Imagine that everything you can think of going wrong, does!

After doing this, consider what you can do to best prepare for an interview.

> *Notes: The goal of this exercise is to allow you to enter the nightmare of a situation where everything goes wrong—in your mind. Through doing so, you should be able to walk away with two key takeaways. First, not everything that could go wrong will, and you will most certainly have a better experience than the nightmare you imagine. Second, you may discover some of your deepest fears and concerns for interviewing, and be able to use these to be proactive in avoiding these mistakes or to consider how to pivot or adapt if a challenge does arise.*

Emotions (© **Rebecca Westerling.**): Your emotions can, and should, be a part of what you reflect on—at work while you're on co-op or on an internship, in class, and in every moment of your life. Take a moment to write down your emotions. Take the time to acknowledge these feelings and allow yourself the space to become very aware of how your emotions are a part of who you are and what you do. Then, if you wish, reflect on what actions you wish to take to help use these emotions for good.

Embracing change (© **Rebecca Westerling.**): "Change is the only constant"—Heraclitus. Think back to a time you have encountered change. Consider all of the good things that came from these changes. New people you met, things you learned (both about what you like/don't like) that you wouldn't have learned otherwise, experiences you were exposed to, and so on.

> *Reference/quote check needed . . . (Many statements paraphrase or extend upon his famous assertions that "everything changes" in ways which arguably diverge from valid translation, and yet have become widely attributed to Heraclitus: Change is the only constant. There is nothing permanent except change. https://en.wikiquote.org/wiki/Heraclitus.)—or Heraclitus, a Greek philosopher, has been quoted as saying "change is the only constant in life."*

Change—past and future (© **Rebecca Westerling.**): Think back to two examples of when big changes occurred in your life. First, outline a time when change was difficult, you encountered many challenges, and did not enjoy the change that occurred. Then, outline a time when change brought about feelings of excitement, curiosity, and/or new beginnings. How did these instances of change differ? What was different in how you anticipated the change, what steps you took to move forward, and how you framed it in your mind. Consider now how you can use these observations to be more successful in embracing change—or seeking out positive change—in the future.

CASE STUDIES

Case Study: Strengths Interview

© Esther C. Chewning and © Anne Wieland.

Annie did a strengths interview with her sister, whom she respected but often clashed with as they grew up. This is what she learned.

"The first thing she said was how strong-willed I am, and she quickly reframed her words to say that I am always trying to resolve conflicts. From there, I was shocked at how many specific examples she came up with, some that I did not even think of as conflict resolution. She emphasized I'm quick to stand up for myself or get other to stand up for themselves. My sister was getting taken advantage of by her landlord. I wrote an email for her outlining a fair resolution. The landlord agreed. The second strength my sister said was that I'm organized. I can tell someone, almost to the inch, exactly where some item of mine is. The third strength she said was that I'm a good communicator. I'm a scuba diving instructor and my sister has watched me teach one of my classes. She said I was good at facilitating a lot of involvement and subtly bringing mistakes to students' attention. I love diving and I want my students to learn to love it too."

What did Annie learn from this interview? What can she use this knowledge for, moving forward? What might you learn from doing a strengths interview with someone you know well? What could this type of interview tell you that you don't already know about yourself?

Case Study—Different (Unexpected) Paths—James and Maria

© Michelle Zaff.

James and Maria were both very strong students academically and both very involved in campus activities and clubs.

James was very interested in working in the environmental sector. He did a lot of work for Divest NU, a coalition of over 20 student groups committed to a university-wide campaign advocating that the university divest its endowment from the fossil fuel industry, and was passionate about environmental causes. He applied to multiple environmental firms and organizations within co-op jobs posted for current students and simultaneously was working to develop his own co-op job at a clean energy firm in Boston. As his work creating his own job was progressing, James landed a job at his top choice through NUCareers, MA-CEC (Massachusetts Clean Energy Center). He was ecstatic, except for one thing. The MA-CEC offered multiple co-op positions, including CleanTech and Water Fellow, Solar Incentive Fellow, Clean Heating and Cooling Fellow, but the only position that they had left to offer James was the Finance and Investment Fellowship. James had absolutely no prior knowledge and no interest in Finance, but James wanted to work for MA-CEC, so he took a risk and he took the job. James ended up loving the job and when he returned to school he took business classes such as Impact Investing and Social Finance. James' second co-op was at a Venture Capital and Private Equity Firm where he learned more about the world of finance and how he can use this to impact the environmental issues he cares about so deeply.

Maria was very interested in finance. She applied to many jobs and went on many interviews, but due in part to her focus of her coursework on the political-science side of her Political Science and Economics combined major, and completing her first co-op in a non–finance-related position in a large law firm, she wasn't getting much traction on her finance co-op job applications. She finally got one offer doing a finance role in a clean energy firm. Maria had no knowledge or interest at all in environmental causes but was happy to have been offered a finance position and accepted it. As Maria learned more and more about how her company was using wind power to make changes in the environment, she became more interested and passionate about this cause. It opened up a whole new sector/industry for future career paths.

What can you learn earn from the paths taken by James and Maria?

Case Study: Forced Adaptation with Merger

© Rebecca Westerling.

Two weeks ago, there was a merger at Zoey's co-op company, a large financial institution in Boston. One Monday morning after the merger became final, her boss called her and informed her that three of the four people she had worked with for the first three months of co-op had been fired. There were new people on the floor by the following Wednesday from the new company. The new leadership style, from what she could see in the first week, was very different; it was less collaborative and there seemed to be more of top-down approach to decision making. She was concerned for her own job every day when she arrived to work and still did not have a boss confirmed. So she was doing projects (when she can get them) from anyone she met. What should she do?

CHAPTER 3 - CREATING AND BELONGING TO A MENTORING COMMUNITY

Class/Activities
Engage (Act Up and Join Up)

Cultivating (Faculty/Research) Relationships

© Sarah Klionsky and Rebecca Westerling.

Cultivating relationships is key to building a network and learning from others in your industry as well as across industries. This can be particularly true in the sciences, which is where this exercise is framed. Students within the sciences are encouraged to join faculty labs, since helping faculty with their research is relevant across disciplines. Learning how to start this process can be daunting, so providing advice on how to approach faculty members and what to put in their emails can be helpful in taking the next step.

While this is framed in the sciences, a similar approach is applicable across disciplines, including social sciences research, market data research, to name just a few.

When reaching out to faculty, your email should include the following sections:

1. **Introduction:** Introduce yourself, what you are studying, and what your interests are.
2. **Why:** Explain why you are *specifically* interested in **their work** and want to work **with them**. You can also add a little bit about specific qualifications that you have, but the paragraph should be focused on them.
3. **Request:** Ask whether they have any room in the lab for an undergraduate assistant during the time period that you are available. Tell them that your résumé is attached and thank them for their time.

Explore (Look Up)

Map Your Network: Map your current network. This step is not specified as your 'professional' network, since personal, professional, civic, and social networks overlap and intertwine. Start with yourself at the center, and map out your connections, people you know they know, and so on. You'll be surprised how many connections you have!

Engage (Act Up and Join Up)

Informational Interviewing Exercise

© Jonathan Andrew and Rebecca Westerling.

An informational interview is a conversation where the goal is to gain information or knowledge. Unlike a job interview where a job is the goal, you are focusing on finding out information—about an industry, about a person's career path, about a role within a company, and any number of other things. Conducting an informational interview involves more than a simple conversation. If done well, there are several steps that can lead you to a great informational interview. The following step-by-step exercise will guide you through the process:

Step 1: Explore

You should first conduct your research in your field of interest to gather relevant information that will help you learn about that specific field.

Remember, you are conducting the informational interview to:

Explore careers and clarify your career goals

Discover employment opportunities that are not advertised

Expand your professional network

Build confidence for your job interviews

Gain information about a career or industry that you may not know or realize

To do:

- **Complete industry research**
  - What is one industry/professional field/cause you are interested in personally or professionally?
  - Do an Internet search to find information on this industry and companies who work in this industry—list three specific companies you found.
  - Search on LinkedIn for companies in your city/town/region that work in this industry—list three companies you found.
  - Search on LinkedIn for alumni of your university within your city/town/region who work at organizations you are interested in.
  - Search for professional organizations related to the field you are interested in—list two of these professional organizations.
  - Within the professional organizations, look on their website for information on companies that are members—list at least two companies.
- **Find three possible contacts:** Find three people you would be interested in meeting, to learn more about their career, industry, or organization where they work. Keep in mind that you do not always need to or want to reach out to the CEO, or someone who has been in the industry for a long time. Often it can be helpful to talk with someone who is newer to the organization and may have more flexibility in their schedule.
  - Name of potential informational interviewee 1
    - Company and title
    - Contact email or phone number
    - Why are you interested in talking with this person?
    - How did you find this person (LinkedIn, Internet search, professional organization webpage, etc.)?
  - Name of potential informational interviewee 2
    - Company and title
    - Contact email or phone number
    - Why are you interested in talking with this person?
    - How did you find this person (LinkedIn, Internet search, professional organization webpage, etc.)?
  - Name of potential informational interviewee 3
    - Company and title
    - Contact email or phone number
    - Why are you interested in talking with this person?
    - How did you find this person (LinkedIn, Internet search, professional organization webpage, etc.)?

Step 2: Reach Out

Reach out to one of your contacts in multiple ways. Don't stop with an email to a generic company website. Email or contact someone through social media, follow up with phone calls. We have found that face-to-face requests for interviews can be the most effective as people will react well to those who show excitement, engagement, and a willingness to learn about what they do.

> **EXAMPLE EMAIL**
>
> **Dear Swati,**
>
> **As a fellow Husky, I was excited to come across your LinkedIn profile and find that you are an Economics major and are now working as a public policy analyst here in Boston. This is a career path that I am very interested in, and I would love to hear more about what you do in your job, and how you were able to build skills in prior roles to get this position. Would you have 15 to 30 minutes to meet for coffee in the next week or two, to share your insights with me? Thank you, in advance, for considering this.**
>
> **Sincerely,**
> **Paxton**

Step 3: Prepare

Read all you can about the field/organization prior to the interview. Make sure you have researched the organization and spent some time on their website. Decide what information you would like to obtain about the occupation/industry. Also research the person with whom you will be conducting the informational interview. Prepare a list of questions that you would like to have answered. Some ideas are listed below:

1. What's your typical day like?
2. What exams, qualifications, education, or certifications are required for this type of work?
3. What personal qualities or abilities make someone successful in the job/field?
4. What do you find most rewarding in this job?
5. How did you get your job?
6. How do individuals advance within this field?
7. Within this field, what entry-level jobs are best for learning skills and gaining as much knowledge as possible?
8. What is the typical salary for someone in this field within an entry-level position? (Do NOT ask someone what their salary is.)
9. How do you see jobs in this field changing in the future?
10. Is the demand for people in this occupation growing, declining, or holding steady?
11. What advice would you give a person entering this field?
12. When you started in the field, what training did you receive? Did you have a mentor?
13. What are the basic prerequisites for jobs in this field?
14. Do you regularly read the professional journals for the field or attend any organization or conference meetings? Where do you get your information pertaining to this job?
15. Given where I am in my education and early career, how can I best gain exposure or experience in this field?

16. From your perspective, what are the problems you see working in this field?
17. If you could do things over again, would you choose a different path for yourself?
18. What other jobs/field would you suggest I research further?
19. How did your major or graduate degree prepare you for your current field?
20. Is there anyone else you could recommend that I speak with regarding a career in X field? When I call him/her, may I use your name?

Step 4: Learn!

Dress appropriately, arrive on time, be polite and professional. Refer to your list of prepared questions: stay on track but allow for spontaneous discussion. Before leaving, ask your contact if they could suggest anyone else who might be willing to meet with you and ask permission to use your contact's name when contacting these new contacts.

Step 5: Follow Up

Immediately following the interview, record the information gathered. Be sure to send a thank you note within 24 hours after the informational interview.

Keeping track: You may wish to create a spreadsheet to track who you met, when, and notes about your conversation. You can then add contacts they suggest you reach out to and note who made the introduction (see Network Tracker exercise below).

Engage (Act Up and Join Up)

Network Tracker Creation

© Rebecca Westerling.

Create a way to track your relationships and networking. Consider what could be "quantitative data"—the who, when, mode of contact (in person, networking event, casual conversation), contact information (email/phone/address), who they offered to introduce you to from their network, when you sent thank you/nice to meet you, last date of contact, as well as the qualitative; for example, feeling you had from the conversation, where you connected most, most interesting thing you learned, how you can help them, and so on. Use a spreadsheet online, such as a google doc, so you can access this information, sort it, refer back to it, and add to it at any time.

Engage (Act Up and Join Up)

LinkedIn

Below is a checklist you may use to update your LinkedIn profile.

©Northeastern Employee Engagement and Career Design

LinkedIn Guide

Follow this checklist to build a strong LinkedIn profile. Click each subtitle for instructions on personalizing that section.

☐ **Professional Headline** can be your current job title ("Project Manager"), your career goal or focus ("Engineering Graduate Student focused on Medical Device R&D) or components of your work ("Communications Professional | Writer & Editor | Creative Writing Instructor").

☐ A **Photo** of yourself, in professional attire, is recommended. Headshots are best so the employer can see your face (avoid hats, glasses, underwater, back to camera, etc.)

☐ **Customize your Public Profile URL** for use on business cards, resume and in your email signature.

☐ **Summary** should express information that can't be found in other areas of your profile. Be sure to include industry-related keywords.

☐ **Sections** can be added (top right corner of webpage). Consider adding sections such as Projects, Courses, Certifications, Languages, and Volunteering Opportunities.

☐ **Experience** section contains a version of your resume. Use targeted key words and accomplishments.

☐ **Skills & Endorsements** is a very important section to customize since others can "endorse" these skills.

☐ **Recommendations** from past supervisors, co-workers, professors, and others who know you well, enhance your profile.

☐ **Posts/Articles** are a great way for viewers of your profile to learn more about you or the expertise you bring to your desired industry.

☐ **Background Photo** can now be added to your free LinkedIn account. Avoid using a picture with people in it.

Engage (Act Up and Join Up)

Job Shadow

© Rebecca Westerling

Shadow a professional contact in the workplace. You will follow similar research and outreach to the informational interviewing preparation; however, when you reach out you will ask whether it may be possible to shadow them in the work they do for a set period of time (few hours, half a day, a day). Be specific with your request, or give a range (for part of a day or a day) and when you are available (during my spring break, which is April 1st to 5th). Do your research ahead of time and be sure to follow up with a thank you email noting how much you appreciated the opportunity and how much you learned.

Look Back (Look In)

Past Mentors

© Rebecca Westerling

Who are the mentors you have had in the past? Keep in mind that it does not need to be a formal or established mentor–mentee relationship—think of those who "believed in you," who "supported you no matter what," or helped guide your way.

Advising Session

© Rebecca Westerling

Look up: Consider what distractions are keeping you from being/staying engaged when you try to make a personal connection with someone? What distractions are keeping others from engaging with you? How can "looking up" help you foster personal relationships and a mentoring community?

Listen up: Consider what advice you have received from people to date in your life. What messages and wisdom stuck with you? Why? Be sure to consider the "random sage"—those who impart wisdom in what are sometimes the most unlikely circumstances, yet can have the most impact on your life. Listen for these voices.

Act up: Seek out a peer mentor. Find someone in your peer group (via social media, clubs, professional organizations, social media groups) whom you admire and think would be interesting to ask for advice. Then, do it—approach them, share why you're impressed with them, and ask if they have time to share their story and provide some advice to you.

Act up: Find someone to mentor—consider what knowledge you have to share with and guide someone you want to mentor. Your experience as a mentor will allow you to give back, to realize the depth of knowledge you have to give, and will build a stronger community for yourself and others.

Look up: What is currently your "dream" goal (job, position of leadership, area of expertise)? Take time to map out three possible ways to get there.

Act up: What are three things you may choose to do while you are on co-op (or in an internship, or in your next leadership role) to ensure you are able to make the most of your time and learn the most?

Look In-Map Your Existing Network

© Rebecca Westerling and Jonathan Andrew

This is not just your professional network, since personal, professional, academic, civic and social networks overlap and intertwine. Start with yourself as the center of your network map, and map out your connections, people you know those people are connected to and so on. Used Linkedin to see 2nd and 3rd connections of your connections. Color coding these by the type of connection they are is helpful as well. You will be surprised at how many connections you have, and could be introduced to.

Look up-Reframing/Reimagining Activity

In advising sessions, we often help students to reimagine or reconsider their thoughts in a given area or situation. Given the concepts that were presented in this chapter on developing personal relationships and belonging to a community of mentors, how could you reimagine the statements below? Consider what limiting thoughts/beliefs you might have in terms of inter- and intra-personal relationships and mentoring—how might you reconsider these to think and act differently and in ways that would help you progress personally and professionally?

- Asking for help is a weakness.
- I need to have it all figured out on my own.
- I don't have enough professional experience to be competitive in my field.
- I have to show that I am a master at the work–life balance.
- I have to be perfect to be taken seriously.

Case Studies

Hugo: Hugo was three months into his co-op and really liked everyone he worked with. He was able to get tasks done well, and quickly, but wasn't getting the opportunities some of the other co-op students in his group were getting. While he did tasks well, he second-guessed his contributions, because he was only a first time co-op student and so much less experienced than the others. In addition, his GPA wasn't as high, and his coursework in Economics didn't align as well with the communications work he was doing, even though he really liked it. What should Hugo do next to get the most out of his co-op? What should he be aware of as he considers his next step?

Sarah: Sarah is struggling to figure out what she wants to do, for co-op and in life in general! She at times feels as if she is able to balance classes and part-time work and activities as well as club obligations, but other times feels overwhelmed. She wants to find a mentor, but doesn't even know where to start. Her interests range from politics to policy, and data analytics to marketing. All of these interests align with her major, International Affairs and Economics; however, there is no one path or roadmap to help her figure out a next step. Rather than pick one area to focus on at a time and networking with her peers, she gets stuck before she reaches out to classmates, thinking that they all have it figured out. What advice do you have for Sarah?

CHAPTER 4 - NAVIGATING DIVERSE LEARNING ENVIRONMENTS

Class/Activities

Explore (Look Up)

Prepare Your Professional References Page

© Jonathan Andrew.

As you prepare to go on with interviews, you will want to have people who can serve as references for you, if this is requested by a potential employer. The following are some basic guidelines for how to prepare and reach out.

1. Choose: Consider who would make a good reference. This may be a former manager, colleague, coach, instructor, professor, or teammate. If possible, it is ideal to have at least three people who are willing to be a reference for you and for them to be from different places. For instance, three managers from one place of work would not be ideal. Having a manager from one prior job, a professor, and a coach would be a good mix. They should be able to speak to your abilities and character.

2. Reach out: Reach out well ahead of time to request permission to share.

   Subject: Co-op Job Reference Request

   Dear Dr. Holmes,

   I hope everything is going well at NHDH! I'm wrapping up my junior year here at Northeastern University and am excited to be going out on co-op (a six-month full-time internship) beginning this July. I plan to explore marketing and communications positions, and know my experience working with social media on your team at the Department of Health has given me great experience to build upon. I was wondering if you would be willing to be a reference for me, if potential co-op employers ask for me to share references. If so, please let me know if the contact information listed below is correct. I look forward to hearing from you, and to keeping in touch.

   Thanks,

   Rebecca

3. Create references page: You will want to create your references page ahead of time and should use the same heading you used on your résumé for this reference page.

AISHA K NELSON

35 Huntington Ave., Boston, MA 02115
617-555-5555, nelson.a@husky.neu.edu

REFERENCES

Professional

Maxwell Holmes, MD
Director, Maternal and Child Health
NH Department of Health
108 Cherry St., P.O. Box 70
Manchester, NH 03467
Tele: 603-555-5555
maxwell.Holmes@ahs.state.nh.us
Known for 2 years

Alice Williamson
Director of Athletics
219 Winthrop St.
Field House, University of Massachusetts
Amherst, MA 05753
Tele: 617-555-5677
Known for 4 years

Academic

Professor Denise Horn
Northeastern University International Affairs Program
200 Renaissance Park
Huntington Ave
Boston, MA 02115
Tele: 617-373-5555
Known for 2 years

Personal

Cassandra Holmes
Youth Group Director
1234 Summit Ave.
Enfield, NH 03748
Tele: 603-632-1111
Known for 8 years

---

4. Update your references: If you share your references with a company where you are interviewing or have interviewed, send a quick email to your reference. Let them know you appreciate their willingness to be a reference. Then share where you interviewed/will interview and why you are excited about the position. Then, once you get a job, update all of your references—whether or not they were contacted—to keep them apprised of where you accepted an offer. They will enjoy the update, and this can help keep them as a part of your network in the future.

Prepare (Listen Up)

Job Description Dissection

© Rebecca Westerling.

This is a quick exercise that will help you dissect and understand a job description from different perspectives. This is a great exercise for pairs or groups in a class setting; however, it can also be done individually or with a mentor or advisee.

Select a job description that you are interested in, and consider the following, and discuss:

- What IS included.
- What IS NOT included.
- Consider who might have written the job description and why they would write it that way.
- Consider what you NEED to know if you interview/speak with someone in the company in order to get a good sense of this specific position (when considering the work environment, schedule, management style, support system, level of uncertainty, and opportunity for growth) would be a fit for YOU. Be mindful of the fact that the answer to this question may be different for different people.

Prepare (Listen Up)

Preparing for an Interview

© Rebecca Westerling.

This is a guide for preparing for an interview. Use this as a general guide to help you begin the preparation process.

Your Name:

➢ Pre-Interview Checklist

This is a guide for preparing for an interview, but you will want to do more/less/different preparation based on each situation. Use this as a general guide to help you begin the preparation process.

BEFORE going to interview

- ☐ *Do your research (below)*
- ☐ *Check directions and commute time*
- ☐ *Bring printed resume copies and notebook for taking notes*

Job/Company Information:

- ☐ **Job #:**
- ☐ **Job Title:**
- ☐ **Company Name:**
- ☐ **Summary of the Company: (in 2-3 sentences what does this company do):**

- ☐ **Industry:**
- ☐ **Location (address):**
- ☐ **Distance from home/campus:**
- ☐ **Commute Time:**
- ☐ **Requirements (list the top 3 requirements for this job)**
    1.
    2.
    3.
- ☐ **Job duties (your understanding of what you would do in this job, in 2-3 sentences)**

- ☐ **Why you are excited about this job**

- ☐ **Why you believe you are a fit for this job (qualifications, skills, interests)**

- ☐ **Who will you be interviewing with (if you know) – Name & Title, background (from LinkedIn, company website)**

Traditional Interview Questions – Preparation:

Remember, they will not always ask these questions, or may ask them in different ways, but preparing general information and stories for your interview will help you be prepared.

- ☐ **Tell me about yourself** *(write notes – what you might say for 30-60 second introduction of yourself)*

- ☐ **What is your greatest strength?** (Highlight something that would be helpful in this specific job)

- ☐ **What is your greatest weakness?** *(Highlight something that is not an essential requirement of this job, and also be sure to share how you have worked on your weakness and show you have improved)*

Your Name:

☐ <u>STAR Examples</u> – These can be used to answer a number of questions, but outline at least 3 that show how **you** took action and achieved results in a past experience.

    1. *Give an example of a time when you took on a leadership role:*
- *Situation:*
- *Task:*
- *Action:*
- *Result:*

    2. *Give an example of when you faced a challenge, and how you dealt with it:*
- *Situation:*
- *Task:*
- *Action:*
- *Result:*

    3. *Give an example of something you accomplished in a past job, or in a leadership role:*
- *Situation:*
- *Task:*
- *Action:*
- *Result:*

☐ **Closing statement** – *If you have the chance to share two or three quick reasons they should hire you as you wrap up, what would they be? 10-15 seconds, tops! ("Thank you again for the opportunity to interview – I am so excited about this job and think that my skills in x, and x, as well as my interest in x could be an excellent fit in this position. I look forward to hearing from you.")*

☐ **Research of company** – **have you reviewed:**
- **LinkedIn** - profiles of anyone you are working with, researched to see if there are other Northeastern co-ops or alumni listed in the company/division
- **Website** – review their website to get a better understanding of their company, mission, size, etc.
- **Recent news** – be sure to check for any recent news (mergers, events, changes in leadership, etc.)

Questions to Ask:

Always have questions ready you would like to ask them – it shows you have prepared, are interested and curious about the job, their company, and the people you are meeting with. Also, be sure you have contact information for everyone you meet with so you can send thank you emails.

1.
2.
3.
4.
5.

AFTER the interview

☐ **Within 24 hours** – thank you email to each person you met with

Additional Resources

➢ **BigInterview** - Online Interviewing
➢ **Northeastern Career Development** – Resume Guide & Interviewing Information

Prepare (Listen Up)

Translate Transferable Skills/Experiences

© Rebecca Westerling.

You have built skills and had diverse experiences throughout your life. While there is a lot of talk about transferrable skills, there is value not only in recognizing that your skills and experiences are transferable but also in translating this to another environment.

- Transferable skill/experience: Think of a skill or experience from one part of your past that you think holds value if transferred to another environment
- Translation: Consider how you would "translate" this when explaining not just that you have the skill but also how it could be used in a new environment. By taking this step into your own hands, you are showing the interviewer that you understand their needs and have been thoughtful of how your past has prepared you well for their needs.

Class/Activity (Look In)

Weekly Reflection Prompts

© Rebecca Westerling and Joani Lamachia.

One way we often begin our classes in the co-op preparatory course is with reflection. Taking the first 5 or 6 minutes to pause, reflect, and consider ideas that will be useful in the session to come. You may recognize some overlap with reflection questions across the chapters—this outlines how you can arrange a set of questions across a semester to have a coordinated approach. The weekly reflection is for the student only and is not collected. Only the final reflection paper is submitted. In addition to the reflection each week, students are asked to keep their writing and do a final reflection paper looking back at their writing each week.

The following are some of the "Starting Six" exercises we have used during our first 6 minutes of class.

- **Co-op hopes and dreams:** Write about everything and anything that comes to mind when you think of co-op. What does co-op mean? What are your hopes for your co-op? Your fears and concerns? What type of words do you associate with co-op (emotions, adjectives, nouns, people, places, etc.)?
- **Your best qualities:** What are the three words to describe the best things about you (your personality, work ethic, style, skills, abilities, etc.)? Who sees these best sides of you? When? What stories would they tell to showcase any one (or all) these three things about you?
- **What animal are you (interviewing)?** Write a list of positive adjectives you could use to describe a co-worker, boss, or employee. Then, make a list of three animals with some of these characteristics and then write as many adjectives about each of the three animals as possible. Now, which animal are you most like?
- **Letter of recommendation:** Think of someone who knows you well and you have worked with in the past. Write a recommendation letter for yourself, in their words. Be sure to use specific examples of your qualities, accomplishments, and reasons why they would recommend someone would hire you for a co-op.
- **Leadership:** Write a story about when you were a leader (at work, in class, in a volunteer organization or club, anywhere). Reflect on some of the following questions:
  - Why do you think you chose this incident? Did your actions fit your values?
  - Who else was involved in this story, and what other perceptions of the situation might they have?

- What type of leadership did you embody (participatory, autocratic, etc.)?
- **Interviewing nightmares!** Write a story about an interview, from the perspective of the interviewer. You are interviewing Nathan Northeastern, a third-year student who is interested in working with your company. Imagine that everything you can think of going wrong, does!
  - *Note for instructor: The goal of this prompt (which I discuss after students write it at the beginning of class) is that often your fears are much worse than how things will likely go, and if you have fears they may help you prepare better ahead of time if you write them down and reflect on them.*
- **Professional network:** Draw your professional network—include where people work or have worked and who you know that they know.
- **Success on co-op:** Think about what you want to learn on co-op, what your strengths are, what your weaknesses are. Now, write a letter to yourself with advice on how to be most successful on your co-op.
- **Best advice:** Write a letter to yourself reminding yourself of the best advice anyone ever gave to you.
- **Dream boss:** What would your dream boss say about you?
- **Emotional check-in:** Your emotions can, and should, be a part of what you reflect on—at work while you're on co-op, in class, and in every moment of your life. Take a moment to write down your emotions. You can then choose to also reflect on what actions you wish to take to help use these emotions for good or just start by writing down your emotions.

Final reflection: At the beginning of each class, you were asked to take time to do reflective writing, with the instructions and prompts listed as follows. For this final reflection assignment, answer the following questions:

1. What did you find most helpful about the reflective writing at the beginning of each class?
2. What was the most challenging part about doing this reflective writing each week?
3. What are three things you learned from doing these reflective writing exercises—be sure to use quotes from your own writing and tie what you learned into concepts we have discussed in class, including at least one quote from each of the readings throughout the course.

Class/Activity (Look Back)

Group Reflection Exercise

© Rebecca Westerling and Jonathan Andrew.

One of the cornerstone activities in reflection within our college is the group reflection session after students return from their co-op experiences. This activity can be adapted to other experiential activities as well, and we often vary our approach semester over semester. The following are some of the questions we have students consider in the group reflection session. You can add, edit, or adjust based on your students and your personal approach to your reflection sessions.

- Introduce yourself—name, year of study, co-op company and job title, a quick introduction to your role.
- If you had to describe the essence of your co-op in one sentence, what would you say?
- Think back to your first day—what is one word to describe how you felt?
- Think back to your last day—what is one word to describe how you felt?
- What is the one thing that you learned?
- What did you find surprising? What did you learn?

- What was one learning objective (goal) you had for yourself on this co-op, and did you accomplish it?
- What advice would you give to yourself going into this job again, or to others going on co-op next semester?
- How does the work your organization does influence social issues and/or policy?
- How did you affect change in the work you did? What barriers did you encounter, or did you find were encountered by others in your organization as they considered or tried to implement change?
- Talk about the pace of change within your office or organization?
- If you could change one thing at your organization, what would it be?
- How does your co-op tie into academic work you have done, or will do?
  - What are skills, habits of mind, insights, or knowledge from your academic coursework that you brought into your co-op?
  - What are skills, habits of mind, insights, or knowledge did you bring from your co-op back into your classes and activities on campus?
- What will you do between now and your next co-op/job to prepare for your next opportunity?
- One fun story!
- What will you do next?

Notes on format:

Students: It often works well to have between 6 and 12 students attend—enough to have good conversation but not so many it doesn't feel like a meaningful conversation. It allows for students to share stories, be vulnerable, take time to make real connections, and network.

Other faculty: It also can be wonderful to have teaching faculty and others who interact with students join the conversation, to hear what the students have to share. They also may jump in with occasional questions, such as how a theory they know students covered in classes overlaps with the experiences the students have had.

Prepare (Listen Up)

Learning Outcomes: What Are Your Learning goals/Outcomes?

© Jonathan Andrew.

Before you develop learning outcomes for a future experience it is helpful to think about outcomes from past positive experiences and challenges.

So begin by brainstorming two different types of previous experiences you had. On one side, chart a positive experience that led to learning and on the other a challenging experience or experience of failure that led to learning a skill or new knowledge upon reflection. After identifying the experience, mindfully describe the course of events or activities and factors that led this to be a learning experience. As the final step, describe the strengths the experience gave you, the weaknesses it exposed, and the skills or knowledge you had to use to traverse the experience. (Be honest and creative; we all have strengths and weaknesses worth examining.)

Positive Experience	Challenging experience or Experience of failure
Mindfully Describe: Examine all details, factors, and environmental causes for the experience.	Mindfully Describe: Examine all details, factors, and environmental causes for the experience.
What does this event reveal about your motivations?	What does this event reveal about your motivations?
What strengths, weaknesses, and skills did you discover through this experience?	What strengths, weaknesses, and skills did you discover through this experience?

Choose a skill area, strength, weakness, or knowledge area you want to develop further in a future experience. Develop a learning outcome around that by using the method below.

Learning Outcome Development

We begin outcome development by thinking of general goals (which are not yet outcomes), objectives (activities that will be accomplished to achieve the goal), and then the outcomes based on these two areas.

Activity: Beginning with the above outline, set a general goal related to something you want to learn or a skill you feel you would like to develop during your next professional, personal, or academic experience.

Goal: This can be a general skill or knowledge area. A goal is not a learning outcome but a general thing you would like to achieve. Learning outcomes are specific, but a goal is often a good starting point to begin the outcome development.

Objectives: After setting a general goal, you want to think about specific things that you can do to accomplish this goal. These are also not outcomes but are action items that can be completed to accomplish the goal. These are your objectives or to-do items for the experience that can lead to an outcome. Describe some activities that you can engage in during that will help you know that this goal has been accomplished and knowledge or skill acquired.

Learning outcome: Once you accomplish the goal and objectives discussed above, what will you be able to do at the end of the experience? (This will be your learning outcome.) The learning outcome should be specific, measurable, attainable, relevant, and timely (able to be accomplished during the timeline of the experience). The outcome is the result, and what you will be able to do once the experience is over.

It is helpful to start it always with the following phrase:

At the end of this experience, I will be able to . . . (it usually helps here to begin this with an active verb that relates to the skill or knowledge you set out to achieve).

*Another way to think of a learning outcome is as a future bullet point for your next résumé in that it starts with a good active verb, is skill focused, and demonstrates specific competency areas.

The following is an example of how to develop goals, objectives, and outcomes for any new experience:

GOALS	OBJECTIVES	OUTCOMES
General Aim or Purpose	The Bullet Points: Clear statements that describe desired benchmarks	Demonstrable Learning Achievements
"I hope to…"	"This is my strategy for taking action…"	"I should now be able to…"
Statement of Purpose	Methodology	Thesis statement/Hypothesis (Reflection=Interpretation/Analysis)

Example:

To enhance my communication abilities by adapting to the workplace culture and models of professional practice	• Review all company handbooks and policy manuals, note any points of confusion. • Observe and take regular notes on the professional behaviors of those around me. • Build an organizational chart that includes my role. • Develop a personalized template and signature for professional emails • Conduct an informational interview with my director • Attend all company meetings and events	I will be able to readily adapt to changing work environments and standards of professional practice and additionally be able to identify different organizational communication models and analyze their impact on institutional culture.

Prepare (Listen Up)

Cultural Bridge Activity

© Jonathan Andrew.

This is a great perspective-shifting activity that prompts you to think about the differences in professional and everyday practice in your destination culture.

Strategies for Developing Cultural Agility during a Global Experience

Step 1: Cultural Assumptions: Please take a moment to fill out the table below with the cultural assumptions/stereotypes that you know are typically referenced about people in the country you are traveling to (left box) and assumptions/stereotypes that others may hold about your home country/culture (right box). In the middle box please outline strategies for things you can to prepare yourself to break down those assumptions upon arrival abroad.

Part 2: Cultivating Cultural Agility

Please Read this First:

The First Steps in developing the "Mega-Competency" of Cultural Agility: Clearing your assumptions and biases"
Developing cultural agility is an important lifelong competency that develops by fine-tuning your skills in intercultural communication, cultural adaptation, professional self-awareness, and conflict management and negotiation.

Typical cultural assumptions for country you are traveling to: _____)	Strategies you will use for breaking down these cultural assumptions	Typical cultural assumptions others may believe about you or your home country: _____
1.	1.	1.
2.	2.	2.
3.	3.	3.
4.	4.	4.
5	5.	5.

Culturally agile professionals are capable of recognizing that cultural differences can be understood as a point of strength in all professional work environments. Those who are culturally agile are capable of engaging and responding effectively and respectfully to co-workers from all backgrounds and skill levels. "Operationally speaking, culturally agile organizations and individuals are able to integrate and transform knowledge about diverse groups of people into 'specific standards, policies, practices and attitudes used in appropriate cultural settings to increase the quality of services; thereby producing better outcomes. (Davis & Donald, 1997)" (Hunt & Orange, 2015).

To begin the process of developing cultural agility one must first examine their own assumptions and barriers that hinder the development of cultural agility. As Paula Caligiuri outlines in *Cultural Agility: Building a Pipeline of Successful Global Professionals*, "The four greatest barriers are:

- Assuming that one possesses cross-cultural competence after only limited exposure to countries or cultures. This assumption produces overconfidence in one's culture-specific knowledge when it is in fact merely superficial.
- Assuming that one's success in a prior global or multicultural role means cross-cultural competence has been achieved. This assumption produces succession plans in which talent is 'anointed' as having cross-cultural competencies when they might not exist.
- Assuming that observed or perceived similarities indicate deeper cultural similarities. This assumption produces an overestimation of commonalities and an underestimation of the influence of cultural differences among people, practices and principles.
- Assuming that technology transcends cultural differences. This assumption produces and overreliance on technology to solve cultural challenges in communication and collaboration." (Caligiuri, 2012)

To begin this process of becoming more culturally agile professionals through your pursuit of a global co-op, we first need to assess our own cultural values, assumptions, and be perceptive enough to recognize how the cultural values and assumptions held by our colleagues shape their perception of us. By doing this you are acknowledging that these differences exist and that you are committing to better understanding the impact of culture on your professional work environment. This exercise will expose you to some of the tools available to you to enhance your knowledge and abilities to communicate with colleagues from many backgrounds and cultures.

PART 3: CREATING YOUR CULTURAL BRIDGE
Important! Before completing the assignment below you will need to have full completed an online Cultural Profile Module through a portal similar to one like Aperian Global's Globesmart technology (Instructions on how to complete this profile

are below if you do have Globesmart access) If you do not have Globesmart then conduct online research about the professional tendencies of your destination culture.

Cultural Bridge Assignment Outline:

1. In order to complete this exercise you will need to have completed your cultural profile via the GlobeSmart cultural profile module. If you have not set up an account and created your profile then please do so with your husky email via this link: https://learning.aperianglobal.com/portal/

   INSTRUCTIONS
   - **Step 1:** Sign in to the learning Portal, https://learning.aperianglobal.com/portal/
   - **Step 2:** Create Globesmart Profile. Button on main page (see screen shots on next 2 pages)
   - **Step 3:** After receiving the results of your profile click on the "learn more" button to find out details about your cultural background
   - **Step 4:** On the profile page click on "compare profile". Select your country of destination and home country from the list and click on "view comparison" (see screen shots on PowerPoint online workshop slides on Blackboard)
   - **Step 5:** Now that you can see how your cultural profile compares to that of the general cultural profile of your home and destination country click on "Get Advice"
   - **Step 6:** In each section explore further by clicking on the "read more" button. Also click on the style switching link in each section. On the left hand side identify areas where you diverge the most from the style of your destination country and read the advice provided on how to "bridge the gap". Take notes on this.
   - **Step 7:** In the read more sections, take notes on topics related to "Training", "leadership", "decision making", "Relationship Building", "Evaluating People", "resolving conflicts" or any other categories that you feel will be helpful and relevant to your international co-op.
   - **Step 8:** Also explore the section called "Learning Paths" At the top of the page, this will link you to learning paths about specific areas.
        i. Cultural Foundations: This overview "cultural dimensions" outlines the cross-cultural models and frameworks to assist in understanding the impact of cultural differences, and provide examples and explanations of the GlobeSmart dimensions of culture.
        ii. Country Specific: You can choose specific countries and from this page can compare your profile & get advice, view the core values and communication styles for this location, and test your knowledge.

2. Now look at your profile in comparison with only the cultural attributes for the country where you will be going on co-op. Where are the biggest differences in these profiles? Dig a little deeper and think about the ways you will need to adapt or prepare personally and professionally in order to bridge this cultural divide effectively.

Now that you have a good grasp of these cultural characteristics, please go to the table below on this document and complete it in the following way:

   a. Section titled, **"Your Cultural Perspective"** Based on your cultural profile results and your analysis of your destination country's profile. What are the top 5 ways that you and your working style could be most unlike to your host country's culture, and what do expect will be your biggest professional challenges?(Be honest as we all hold some basic expectations and assumptions of what things will be like). Try to think of things that may come up as barriers or points of disorientation in your adaptation to your new work environment.

   b. Section Titled, **"Cultural Perspective of Destination Country"** Based on the general cultural profile results and analysis of your destination countries profile. What are the top 5 ways your new employer or co-workers will need to adapt to your working style? What expectations may they hold about you?

   c. Section Titled **"Strategies for how you will bridge the divide"** – In this section please develop your top 5 strategies/action items for what you will do to bridge the cultural divide as a culturally agile professional. Try to be as specific as possible in terms of not only what you can do to adapt to the culture, learn the language, and meet people, but try to hone in on specific soft skills you can utilize to negotiate the impact your own cultural norms have on your work and expectations of new colleagues. Here tell us how you will integrate your understanding of your own cultural values to confidently and appropriately integrate within the shifting cultural context of your new working environment(s) (Please feel free to use a second page for this if there is not enough room on the table for details).

a. Your cultural perspective	b. Cultural perspective of destination country	c. Strategies for how you will bridge the divide
1.	1.	1.
2.	2.	2.
3.	3.	3.
4.	4.	4.
5.	5.	5.

Final Step: Take it one step further and compare your strategies from the table on page one and the strategies from this chart. Please add a few notes on the cultural assumptions you still hold after completing this exercise and in the bridge image, on the last page, please fill each block with one goal or action strategy for your global co-op that will help you negotiate or overcome these points of potential bias and false expectations in order to be more culturally agile on co-op. Let these goals help to guide you during your cultural transition.

Notes:

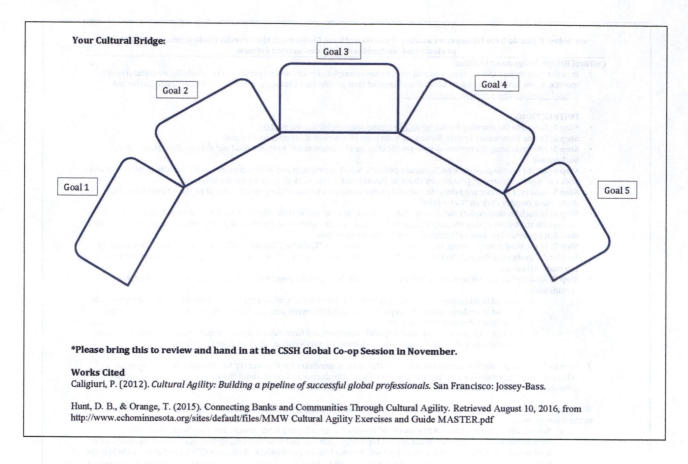

Your Cultural Bridge:

Goal 1 · Goal 2 · Goal 3 · Goal 4 · Goal 5

*Please bring this to review and hand in at the CSSH Global Co-op Session in November.

Works Cited

Caligiuri, P. (2012). *Cultural Agility: Building a pipeline of successful global professionals.* San Francisco: Jossey-Bass.

Hunt, D. B., & Orange, T. (2015). Connecting Banks and Communities Through Cultural Agility. Retrieved August 10, 2016, from http://www.echominnesota.org/sites/default/files/MMW Cultural Agility Exercises and Guide MASTER.pdf

Advising Session

© Rebecca Westerling

Look in: What is your baseline/compass/basis for understanding the world? Consider what has influenced you in your culture, language, community, family, school, and work identities. Consider these elements as you endeavor to interact with new people, communities, and cultures.

Look up: Take a moment to observe your environment. How do people communicate? Is it a formal/ informal setting? Body language? Interactions? Ways people work? Ethics?

Listen up: Literally, listen. In a new environment—whether it is a new club meeting you are attending, a new office you now work in, a new activist march you have joined, or a new part of the city you have decided to explore. What do you hear? What is the pace? What is the vibe?

Look back/in: Look back to a formative experience that changed your perception of yourself, or moved you to do something. What was it in that situation that caused the change?

Look up-perception: How do you think you are perceived by others in terms of power/knowledge/belonging? Are you inside or outside of communities, and why?

CASE STUDIES

Tony: Tony is considering a co-op in Eastern Europe. He is excited about the possibility of a few specific co-ops in three different countries; however, given some of his personal values (religion, lifestyle, etc.) and some recent political unrest, he is unsure of how to get the best information. He interviewed with his top choice, and the manager of the position assured him that he would be fully welcomed in relation to all of his concerns. In conversation with former co-op students, however, he is not certain if he is comfortable. How can he best assess what may be the best fit, and a safe option. From there, what steps can he take before arrival and during his co-op?

Ethics Case Study (Experience Versus Personal Beliefs/Values)

© Rebecca Westerling.

This case study is viewed from two different perspectives: Sasha and Arjun. Read both perspectives and consider what you know about each, what you still don't know, and what Sasha may not understand about the other person's perspective.

Sasha, a co-op student, has been on the job for six weeks and generally likes the position and all of her colleagues. This said, she is frustrated that she keeps asking for more work and knows that her colleagues are busy, meaning that they could likely use the help. She is starting to feel like a broken record, asking the same people, day after day. She may just give up, since no one seems to want to give her additional work, even though she has time. What can she do?

Arjun is Sasha's direct manager. He recently took on managing twice as many employees, and while he is happy to have Sasha on board and helping with projects, he doesn't have a lot of capacity to direct her in new projects. This said, he knows there is plenty of work for her to take on once she shows full competency in her daily tasks, and takes initiative. His last co-op sent weekly updates on what they accomplished, and set time on his calendar to not only discuss goals but also came up with ideas based on projects they found interesting across the teams. Arjun wants Sasha to learn and be challenged, but does not want to hand her work she is not prepared to do, or that she doesn't show initiative to take on. How should he handle this?

CHAPTER 5 - LET'S TALK! BOUNDARYLESS COMMUNICATION

Class/Activities

Prepare (Listen Up)

Activity: Cover Letter Outline

© Rebecca Westerling.

There are many ways to write a great cover letter, and there are resources available to coach you on the details of various approaches; however, getting to the essence of an excellent cover letter is the focus of this exercise. Use this to ensure you have thought about the company and position you are applying for, your strengths as a candidate, and have organized your thoughts in a way that are compelling.

Step 1: Read the description of the employer, research the employer (website, LinkedIn information including profiles of current employees, news articles, and other sources available), and identify the company's values and strategic goals via their mission or vision statements.

Company Values

Company Goals

Step 2: Write out two to three sentences on how your personal values, goals, and experiences connect with the company's values and goals.

Step 3: Scan the job description and identify the requisite skills and qualifications for this position and write down two to four experiences or personal skills that will fulfill each of the qualification.

1. Qualification 1:_____

   a. Skill/Experience 1:_____
   _____

   b. Skill/Experience 2:_____
   _____

   c. Skill/Experience 3:_____
   _____

2. Qualification 2:_____

   a. Skill/Experience 1:_____
   _____

   b. Skill/Experience 2:_____
   _____

   c. Skill/Experience 3:_____
   _____

3. Qualification 3: _____

    a. Skill/Experience 1: _____

    b. Skill/Experience 2: _____

    c. Skill/Experience 3: _____

_____

Step 4: Use the information outlined above to create a cover letter that conveys your interest in the position, your understanding of what they are looking for, and translates for the person reading the cover letter why you are a great candidate for this position and their organization.

Prepare (Listen Up)

Good Cover Letter Writing Principles and Sample

© Jonathan Andrew.

Cover letter writing is fairly formulaic, but the communication style of a cover letter is fairly nuanced. Writing a good cover letter is similar to constructing a convincing and compelling story. You don't want your cover letter to simply read as a list of skills and accomplishments; instead, it should weave a narrative of your past experiences in a way that captures the reader's attention, has a good flow and transitions between thoughts, and uses real-world examples to accentuate the skills you would bring to the job you are applying for. A cover letter, like the résumé, should be employer centric in that it is tailored specifically to the job you are applying for (no cutting and pasting one letter to the next), and should be written in a way that demonstrates how your past experiences fit the needs outlined by the employer's job description. In addition, it requires researching the employer's values and getting a sense of the company culture, the language of the field, and an understanding of the professional expectations. Constructing a good cover letter is great practice for boundaryless communication, as it requires shifting to the prospective employer's perspective and anticipating their recruitment process and needs.

The following is an overview of the formula for writing a good cover letter:

1. **Professional heading:** A good cover letter will have a professional look. A good way to start is to make all application materials consistent in appearance. So begin the cover letter by using your name and contact information at the top and in exactly the same format as it appears on your résumé.

2. **Business letter format:** Your cover letter will appear professional if left aligned, includes the address information of the employer, and a date. Also remember that a business letter has a colon after the salutation instead of a comma.

3. **Salutation:** It is always more effective if you can address it to a specific individual when possible as it adds a personal touch. For this, be mindful of the gender of the reader. If you do not know the employers preference of "Ms.," "Mr.," "Dr.," and so on, then it is best to simply write out the full name of the individual. If you do not know the name or gender of the recipient of the letter then "To whom it may concern":, "Dear hiring manager":, "Dear search committee:," and so on are acceptable salutations.

4. **Introductory paragraph:** It is always recommended to begin with a line like, "It is with great excitement . . ." or "It is with great anticipation . . ." to instantly show your engagement, excitement, and interest. This first paragraph should be short, concise, and to the point. It should always reference the job title you are applying to, indicate how you found the job, and have one or two sentences on who you are and an introduction to the skills and experiences you feel make you a good fit for the job. Remember the introduction is also a preview to what the employer can expect to find in the remainder of the letter. So, your concluding sentence of the paragraph should highlight areas that you will be describing in more detail in the body paragraphs.

5. **Two to three body paragraphs:** These are paragraphs where you tell your story. It is important here to introduce one of your past experiences and explain why it is relevant to the skills and qualifications outlined in the job description. Here you also communicate how your values and interests are in good alignment with the values and interests of the employer. Each body paragraph should not list skills or accomplishments but should be constructed around one relevant experience and explain how that experience gave you the skills, values, and interests that fit the needs of the employer. A good cover letter will include body paragraphs that are well constructed with introductory and concluding sentences that wrap up the paragraphs nicely and provide transitions between thoughts. Read your cover letter out loud to yourself to ensure you have a good flow and that your story will be communicated in a way that does not come across as choppy or awkward.

6. **Concluding paragraph:** This paragraph (like the introductory paragraph) should be short, concise, to the point, and leave the employer excited to read your résumé or hear more from you in an interview. Here you should reemphasize your enthusiasm and fit for the position. Hit on the main skill and qualification points that you touched on in the body paragraphs and finish with a short overview on how you can be best contacted for an interview. This is followed by the appropriate letter closure of "Sincerely," "Kind Regards," "All the Best," and your name/signature at the bottom.

As with the résumé, it is very important for you to have as many proofreaders and editors you can find to ensure that there are no grammatical errors and that the cover letter communicates your story in an effective way to match the job. So it is helpful to have your editors first read the job description and then the cover letter to ensure it match the employer's needs and expectations.

Cover letters are a gateway to the employer reading your résumé and inviting you to an interview. Keep your document professional, concise, and as perfect as you can make it. Always run the spell and grammar check and take the time to really ensure you are connecting well with the expectations of the job.

The following is an example cover letter that demonstrates the application of the cover letter formula outlined above. In addition, you will also find a sample cover letter outline that can be helpful in designing your body paragraphs to be focused on the desired values and skills of the employer's job description.

ANDRE BRIGHAM

39 Forsyth St., Boston, MA 02115
802-255-3218, aisha.nelson@husky.neu.edu

Dewey Square Group
100 Cambridge Street, Suite 1301
Boston, MA 02114

October 28, 2014

To whom it may concern:

It is with great excitement that I am writing to express my interest in the Administrative Intern position with Dewey Square Group listed on Northeastern University's co-op website. I am a second year International Affairs student with a minor in Communication Studies. This coursework has sparked a passion for the field of political consulting and public relations, and I believe that this coursework combined with my previous professional level research and writing experiences make me an ideal candidate for the position.

As an International Affairs major, politics – both global and local – play a central role in my education. My coursework, which has ranged from political theory to environmental science, equips me with solid structural understanding of both American government as well as more abstract political and social issues currently affecting American society. Various political science courses, in particular, have informed me about the legislative process in the United States so that I am familiar with the processes by which bills are introduced and enacted (or not). Most recently, I attended a lobbying day at the Massachusetts Statehouse earlier this year where I lobbied my representatives to co-sponsor four bills. My familiarity with the American governmental system and particularly with state politics from both my academic and my personal experience would make me a valuable asset at Dewey Square Group.

In researching the work that your organization has accomplished in Boston, I was struck by the efficacy of Dewey Square Group at maneuvering complex legal and political frameworks on behalf of clients. In addition to the political activism experience I've gained, my position as treasurer in student government has also provided me with valuable experience navigating the regulatory framework of a large organization. A vital part of my role as treasurer involves advocating for our student organization and maneuvering university requirements so that we continue to receive funding and may pursue our organization goals to the fullest. Each semester I must present our funding requests to the financial board, a skill that requires not only significant planning and organization, but also strong argumentation and advocacy skills. I believe that due to my experience navigating "legislation" within the microcosmic example of Northeastern University, I will contribute significantly to the larger-scale advocacy efforts of the Dewey Square Group.

Lastly, I would like to draw attention to my written skills. Though I have always been strong writer, as indicated by the publication and awards of my creative writing in my high school literary magazine, it was not until this past summer that I gained experience writing in a professional environment. During my internship with Mærsk Line Shipping, I was required to draft material about the Key Client Programme, a group of benefits offered to Mærsk's most elite clients, to be released both internally and externally. Thanks to this experience, I was able to hone my writing and public relations skills, as certain information necessitated diplomacy and sensitivity. Ultimately, my efforts culminated in an eight-page document detailing the benefits of the Key Client Programme as well as numerous other smaller documents.

I believe I would be a good addition to Dewey Square Group due to my knowledge of the American legal-political system, experience with advocacy, and strong writing skills. I am eager to speak with you more about the position and my qualifications, and can be reached at the above contact information. I will be on the West Coast until March 7th, but after that please feel free to contact me at your convenience. Thank you very much for your time and consideration, and I look forward to hearing from you!

Sincerely,

Andre Brigham

Prepare (Listen Up)

Building Awareness

© Rebecca Westerling

Consider an upcoming new experience (activity, job, class, social event, travel experience, etc.). What are the verbal and nonverbal cues you can learn from in a new experience? What are ways you can prepare ahead of time? What are details you may only be able to gather when you are there? How can you show to others that you are open to participating, engaging, and learning? What does this look, sound, and feel like? What are some of the preconceived stereotypes (positive, negative, and neutral) that you realize you are bringing into the situation?

Engage (Act Up and Join Up)

Perspective Taking

© Rebecca Westerling

As was discussed in the chapter, perspective taking is a key step.

What are the things that you would want the interviewer to know about you apart from your job qualifications? What are the personal characteristics that you would like to come across about your work ethic, attitude, and personality? What are the things you would try to minimize? After answering these questions, rework them according to the perspective of the employer. What are the cultures and values of the workplace you are joining? How will the employer expect you to act and communicate in the job interview? How will your skills be framed in the context of the needs of the employer? By thinking about your qualifications from the perspective of the employer you are beginning the process of relating to their needs and beginning the conversation of the job with an employer-centric lens instead of a self-centric lens.

Engage (Act Up and Join Up)

Perspective Taking: Employer for a Day

© Rebecca Westerling

This activity was created by colleagues across Northeastern University and has been adapted to fit different needs pedagogically at different points in the semester. This format is intended to focus on taking the perspective of others and understanding the many factors in the decision-making process for hiring, whether for internships, co-op, or for full-time employment.

Preparation for instructor: Prepare enough job descriptions for students to review distinct jobs in groups of three to five students. Also, prepare a set of résumés that are in line with the candidates expected to apply for the positions you are reviewing (likely similar to the students in your class).

1. **Set the stage:** Let the students know that today, they are the employer! They have the power to choose the candidate they wish to hire for their job, and with that also comes responsibility. Let them know that this should be fun, and will help them as they dive into the application process for their own job search.

2. **Review the jobs:** Have each student group read and review the job description in front of them. Give them time to review and decide who will share a summary of the position, including the top qualities they are looking for in a candidate. One team member can share:
   - Name of organization, title of the job/position, relevant information (location, technical or language requirements, etc.)
   - Also ask them to note what was, or was not, included in the job description. They may share observations including the following: company culture, expected work hours, types of projects the employee would do, who the employee would work with, and so on. This can lead to a discussion about who writes the job descriptions, how they are updated, and why certain information may or may not be included.

3. **Review résumés:** Have each "hiring team" review the packet of résumés (same across all teams) and choose their top three candidates. Then, have them share their rankings, noting that they cannot change their minds based on what they hear from other companies, since this does not happen in the real world.

4. **Hiring process:** Randomly choose one student or company to move forward with first, and determine what job they chose and why. Continue this process until all companies and candidates have a match—or do not and need to go into a second round of applying and hiring. Have students consider the following:
   - Did some of the hiring groups want the same candidate, but the candidate was overqualified for some positions so would choose a different position?
   - Were some hiring teams focused more on potential while others focused on proven skills?
   - Were some hiring teams were more stringent on formatting and accuracy of the résumé than others?
   - How do hiring managers determine who is likely to accept their offer if it is given?
   - How do candidates know what positions to apply for in terms of level, challenge, and so on?

5. **Discuss:** Discuss in this session and throughout the job search process the lessons learned in this exercise.

*There are many different variations of this exercise, so adjust the group size and focus area that works best for you and your group.

Engage (Act Up and Join Up)

Professional Portfolio Website Assignment

© Jonathan Andrew.

This activity is framed as a class assignment for a group of students to complete within a set timeframe, in this case one semester as students prepare to go out on co-op for the first time. It can be adapted for use in a different type of course, while students are on work experiences (co-op or internships), and more.

Platform: Free Online Site of Your Choosing: Wix, Weebly, WordPress, etc.

Description

A professional website is an online platform for you to showcase your professional skills, knowledge, interests, and motivations. It also provides you an opportunity to begin the process of defining your own professional "online brand" for future employers. In the digital age we live in, employers will frequently (if not always) seek information about you online before deciding to hire you to work with them. Developing a LinkedIn page is very important, but it is important to be able to differentiate yourself further by featuring examples of your work portfolio in unique and personal ways. The purpose of developing this professional online presence is to create a positive image of your professional accomplishments to a potentially very broad audience and to take control of what potential employers will see when searching for you on the Internet. The website portfolio will allow you to integrate your previous experiences and knowledge in a thoughtful and meaningful way. Through the process of creating this website you may also improve your abilities to describe your experiences more thoroughly and articulate your abilities for future employment opportunities.

Eventually, the professional website you create is intended to be a running online repository for all of your professional accomplishments across professional experiences

Professional Portfolio Website Requirements

Carefully consider your website's design and professional message and tailor it for a broad audience of potential employers. This requires some careful consideration of your personal, academic, and career goals, and desired learning outcomes from co-op. Your website is intended to be unique to you, but there are some graded elements (professional statement, sections on your educational background, experiences, etc.) required to be uploaded to your website, which will be accomplished in the normal schedule of the co-op course.

1. **Sections of Professional Portfolio Website**
   A. **Introductory homepage:** Displays a professional picture and statement that introduces the reader to the site.
   B. **About me page or purpose statement:** This statement should provide the audience with your interpretation of your overall purpose and motivation, including why you have chosen your major, a field of work that will give you a sense of purpose, and a plan of what you hope to do in the future.
   C. **Education section:** This section is intended to provide a narrative overview of your educational background and details on the skills and abilities you have developed via your education over time.
   D. **Experience section:** This section should detail your various out-of-classroom and professional experiences with an overview and timeline of your skills and accomplishments professionally and personally
   E. **Skills sections** (could include separate sections on research, leadership, writing, computer, languages, etc.): This should provide visual representations of things you consider professional and personal strength areas.
   F. **Writing or work samples:** Posted according to disciplinary focus or professional industry interest.
   G. **Interests section:** This gives the employer a chance to know your personality. Examples to be included here could be writing blogs, photography, and videos you have created, other multimedia examples of your work, and so on.
2. **Other Optional Sections of Website**
   A. **International experience**: Introduction to your cross-cultural educational background.
   B. **Evidence of awards/honors or substantial professional/research accomplishments**
   C. **Professional evidence:** Includes examples/artifacts of materials written for past jobs that will contribute to enhancing your professional image ideally broken into discipline-specific sections. (Note: be mindful of not sharing confidential or proprietary information from previous employers on the Internet, especially if you signed a nondisclosure agreement. Always check with your prior employers about the appropriateness of material shared online before doing this.)

D. **Other:** This website is your creation and your chance to convey your professional style and your personality to future employers. Be Unique!

Guidelines for the Composition and Design of Your Website

The creation and selection process for what to feature and how to feature it on the website is a very individual process, and some students will feel more comfortable making this a public online site sooner than others. Whatever your comfort level, our end goal for this semester will be for you to have a final professional online website completed by the end of the semester. This can be composed in the following stages for best effectiveness:

Stage 1: Outlining and establishing a front page design for the website:

- Discuss the front page of the website with a trusted mentor and work on creating a front page introduction that not only makes a great professional first impression but will also lead your intended audience in navigating your website in an intentional way.
- Simultaneously work on finalizing your career portfolio items (résumé, cover letter, list of references, etc.) that will aid you in your job search, application, and interview process. All of these items will contribute to the composition of your website.

Stage 2: Articulating and showcasing your professional skills, interests, and motivations:

- After determining the design and outline for your website, spend some time discussing your professional motivations and workplace values with a mentor. This work will assist you in making determinations of how to feature your disciplinary and professional, industry-specific content areas. These unique components of the website will allow your audience to get to know you better personally, academically, and professionally.

Stage 3: Self- and peer assessment

- Take some time to critically examine your website and the websites of others from the perspective of an outside party or employer. This ideally will help you fine-tune your professional online presence and website from an employer's perspective.

Stage 4: Peer feedback and the creation of co-op work experience learning outcomes

- The final step of designing your website is to incorporate peer and mentor feedback into the design of your website before making it public. The website will then become a place for you to further develop as you create artifacts of your professional accomplishments. Always keep a live website current and up to date.

Visit the following website to see an example of a student's professional website: https://sorensono.wixsite.com/mysite

Also provided below is a peer-review form that you can give to others when reviewing your draft website.

Website Peer Assessment Activity

Have a mentor or trusted peer go through your website to answer the following questions:

Please go into the website and answer the following questions in a critical, positively framed, and honest way. Please answer all of the questions completely with details focused on helping to improve the site.

1. **Assessment metric: Who is this student becoming?**

   What are your first impressions about the student's professionalism and personality through their front page, about me page, or welcome page? What does the website structure and format communicate to you about this as a young professional? What does this student's page communicate about what kind of professional they would like to become?

2. **Assessment metric: What are this student's values, strengths, and capacities?**

   Read the student's professional and/or about me statements, experiences, and education pages. Visually and in writing what can you tell about this student's abilities, professional strengths, and personal or workplace values? What is one good thing and one thing that needs to be improved about the professional statement? Does the student do a good job of directing the reader on where to find important information about their skills and abilities? Why or why not?

3. **Assessment metric: What and how are they learning?**

   Take a look at the student's Writing Samples and Education sections. As a potential employer what does this website tell me about this student's academic interests and knowledge areas? What do you feel that this student's strengths are academically or with discipline-specific research?

4. **Assessment metric: How will this student contribute to their professional community or society in general?**

   On the whole, what do you feel that this student will contribute to their new community of practice? From this website, do you get a sense of the student's broader hopes and goals for society? Why or why not?

5. **In conclusion:** Is there anything on this website that you think you would want on your own professional website. Why or why not? What suggestions would you give to this student before making this a public online professional show piece?

Advising Session

Look in (© Rebecca Westerling.)**:** How do you communicate nonverbally? What is your verbal communication like? Consider where your style of communication is most effective? Are there places where you feel you are not as effective—why? Now, imagine transporting yourself to another setting—a new location (across town, across the globe, in a different type of setting work vs. play vs. discussion vs. public speaking vs. student)—how would you choose to alter your verbal and nonverbal communication in these settings?

Look up: Observe others' verbal and nonverbal communication styles. What do you notice when this is all you focus on? What works well and what could you adapt to use yourself?

Listen up: Listen to a conversation in a language other than your native language—one you either don't know or don't know well. Do this in person if possible, and if it isn't, then find an online talk show, such as TED talk, in another language. What do you believe you understand, based on their communication style?

Act up: Go somewhere outside of your comfort zone—where you will be the minority in some way, and where you will need to confront a difference that will stretch your comfort level.

Listen up-modes of communication: (© Jonathan Andrew.)**:** How do different modes of communication help or hinder the intent or reception of communications. How can different forms be used to create deeper more trusting human connections and which can be used for the sake of efficiency? How do you approach the uses of these technologies with the notion of respecting another's time without it being distracting to human connections (e.g., cell phones on the table, student fidgeting and clearly anxious about not having a phone to communicate with others at the table)? How are some modes better for some tasks and not for others, and how do these change according to your role and relationships?

CASE STUDIES

Case Study—Perspective and Ethical (or Unethical) Action

This case study is viewed from two different perspectives, Pat and Sergio. Read both perspectives and consider what you know about each, what you still don't know, and what Pat and Sergio may not understand about the other person's perspective.

Pat works at a successful lobbying firm in Boston and often works with clients from both sides of the political spectrum and many clients who have different views and values than she does, and this is required of everyone who works at the firm. The co-op student she manages, Sergio, has been assigned to work on a controversial client case that should give him excellent professional experience, but will stretch his analytical abilities and challenge him to be more concise than he has been in the past with other projects. She believes it should be a great learning experience for him! Is there anything she could do to best prepare Sergio for the level of work expected on this big project?

Sergio works at a lobbying firm that often works with clients from both sides of the political spectrum and many clients who have different views and values than his. He understood when he took this job that this is required of everyone who works at the firm. There is one client project, however, that his manager, Pat, requested he work on that is in direct conflict with his personal beliefs and he does not feel comfortable participating on this project. Can he bring this up professionally, and if so, how? Is this appropriate, given the expectations set when he was hired?

Case Study—Communicating Your "Self"

Sam plans to apply for co-ops for the next cycle and hopes to find novel ways to present himself to potential employers. He has heard advice regarding updating his résumé, LinkedIn account, creating a professional website, writing a blog, showcasing his photography on a personal website, among others.

How would you suggest Sam work to present himself? What formats would you suggest, depending on the type of job he is seeking? Are there other factors that would influence your advice to Sam? How should he prioritize his time spent on his professional presence, both online and offline?

CHAPTER 6 – DEVELOPING AGENCY FOR ETHICAL AND IMPACTFUL PROFESSIONAL AND CIVIC ENGAGEMENT

Class/Activities
Engage (Act Up and Join Up)

Agent of Social Change Reflection Activity

© Jonathan Andrew.

If you want to someday enact a social change it is helpful to learn from those who have done this before. The following exercise can be used as a preliminary activity to begin the research phase of an informational interview.

Write a two- to three-page reflection and profile as a social change agent in the following way.

1. **Brainstorm:** Please start the reflection paper by listing the three most critical global or social issues that are important to you. These can be issues you have learned about in your coursework, stumbled across in the news/social media, or it could also be unrelated entirely to what you are studying, but still an important issue for you that you think about regularly

2. **Focus on one issue for now:** Now that you have your list, select the critical issue that you are most passionate about or gives you the greatest sense of personal purpose in your academics or professional pursuits. Please briefly write me a short story (one to two paragraphs) about why this issue is meaningful to you and reflect on how you would like to change or help to fix that problem in some way now or in the future.

3. **Research:** Now research organizations/companies/institutions that are in some way dealing with this issue. Below are some suggested websites to find lists or links to these types of organizations (there is no need to limit your search to these websites in order to find an organization that speaks to you in some way).

   Skoll Foundation (Awardees Page):
   http://skoll.org/community/awardees/

   Oslo Freedom Forum (Speakers Page):
   https://oslofreedomforum.com/speakers/

4. **Focus on a particular organization:** Please list three organizations/companies/institutions that you found are particularly interesting to you. In this list, include their website URL, mission statement, and whether or not they hire interns.

   Last, choose one person who is affiliated in a leadership role with only one of these organizations (this could be the founder, the CEO, executive director, or even someone you personally know at the organization), research into their background using LinkedIn and other online sources, and in one to two pages, in double-spaced line spaces, answer the following questions.

   - What has this person accomplished as an agent of social change?
   - How long has it taken this person to get to where they are (if you can find this)? What does this person's actions and life experiences tell you about the skills and abilities they have? In what way will you seek to use your experiences to help you develop a similar set of abilities that will help you to become an agent of social change?

5. **Informational interview**: Take this one step further by trying to contact the organization via email, phone, social media, or in person to see if someone could talk to you about their background, how they became involved, and how the vision for social change is being organized and enacted by the organization. Focus on ethical dilemmas, unintended consequences, and the model through which the organization enacts change. By following the steps of those who have been there before you may learn the skills and attributes you will need to tackle an issue important to you someday. Be bold, ask good questions, and follow up by showing gratitude and paying it forward!

Engage (Act Up and Join Up)

Policy Memo

© Jonathan Andrew.

While the following activity is framed as a hypothetical memo, and is not necessarily intended to be sent, it allows you the space to choose an issue, research, frame your policy suggestion, and consider possible outcomes for internal or external stakeholders. In the "if you build it they will come" approach, if you never consider what policy may be necessary to implement change, it is extremely unlikely that the change will happen spontaneously. Take this chance to consider how meaningful change might be possibly related to a cause that you care about.

Assignment purpose: Good memo writing is an important skill set that connects classroom assignments with professional practice. Those who can concisely introduce a problem, effectively analyze the organizational situation, and can succinctly provide recommendations on resolving the issues at hand will excel both academically and professionally.

Assignment description: Write a three-page draft memo that would be intended for a head of a company/organization you work with or care about. Or choose to write this as a piece of advocacy to someone external to your organization (government official, potential donor, etc.) that may be impacting your organizational activities. You should begin with a brief introduction to your organization/departments mission, your role in the organization/department, and provide an analysis of a current situation or problem affecting your organization. Good data and outside research should support your analysis of the problem and the potential impact on critical strategic goals of the organization. Finally, provide recommendations for strategic actions either internally or externally that could help solve your organization or company's problem and help in the more efficient fulfillment of the organizational mission. Your recommendations should be supported by data and research on the best practices in the field for the type of work that you are doing.

For tips on good policy memo writing, consult online resources through a simple Google search.

A successful memo will have the following four elements:

1. A strong and convincing introduction that has been written appropriately for the intended audience and provides a concise statement of the problem affecting your company or organization. (Tip: It often helps to state the purpose of the document and your conclusions and recommendations first, as this document is typically used to provide succinct advice to the intended audience.)

2. Appropriate background on the situation or problem is provided that clarifies any technical information or insider jargon that may only be relevant to your organization.

3. Analysis and arguments should make logical connections to why your recommendations will have a positive impact on the problem situation. Analyses should always be given appropriate support with

real-world examples (I would like you to use at least two relevant outside sources that reflect the best practices in the field as it relates to the issue you are analyzing) and should be cited when necessary utilizing APA-style citation format (http://www.apastyle.org/).

4. Your memo should include a strong implementation plan that takes into consideration any future issues that could arise from your recommendations.

Remember to avoid plagiarism and add to the convincing nature of your memo by citing gathered material and supporting evidence appropriately and professionally.

Engage (Act Up and Join Up)

Creating a Code of Ethics

© Rebecca Westerling.

First, consider these three scenarios:

1. Engineering

The Engineers Ring is issued by the Order of the Engineers. It is worn on the little finger of the dominant hand of members of the Order of the Engineer, and symbolizes the oath taken by the wearer. "The Obligation is a creed similar to the oath attributed to Hippocrates (460-377 B.C.) that is generally taken by medical graduates and which sets forth an ethical code. The Obligation likewise, contains parts of the Canon of Ethics of major engineering societies. Initiates, as they accept it voluntarily, pledge to uphold the standards and dignity of the engineering profession and to serve humanity by making the best use of Earth's precious wealth."

> 1. I am an Engineer. In my profession I take deep pride. To it I owe solemn obligations. As an Engineer, I pledge to practice integrity and fair dealing, tolerance and respect; and to uphold devotion to the standards and the dignity of my profession, conscious always that my skill carries with it the obligation to serve humanity by making the best use of the Earth's precious wealth. As an Engineer, I shall participate in none but honest enterprises. When needed, my skill and knowledge shall be given without reservation for the public good. In the performance of duty and infidelity to my profession, I shall give my utmost.
>
> Sources: http://www.order-of-the-engineer.orghttp://www.order-of-the-engineer.org/wp-content/uploads/2009/10/Ceremony.pdf (check citations from these sources)

2. Medicine

The Hippocratic Oath is a well-known concept, related to professionals in the field of medicine and beyond. This oath, to whom the actual writer is not known, "is often cited as one of the oldest binding documents in history. Most graduating medical school students swear to some form of the oath, usually a modernized version."

- http://www.pbs.org/wgbh/nova/body/hippocratic-oath-today.html
- https://www.bioedge.org/bioethics/new-hippocratic-oath-for-doctors-approved/12496

3. Management

In his article "A Wallet-Sized Code of Ethics," Bob Stone argues that "ethical grounding of an organization demands a statement of principles that its members can understand and remember. It should be no longer than what you can fit on a wallet-sized card." He posits that rather than working within a system of rules, regulation, and enforcement, finding a sense of shared mission and ethics across the board and finding language that is accessible is important.

http://www.governing.com/columns/mgmt-insights/A-Wallet-Sized-Code-of.html

Built upon this concept—whether based in medicine, engineering, or in management—committing to an ethical approach to your profession, your organization, or yourself, we would argue, leads to better outcomes overall and leads to an intentional approach to ethical engagement with your community.

Take the time to create your own "Code of Ethics." Activity:

- Pick the organization, community, or group that will be your target.
- Write out your Code of Ethics
  - Aim for each statement to be clear and concise
  - Aim for the Code of Ethics to be easy to understand
  - Aim for it to be something you can live by
  - Aim to carry a copy with you
    (check proper citation for articles/source materials)

Look Back (Look In)

Purpose-Mapping Exercise

© Rebecca Westerling.

What is the purpose of what you are doing? What impact do you hope to have? How can you be most effective at doing this? How does it connect to the greater good? How does it connect to the idea of having a common purpose with others?

Take time to map out the answers to these questions for three to five activities you are currently involved in or are about to begin (jobs, internship, co-op, upcoming co-op, service activities, etc.).

If you are doing this in a classroom setting, pair up and share what you have found. Consider ideas from your partner and what steps you could take to be more effective, or hear how they imagine your actions connect with the greater good. If doing this independently, find a mentor, friend, or colleague to discuss these ideas with.

Advising Session

Look in: What is your purpose? What are your purposes? If you have a set idea for this right now, great! If you don't, great! If this changes tomorrow, next year, or in five years, great! This said, being mindful of what drives you and why is important. Look inside and reflect on what you find to be important to *you*. How will this drive what choices you make going forward?

Look up: It is said that the world is becoming a global world. Look up, and look around you. What are the signs of a global economy/interconnected global society in your daily life?

Civic engagement decision making: How do you decide how, when, and to what extent to get involved? What choices are you making now? What do you want to do in the future?

Five-year reflection: Instead of the question "Where do you want to be in 5 years?," which is a classic interview question, consider this question, "What do you wish could be different in the world in five years?" Then consider how you can take actions to contribute to this change.

Hindsight is 20/20: Often it is easier to look back on a decision and clearly state that something unethical happened, and this is what I would have or could have done differently. Consider a scenario in which you know unethical decisions were made. This could be in your past (a company decision where you worked, a colleague you worked with, a decision you made, etc.), or an example of unethical behavior in an industry you are interested in. *Write about what you would have done differently in the situation, if you were directly involved, or what you imagine you would have done to influence the outcome to find an ethical solution.* Use this knowledge as you encounter questionable situations in your future.

Set up for success: Think about what you want to learn in co-op (or in an internship or in your next leadership role). Also consider what your strengths are and what your weaknesses are. Now, write a letter to yourself with advice on how to be most successful in this endeavor. © Rebecca Westerling & Joani Lamachia

CASE STUDIES

Case Study—Offer Acceptance Versus Renege

Lynn is interviewing for co-op and has just finished her fourth interview. When she arrives home, the phone rings, and it is an employer from Amazing Company that offers work with a pay of $15 an hour. She is so excited she has obtained a co-op with a good organization and accepts the position immediately. A few hours later, MoreAmazing Company calls and offers her a job that she really wanted and offers her $20 an hour. What should she do?

Case Study—HR Policy Versus Practice

Craig works at a nonprofit that is very laid back, but he was told in the interview that they have a strict policy of no personal emails, phone, or Internet use. Craig sees his coworkers texting and on Facebook all the time. They even requested to be friends with him. Would it be OK for Craig to do the same if everyone else is doing it? Even if the boss doesn't see?

Case Study—Experience Versus Personal Beliefs and Values

This case study is viewed from two different perspectives, Jane and Alex. Read both perspectives and consider what you know about each, what you still don't know, and what Jane and Alex may not understand about the other person's perspective.

Jane, a co-op student, is a research assistant at University Hospital. The head research assistant asks Jane for a date. Jane politely declines the invitation. The next day the research associate acts coldly toward Jane. Soon, Jane finds that some of her key responsibilities have been taken away from her. What should she do?

Alex is Head Research Assistant at a busy hospital, and they have great co-op students working on the team. Alex is the same age as many of the co-op students since they graduated from college back home in Australia three years ago. Alex really enjoys the presence of Jane on the team and asks her out on a date. Alex realizes he might need to seek permission of HR if the two of them do end up dating, but they just want to go out once and get to know more people here in the states. Jane declines, which is unfortunate but there are now more pressing issues for Alex to worry about, between a troubling call from family at home and cutbacks on funding in the lab. Jane seems removed in her interactions with Alex the next day, but Alex is quite busy to notice that. What does Alex need to do?

==

Note on sources of activities in the toolkit: *The activities and advising content shared in this section comes from a deep pool of experience in the field. Activities, advising prompts, and case studies that were created, written up, or framed by a specific person or departmental group are noted in the text. The ideas behind many of these attributed sections are built upon ideas from across Northeastern University, and beyond. Thank you to all, named and not, whose work contributed to the activities and best practices shared and improvised upon in this book.*